Apple Pie and Enchiladas

Apple Pie
& Enchiladas

Latino Newcomers in the Rural Midwest

Ann V. Millard and Jorge Chapa

with Catalina Burillo, Ken R. Crane, Isidore Flores, Jeremy Hogan,
Maríaelena D. Jefferds, Eileen Diaz McConnell, Refugio I. Rochín, & Rogelio Saenz

University of Texas Press *Austin*

We gratefully acknowledge permission to reproduce lyrics from the song/poem "En Michigan," © 2001 Lualyric Pub. Co. / Transom Music Co. From the CD *La Onda del Midwest/Los Bandits,* © 2001 LaBianca Recordings. Words: Guillermo Martínez. Music: René Meave. All rights reserved.

Second paperback printing, 2005

Requests for permission to reproduce material from this work should be sent to Permissions, University of Texas Press, Box 7819, Austin, TX 78713-7819.

www.utexas.edu/utpress/about/bpermission.html

♾The paper used in this book meets the minimum requirements of ANSI/NISO Z39.48-1992 (R1997) (Permanence of Paper).

Library of Congress Cataloging-in-Publication Data

Apple pie and enchiladas : Latino newcomers in the rural Midwest / Ann V. Millard and Jorge Chapa, with Catalina Burillo . . . [et al.].
    p.   cm.
  ISBN 0-292-70277-9 (hardcover : alk. paper)—ISBN 0-292-70568-9 (pbk. : alk. paper)
  1. Hispanic Americans—Middle West—Social conditions.   2. Community life—Middle West.   3. Immigrants—Middle West—Social conditions.   4. Migration, Internal—United States.   5. Middle West—Rural conditions.   6. Middle West—Ethnic relations.   I. Millard, Ann V.   II. Chapa, Jorge, 1953–   III. Burillo, Catalina.
  F358.2.S75I38   2004
  977'.00468—dc22

                                                    2004006920

We dedicate this volume to Manuel (Manny) Gonzalez, former head of the Inter-Agency Migrant Council, Family Independence Agency, State of Michigan. He inspired many researchers, volunteers, and legislators concerned with the living conditions of low-income Latino newcomers. By organizing regional and state Migrant Councils to coordinate services for migrant farmworkers, he fostered cooperation among many stakeholders in Michigan, providing a model of service and policy coordination that would be useful to those dealing with the Latinos in this book. Manny passed on from this world September 8, 2002, after participating in a march to the capitol building in Lansing, Michigan, in support of migrant farmworkers.

Contents

Tables

Figures

Photographs following page xiv

Preface

This volume is the product of many hands, including the principal investigators, researchers, study participants, and photographers. While we studied the process of migration of Latinos to the rural Midwest, nearly all members of our research team also migrated.

The authors have shared a common bond for years in producing this work and continue to bring a vibrant cross section of interdisciplinary experience to research on contemporary Latino issues. The authors maintain a strong commitment to understanding and accurately reporting the dimensions and significance of Latino sojourners and Latino communities. The interest in rural Latinos is growing today, as well as the need to keep abreast of the changes brought forth as Latinos become established workers, new neighbors, and civic participants in local governance. For the authors, the prospects look good and very promising for the rural United States. The country's old citizenry has always welcomed the nation's newcomers, and together they have maintained a creative and vital society for all.

This project began with a research proposal, "Latinos in the Rural Midwest: Community Development Implications," submitted to the United States Department of Agriculture by Refugio Rochín and Rogelio Saenz. The proposal focused on various aspects of immigration from Mexico to the United States and in-migration from the Southwest to the Midwest. When the proposal was submitted, Dr. Rochín was director of the Julian Samora Research Institute (JSRI) at Michigan State University; he later moved to the Smithsonian Institution in Washington, D.C., and he is now a senior fellow and Washington, D.C., liaison for the Inter-University Program for Latino Research at Notre Dame University.

Throughout the project, Rogelio Saenz has been the co–principal investigator, as well as a professor and head of the Department of Sociology at Texas A&M University. The grant supported Dr. Saenz's demographic research and sociological studies with Lourdes Gouveia and students at the University of Nebraska, Omaha, which is being published elsewhere.

Jorge Chapa succeeded Dr. Rochín as acting director of JSRI and was the principal researcher coordinating the project for a year. Dr. Chapa carried out the demographic analysis of rural population dynamics published in this volume, left JSRI to start the Latino Studies Program at Indiana University, and continued work on this project throughout all remaining phases. In Bloomington, Chapa met Jeremy Hogan, a photographer with the *Bloomington Herald-Times* nominated for a Pulitzer Prize. Hogan has a long-standing interest in using photography to portray the Latino condition. Eileen Diaz McConnell, a visiting professor in Latino Studies at Indiana University at the time, extended her dissertation research to the subjects covered in this book. She has moved on to join the faculty at the University of Illinois at Urbana-Champaign.

Ann Millard started working on the ethnographic component of the project when Dr. Chapa was at JSRI and, when he left, she became the principal investigator of the project. She worked closely with Maríaelena D. Jefferds and Ken R. Crane, who were ethnographic research assistants and graduate students at Michigan State University. After finishing her Ph.D. in anthropology, Jefferds moved to the Centers for Disease Control and Prevention, while Crane finished his Ph.D. in sociology and moved to Ancilla University in Indiana. Catalina Burillo, who has worked with some of us on a number of research projects on Latinos in rural Michigan, finished her undergraduate education at Michigan State University and moved to Hart, Michigan. In the final year of the grant, Ann Millard moved to the South Texas Center for Rural Public Health in McAllen, Texas, which is part of the School of Rural Public Health, Texas A&M University System Health Science Center. Isidore Flores also moved from JSRI to the South Texas Center.

As is evident, every author in this volume, except Saenz, moved to a new community and began a new job as we completed work on the manuscript. As academics, we tend not to be called migrants, but like the people in our book our moves were related to learning more and to employment; and like a *familia* of colleagues, we have stayed in close contact.

The contrast of our experiences as migrants—many of us Latinos—with those of many people in this book reminds us of the importance of social class and its many ramifications in making us acceptable to and comfortable in our new communities. It is the wish of the authors of this book that the legitimacy and respect we receive as newcomers will be extended to those who follow in the footsteps of the Latinos in this book, in recognition of what they bring to many of the faltering rural communities in the Midwest.

AVM, JC, RS, and RIR

Acknowledgments

We thank the United States Department of Agriculture for the grant "Latinos in the Rural Midwest: Community Development Implications" (USDA grant no. 97-36200-5207). This support was crucial to funding graduate students while they carried out fieldwork and faculty while they contributed to focus-group, ethnographic, sociological, and demographic investigations. We thank the following faculty from Michigan State University for their encouragement: Lynne Goldstein (chair of the Department of Anthropology), Chris Vanderpool (former chair of the Department of Sociology, now deceased), and Israel Cuellar (director of the Julian Samora Research Institute).

We also thank Patricia Whittier, editor extraordinaire, for editorial, philosophical, and moral support, and Theresa May, editor at the University of Texas Press, whose interest, goodwill, and energy have been an inspiration to us. For her assistance with copyediting, we thank Crystal Brim. For her skillful and diplomatic corrections and queries, we thank Letitia Blalock. For her assistance in final preparation of the manuscript, we thank Esmeralda Sanchez. We are also grateful to Juana Watson and Elizabeth Chapa for their assistance in making contact with the subjects of many of the photographs.

Muchas gracias to the many Latinos and Anglos in the Midwest who assisted us in this project, whether as advisers or participants in the study. Nearly all of those who worked with us did so in the interest of advancing relations between Anglos and Latinos, and we designed this book to serve that purpose. We also enthusiastically thank Ruby Acosta, Armando Cordero, José Alonso Guzmán, Laura Guzmán, Juan A. Lopez Tovar, Juan and Marta Manzanares and family, José Pizaña, Luis Reyes, María Rodriguez, and Rigoberto Silva Campos. There is great need for increased understanding among ethnic groups, especially Anglos and Latinos, in the rural Midwest, and we applaud all of those engaged in creating better relationships and thus constructing pathways toward a better future for the rural Midwest.

AVM, JC, RS, and RIR

1. Latino couple working on a small chicken farm in southern Indiana. (Published by permission of Jeremy Hogan)

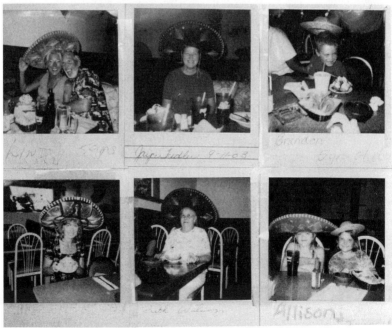

2. Businesses in downtown Ligonier, Indiana, that cater to Latinos. The second-story apartments are rented mostly to Latino tenants. (Photo courtesy of Ken R. Crane)

3. Anglos at a Mexican restaurant in Linton, Indiana, where these snapshots were posted. (Published with permission of Jeremy Hogan)

4. Mural painted in the 1930's by Carlos Fuentes in the post office in Paw Paw, Michigan. Fuentes came to Michigan as a migrant farmworker and painted the mural as part of a Works Progress Administration (WPA) program. (Photo courtesy of Ken R. Crane)

5. Family room in a double-wide mobile home of an immigrant family in central Indiana. (Published with permission of Jeremy Hogan)

6. Ligia Zavala holds three-month-old Héctor Gaitán as Jaime Zavala looks on during Baile Latino, a Latino dance at the Cascades Park Clubhouse in Bloomington. (Reprinted with permission of Jeremy Hogan/The Bloomington Herald-Times)

7. The family of Homero Hernández received a beautification award from the city of Goshen for their great work on their house and garden. (Reprinted with permission of El Puente, Goshen, Indiana)

8. Work in meat processing. A Latino man carries a dressed hog into a grocery store stocked with goods that would appeal to Latinos of many origins in Columbus, Indiana. (Published with permission of Jeremy Hogan)

9. Changing chicken bedding on a small chicken farm in southern Indiana. The worker is a Latino immigrant. (Published with permission of Jeremy Hogan)

10. On the job, washing dishes in a southern Indiana home. The worker is a Latina immigrant. (Published with permission of Jeremy Hogan)

11. At work, burning trash. The worker is a Latino immigrant. (Published with permission of Jeremy Hogan)

12. Adult students before their English class in central Indiana. (Published with permission of Jeremy Hogan)

13. High school medal for academic excellence. The medal was awarded to Jaime Muñoz, the only Latino in his 2003 high school class to graduate with "high distinction." (Reprinted with permission of El Puente, Goshen, Indiana)

14. Feeding baby during English class in central Indiana. (Published with permission of Jeremy Hogan)

15. *Faldas volando* (skirts flying). High school students performing folkloric Mexican dances on Diversity Day. (Photo by Jesús Mujica/Reprinted with permission of El Puente, Goshen, Indiana)

16. Grocery store window of a Latino-owned shop in Columbus, Indiana. (Published with permission of Jeremy Hogan)

17. Latino family at church in central Indiana. (Published with permission of Jeremy Hogan)

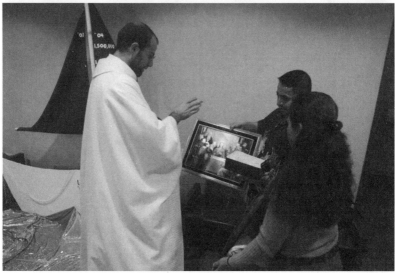

18. Men chatting at church breakfast in central Indiana. (Published with permission of Jeremy Hogan)

19. Priest blessing picture and nativity set in central Indiana. (Published with permission of Jeremy Hogan)

20. Procession on Palm Sunday (Domingo de Ramos), Immaculate Conception Catholic Church in Hartford, Michigan. (Photo courtesy of Ken R. Crane)
21. Christmas in a double-wide mobile home in central Indiana. (Published with permission of Jeremy Hogan)

22. Saint Valentine's Day party. Edgar Gaitán, who was born in Illinois but spent 21 years living in Mexico and recently moved to Bloomington, Indiana, from Chicago, feeds his son during a celebration that was mostly attended by Latinos. (Reprinted with permission of Jeremy Hogan/The Bloomington Herald-Times)

23. Billboard in north central Indiana. The billboard states, "Let our family help your family/Superior Auto/We finance." (Photo courtesy of Ken R. Crane)

24. Rephrased welcome sign in Ligonier, Indiana. "Mexico" is painted over "Ligonier."
Published in the *Ligonier Advance Leader* (September 1994) with the caption "With a
growing Mexican population, is this a sign of the times?" (Copyright Kendallville Publishing Company, used by permission)

25. A Latino worker at his flooded mobile home. Benino Rodríguez stands outside the trailer where he lives, inundated by the White River in Spencer, Indiana. (Reprinted with permission of Jeremy Hogan/The Bloomington Herald-Times)

Apple Pie and Enchiladas

Aquí in the Midwest [Here in the Midwest]

Ann V. Millard and Jorge Chapa

Apple pie and enchiladas symbolize a new combination in the dynamic contemporary encounter of peoples and cultures in the rural Midwest. In the late 1980s, Latinos began to pour into Midwestern villages and towns, living there year-round, working, going to school, attending church, and generally becoming members of local communities. Although some of them work in agriculture-related industries, the newcomers are permanent residents, not the migrant workers familiar in much of the rural Midwest. Latinos settle in the region to raise their income by working year-round instead of seasonally or, in some cases, for higher hourly wages and better benefits than they find elsewhere. Some of the newcomers also mention seeking a place to live where their children can attend school and the family can live in peace.

Some workers come directly from Mexico, informally recruited by factories through employees' social networks. Others come from the southwestern United States and, in some cases, visit the Midwest as migrant farmworkers before settling there to live year-round. Their employers range from small family-owned companies to huge multinational corporations.

Anglos and Latinos easily enjoy one another's culture when it comes to food—apple pie and enchiladas—giving an impression of smooth social integration, that all is well in the new social encounter. Our research, however, finds many problems, especially prejudice against Latinos, as it shapes their low-income niche in local economies and disrupts neighborhoods, schools, and churches. Our analysis explains the causes and consequences of the Latino influx and points out successes and failures of rural Midwestern communities in accommodating the newcomers.

This volume presents research by a bilingual team of sociologists and anthropologists comprised of Anglos and Latinos. Our demographic analysis quantifies the extent of the Latino influx and its relationship to rural population trends. Our ethnographic studies of clusters of rural communities in Indiana, Michigan, Nebraska, and Ohio explore the human dimensions of

the process of change, particularly regarding interactions of Anglos and Latinos in daily life and their division of labor in local economies.

Apple Pie

Anytime the Village Hall wants to do something for the town, the growers [farm owners] don't want to participate. Last year, we had an apple pie
contest to help the hospital. None of the growers bid on the pies. They
would've been really upset, though, if we had had a *pecan* pie contest
[because pecans are not grown locally]. The Village Hall and Chamber
of Commerce promote local crops and local businesses, but the growers
don't support our efforts. But they'll be pissed off if the local government
and others don't support their crops!
An Anglo townswoman in Fox, Michigan

This statement is related to one of many divisions among Anglos
("whites") that are typical of the villages and towns in the rural Midwest.
As researchers, we were surprised at the strong Anglo sense of difference
among "white" townspeople. We had anticipated that Latino newcomers
would bring variation to homogeneous communities; however, they have
simply become a new category in an already fractured social landscape.

In general, public opinion is concerned about the business district,
but growers only care about their farms. They are a tight-knit group,
conservative. A lot of them will go drinking at the bar; they're not all
alcoholics, but they do tend to drink a lot. That's mostly where we
see them.
An Anglo townsperson in Mapleville, Michigan

Conflicts between townspeople and farm owners have a long history, tied
in part to farmers' bringing migrant workers to the region and polluting air
and water with waste from food processing plants. The split between townspeople and farmers, and other divisions among Anglos, are acted out partly
through contrasting Anglo reactions to Latino newcomers.

Anglos commonly refer to their division between "old-timers" and "newcomers." An Anglo man who has lived in Fox, Michigan, for seven years and

holds an important position in the community says that he is not really accepted in the town because he does not have "the right name and history."

> I've only been here in Mapleville for 23 years—I've raised four children here. So I'm not really from here. You have to live here for five generations for people to say you're from here.
> *An Anglo village official in Mapleville, Michigan*

> Generations of founding farm families have lived here, and they've intermarried over the generations. Most are related, so it can be difficult to become an insider. People won't perceive you as being from the area and belonging. This may be one reason that Mexicans generally have social circles separate from whites.
> *An Anglo in Mapleville, Michigan*

Anglos remember an earlier time when marriage between Catholics and Protestants was unthinkable, and divisions among Anglos still follow the lines of religion, ethnicity (e.g., Belgians versus Scots), and social class, in addition to occupation and length of time in the local community. Anglos portray their divisions as weaker than in the past, but controversies still prompt the fading divisions to reemerge.

Anglo Perspectives on Latino Newcomers

Anglos tend to view Latino newcomers as undergoing the hardships of past immigrants to the United States, as though an inexorable historical force works to improve the fortunes of the children of immigrants (and as though the Latino newcomers are all immigrants). Anglos are vaguely aware of the newcomers' poverty and poor living and working conditions, but tend to see them as transitory. From the perspective of most Anglos, the newcomers bring problems with them, rather than encounter them locally through systematic exploitation by local business people and "corporate culture." Anglos' misleading stereotypes about Latinos, moreover, tend to block joint efforts by Anglos and Latinos to solve community problems. The schisms in Anglo communities also create major impediments to addressing changes associated with the newcomers. Perhaps the only grounds for optimism lie in the opposition of many Anglos to ethnic prejudice and racism, their view of themselves as fair-minded people, and the conviction of many Latinos that they are headed for a better future.

Enchiladas

Mi Casa Number 2 was a Mexican restaurant attempting crossover appeal to Anglos with a sports bar, until it was closed in the early 2000s. The "Mexican restaurant" character of the place included "Mexican" trappings, menu, and staff. Sombreros, pottery, weavings, paper flowers, posters of the Tejana singer Selena, and piñatas decorated the walls. A second, large room in the restaurant was the epitome of the sports bar, a type of dining and drinking establishment that became popular in the Midwest in the 1990s—a casual, noisy place serving food at reasonable prices and providing a gathering place with big-screen TVs, tuned to sports channels, sometimes showing expensive pay-per-view contests. The two rooms in the restaurant suggested a rare and sophisticated attempt to appeal broadly to both Latinos and the general Anglo, Midwestern sports enthusiast public.

As Mexican food became popular in the Midwest, Anglos opened their own Mexican restaurants, ranging from Taco Bell to more distinctive and expensive restaurant-bars. This expansion of Anglo entrepreneurship suggests cultural integration, and it does seem to be a step in that direction; however, Latinos appear in most Anglo-owned restaurants only as dishwashers, not patrons.

Restaurants account for a small but highly visible part of small-town commerce. At first sight, Latinos and Anglos seem to have intertwined relationships, as suggested by Anglo appreciation of Mexican food and Anglo ownership of Mexican restaurants. As they eat enchiladas in a Mexican restaurant in the typical small town in this study, Anglos see themselves as open-minded about Latinos and their culture. In examining the ownership and workforce at the restaurants, though, we found a rigid separation of Anglos from Latinos.

A Mexican-owned restaurant is typically small, owned and staffed by a family, low budget, and low profit. In a few cases, over the course of many years, such enterprises have grown enough to hire staff from outside the family. Latino newcomers feel comfortable in these eateries; the staff speak Spanish fluently, and the food is familiar and relatively cheap. Anglos usually feel out of place and sometimes have difficulty ordering food. An Anglo-owned restaurant is generally either a fast-food eatery, open to all ethnic groups and classes, or a restaurant patronized almost entirely by Anglo old-timers, who tend to make newcomers feel unwelcome, regardless of ethnic identity.

We had expected greater integration of Latinos and Anglos in the workforce of Midwestern villages and towns than we found in our research. The two groups are quite separate in all sectors of the workforce, including factories, commerce, and services. In this volume, we trace the lines of demarcation between Anglos and Latinos in the workforce, at school, and at church. We show that Latino newcomers face considerable hardship in many cases, and that Anglos are too distracted by their own internal, factional disputes to engage constructively with Latinos in adjusting the social and economic conditions of their small towns for the common good. Anglos generally pay little attention to Latino newcomers, who are often left to the practices and prejudices of an Anglo minority that exploits them and another, larger group of Anglos that rebuffs them. Poor treatment of Latinos on the job, in school, at church, and generally in daily life occurs in a climate of inattention on the part of the Anglo majority, coupled with the greed and ill will of some.

The rest of this chapter introduces the main points in our analysis as follows. Although many Latinos and Anglos cross the cultural divide sufficiently to enjoy both "American" and "Mexican" food—apple pie and enchiladas—in other ways the two ethnic groups tend to be segregated and polarized. Many Anglos assume, however, that welfare benefits are the goal of Latino newcomers. This assumption flows out of Anglo stereotypes about "Mexicans," and the welfare issue is inflammatory among both Anglos and Latinos. Latino newcomers, however, move to the Midwest for jobs, not to go on welfare; many apply for welfare because their jobs pay poorly and provide few benefits. Few Anglos see the employers of the newcomers as exploiters of the welfare system; however, low-wage jobs enhance employers' profits and are designed with employee welfare dependence in mind.

Few Anglos, moreover, realize that the movement of workers from Mexico and Texas to the Midwest has a long history, extending through much of the twentieth century (see Chapter 2). Currently, the Midwestern Latino population is growing much more rapidly than the general population, and few Anglos realize that their towns would lose population if not for Latino newcomers (see Chapter 3).

To characterize the impact of the sudden Latino influx on small town life, we used ethnographic methods, semistructured interviews, and focus groups with rural Anglos and Latinos in several Midwestern states (see Chapter 4 and Appendixes A–C). The communities encountered by Latino newcomers vary in the extent of difficulties that townspeople create for Latinos in daily life, at work, school, and church (see Chapters 6 through 8). Although our research clearly finds that most Latino newcomers are heavily exploited, Anglos tend not to see this dynamic and instead stereotype Latinos as bringing poverty with them (see Chapters 4 and 5). Among a few rural Midwestern communities, the issues raised by the influx of newcomers have been addressed successfully, but their innovations have not spread to other communities (see Chapter 9). One purpose of this book is to characterize the issues created by the influx to make the positive innovations available to rural Midwesterners in general.

Latinos' Quest for Jobs and a Better Life

Alicia and her family first came to Michigan from south Texas in the late 1970s to work in the fields during the summer. Alicia had moved to Texas from Mexico with her parents as a child; her husband, Rubén, had arrived from Mexico as an adult, and they were working as migrant farmworkers when they met and married in the early 1980s. In 1990, Alicia and her family lived in a two-room shack and shared a toilet with 30 other people in a farm labor "camp" of 150 residents. Alicia did not complain about her living quarters, but she confided that the sheer misery of working long days harvesting in the fields sometimes made her weep as she reached the end of a row. From time to time, other women also commented that the misery of working in the fields drove them to tears.

Alicia and her husband, Rubén, had driven to Michigan in their pickup truck, with their children and all their earthly belongings. Packing for the road trip, they slid a 4-by-8-foot sheet of plywood into the back of the truck to rest on the wheel wells and cover their belongings; their children rode on the plywood, under the truck cap. On the road, they traveled in a caravan of trucks owned by various family members, enabling them to provide assistance when one of their vehicles broke down on the road.

Midwestern townspeople sometimes describe farmworkers as doing well by earning large quantities of money at harvesttime. Migrant workers tend to travel in relatively new pickup trucks that are kept immaculately clean. When they shop, farmworkers wear much the same clothing as the general public. Thus, they appear to be as prosperous as anyone else. The reality, however, is that their truck and its contents are generally their only property and that they may earn nothing in the month or two before the harvest, resulting in annual household incomes well below the poverty line. Although well attired while shopping, they have very few presentable clothes.

At the farm in Michigan, Alicia and Rubén worked quarter-mile-long rows of cucumbers, a particularly back-breaking crop. The hardest labor was during the three-week harvest peak, when they worked from dawn to well after sundown—picking, hauling, and overseeing the sorting of the harvest to ensure they got credit for their hard work. In the winter months, Alicia and Rubén lived and worked at a large truck farm in the Belle Glade area of Florida, inland from Palm Beach, where they labored six days a week through most of the period from October through May.

As migrant workers, they were surviving, but they sought a better life. They wanted to move away from Florida, as they were worried about their children getting into trouble with other kids in Belle Glade. Eventually, Alicia and most of her extended family settled down in northern Indiana after working seasonally, off and on, in the fields, at farm produce packing sheds, and in small factories in western Michigan and northern Indiana. She and Rubén obtained factory jobs in the late 1990s, settled permanently, and moved into the middle class.

They now work different shifts in a small automotive parts plant. They bought a modest four-bedroom house, two new cars, which they park in their two-car garage, and a large, above-ground swimming pool. Their house is immaculate, without a weed in their lawn. Alicia and Rubén coordinate their shifts at work to take care of the children and take them to football games, soccer practice, and the church youth group.

Their oldest child, Gabina, dropped out of school, pregnant, last year. She married at age 17, now has a baby, and lives in a trailer park, home to many low-income Latino newcomers and, unfortunately, contaminated with toxic waste. (Although the authorities have tried at times to get the waste cleaned up, they have not yet succeeded in pinning that responsibility on either the current or past owners.)

"I cried for three days when Gabina dropped out of school," Alicia said. "My greatest ambition is that the children finish high school and possibly get even more education."

Her oldest son, though, is not particularly concerned about studying. "My parents didn't finish high school. Still, they're doing OK," he commented.

Alicia and her husband are living the American dream, in a modest way, although their prosperity is somewhat precarious—it depends on their working two jobs, which depend on their health and the prosperity of the automotive industry.

Millard, field notes

Alicia and Rubén typify Latino newcomers to the rural Midwest in that they came for work and arrived with their family. Their pathway to settlement, beginning with migrant farmwork, is followed by some but not all Latino newcomers. As in their case, jobs are the main reason that Latinos settle in the rural Midwest. Most newcomers have jobs lined up before they arrive; they are recruited informally by Anglo employers, who advertise jobs by word of mouth among employees. The jobs with the best pay and benefits, like those of Alicia and Rubén, are in light industrial plants, mostly auto parts factories. The least desirable and lowest-paying jobs are in food processing, where Latinos wash, chop, can, freeze, slaughter, and pack food under arduous conditions requiring physical strength and endurance.

The success of Alicia and Rubén, their extended family members, and friends who have settled down to work in light industry is powerful testimony to the continuation of the American dream. It is moving to see the transformation in their lives from poor, migrant farmworkers to middle-class factory workers living comfortably and trying to provide their children with a better life. Their success story, however, holds for only a small segment of Latino newcomers. Most belong to the working poor, live in dilapidated housing, and work hard in heavy labor under dangerous conditions.

This has been the worst year of my life!
Sofía, a Latina, discussing work in food processing in Mapleville, Michigan

Factory jobs are often assumed to provide excellent compensation to unskilled workers; however, employment in manufacturing is highly stratified, ranging from ill-paid work without medical or retirement benefits to well-paid jobs with comprehensive benefit packages. Above, Sofia was recounting her experiences in a plant as discussed further in Chapter 6. She found the working conditions inhumane, the worst she had ever seen, even compared to her former work in Mexico and her many years of harvesting crops in the United States.

Latino Migration to the Rural Midwest
Population Dynamics

While Latinos have resided in parts of the rural Midwest for more than a century, the 1990s brought a great increase in the number of Latinos and in the number of rural areas with noticeable Latino populations (see Chapters 2 and 3). During that decade, the total population of the Midwest increased by about 8 percent and Midwestern Latinos by 80 percent. Rural counties outran metropolitan counties in the growth rate and numbers of Latinos. In the year 2000, nonetheless, Latinos residing in the rural Midwest accounted for less than 2 percent of the total rural population. The Latino influx reached only some communities rather than spreading evenly through the countryside. Much of the Latino population growth occurred in the last years of the 1990s, and the major component was a rapid increase in immigrants from Mexico. The demographic context for our study is Midwestern rural areas that have recently experienced a significant increase of Latinos, particularly Mexican immigrants, regardless of any preexisting Latino population.

Industry and Migration

Cities in the Midwest are well known for their long history of highly productive industrial development. The incursion of industry into the rural areas has grown rapidly in the last few decades, with the relocation of plants close to raw materials in some cases and away from pressures to unionize or to control pollution in others. Many employers see Latino immigrants as particularly desirable employees. Employers typically commented, "Nobody works like a Mexican."

While Flint, Detroit, and other cities in Michigan have lost automobile manufacturing jobs, small automobile parts plants have been built in rural southern Michigan and northern Indiana to employ hundreds of workers, partly replacing the lost industrial capacity of the large cities. The concept of the "de-industrialization" of the Midwest thus applies more to cities than to rural areas. Moreover, the tendency of companies to move factories to Mexico is being moderated in part by bringing Mexican workers to the rural Midwest to work for wages and benefits below union scale.

Generally, the rural Midwest has two paths leading Latinos to settle there. Some Latinos arrive first as migrant farmworkers, returning annually for many years and eventually settling in the region, often to work in food processing. This was the pattern of settlement of Alicia, Rubén, and their relatives, except that they moved to better-paying jobs in light industry. Others, with no previous Midwestern experience, move directly to a Midwestern town to work in a specific plant, whether in light industry or food processing. Newcomers of the first type are often Mexican Americans, whereas those of the second type, in many cases, arrive directly from Mexico.

Comparison with Rural California

Rural areas of the Midwest resemble those in California regarding their mixtures of Latino populations of different national origins and legal statuses. In both regions, some employers recruit workers by ethnicity, nationality, and gender to enforce policies of low wages and benefits (on California, see Menchaca 1995; Ruiz 1987, 1998; Wells 1996; Zavella 1987; see also Chapa 1988, 1995). Rural California has received a major influx of immigrants from Mexico, some of whom moved to the Midwest in the 1980s and 1990s. Many were citizens or had worked in the United States for more than a decade (Kerr 2000; Gonzales and Gonzales 2000; Healy 1995; Valdés 1991, 2000a,b; Vargas 1993). As in rural California (Allensworth and Rochín 1999), however, some Midwestern communities rely on a workforce recently arrived from Mexico (Gouveia and Stull 1995; see also Martin et al. 1996; Massey 1998).

The Midwest differs from California regarding the types of work available. California's mild climate and long expanse of farmland from north to south give it a long growing season, with more than one crop annually in many regions. The result is that farmworkers can follow the crops year-round and have nearly 12 months of employment without leaving the state. The Midwest, however, has a relatively short growing season, tends to process food through drying, freezing, or canning, and has many more beef cattle, meatpacking plants, and factories devoted to light industry. Various geographic areas offer different types of employment that draw Latinos; for example, in Fall County, Michigan, the main Latino employers are fruit and vegetable processors, whereas in Nebraska they are meat processors (butchering and meatpacking) (Gouveia and Stull 1995). All these employers pay low wages compared with those paid to urban factory workers. Light industrial plants tend to cluster in areas close to the factories they serve (see also Martin et al. 1996). The higher wages in light industry allow two-earner families to reach the solid middle class, a major contrast with the typical Latino newcomer's situation.

Social Services and Government Policies

To stretch their low wages, many Latino factory workers rely on government services to help support their households, a phenomenon resented by many local Anglos. In a Nebraska meatpacking community, however, only 27 percent of households used such programs, including immunizations, Medicaid, and food stamps (Gouveia and Stull 1997; see also Healy 1995). In California, Anglo resentment of Latino use of government resources was one of the factors leading to Proposition 187, passed in the mid-1990s as a backlash against Mexican immigrants, whom it prohibited from using a long list of government services (Rochín, quoted in Healy 1995; see also Allensworth and Rochín 1998a, 1998b; Rochín 1995; Salgado de Snyder et al. 1996; Foley 1997; Menchaca 1995; and Valdés 2000a,b on the roots of pejorative Anglo views of "Mexicans").

As we began this study, we anticipated that we would meet many families among Latino newcomers, but we did not realize the great extent to which children would provide crucial services to their parents and other adults. For example, many community and state organizations do not provide interpreters, a service often provided by children. It is not unusual for children six or eight years of age to interpret for their mothers as they apply for food stamps or seek medical treatment. Organizations that tend to provide interpreters include huge chain stores (such as Wal-Mart), community health clinics (funded by the federal government to offer health care to low-income people on a sliding scale), and, in a limited way, state welfare departments, especially in their outreach to Spanish-speaking migrant farmworkers. Organizations not typically providing interpreters are ordinary stores, schools, state unemployment offices, and hospitals, including emergency rooms. All of these organizations, in not providing interpreters, ensure that Spanish monolingual clients will receive fewer services than do Anglos. Inability to communicate tends to eliminate all but the most desperate clients.

We also did not anticipate that Latinos would take the initiative to establish their own religious congregations, in many cases recruiting pastors from other parts of the U.S. and Latin America. Latino churches provide many crucial social services, including emergency food and clothing. Important to many newcomer families, bilingual church staff provide crucial referrals to health and social service agencies; that is, they connect newcomers to ongoing assistance in the form of food stamps, children's Medicaid, and other benefits. Some pastors also informally represent their congregations to the local mayor and other town officials. These activities undoubtedly contribute to the vitality of many of the newly founded Spanish-speaking congregations in the Midwest.

Community Variation in Racism, Employment, History, and Economy

Rural Midwestern communities vary dramatically in the nature of Latino-Anglo relations, and many towns waver back and forth over time. To provide an overview, we describe some of the dimensions of the variation among communities that we found through ethnographic fieldwork.

Racist and Nonracist People and Communities

In this study, racism emerged as an important aspect of Latino experience in the Midwest. In conversations, Latinos freely referred to "racist" people and communities, described as those who violently attack Latinos because of their ethnicity. (*Racista* [racist] is the term used in these discussions, and it is part of the ordinary Spanish vocabulary of newcomers, not a term introduced by our research team.) All the Latinos with whom we raised the issue of discrimination had, at one time or another, been the target of anti-"Mexican" taunts, police harassment, or graffiti suggesting they "go back to Mexico."

Latinos described the "racist community" as a place where Latinos should not go and are not welcome to settle. Perhaps as many as 10 percent of rural communities in Michigan, Indiana, and Illinois are in this category, according to those we interviewed. Some communities are associated with organizations such as the Ku Klux Klan; however, others do not have any obvious identity or reputation among Anglos to suggest that they are racist. Latinos avoid spending time in such communities, and they neither live nor work in them. In taking up issues of racism in this book, we do not explore any specific communities considered racist by the Latinos we interviewed, but it is important to understand that they are part of the Midwestern backdrop for Latino newcomers.

In our studies of communities where Latinos settled, we found that racism against them was not a fixed characteristic of a village or town. Progress against discrimination often fit the sequence of two steps forward, one step backward. Extreme racist incidents occurred from time to time in various places, but they were often followed by a positive local response.

This seesawing back and forth between outbursts of racism and periods of improved relations was evident in interview data and newspaper accounts. In discussing the experiences of Latinos with racism, we are dealing with situations in which we cannot know much about what really happened, but we analyze Latino and Anglo renditions of their experiences and how they strategized in response. In this study, we did not find that discrimination was gradually abating; rather we found a pendulum of change at work, making it difficult to trace progress against discrimination with any confidence.

Among Latinos, we found some optimism about social relations between Anglos and Latinos.

Saben convivir. [They enjoy getting along well with others.]
Rubén, a Latino, describing Anglos in his town

Rubén made this comment as he discussed Latino-Anglo relations in his town. He was describing Anglos as people who make good neighbors, and he was responding to comments about problems with racism in the region. Rubén, introduced earlier in this chapter, worked with his wife in an auto parts plant, and they lived in a lower-middle-class neighborhood of Latinos and Anglos in a northern Indiana town.

The nuances of Rubén's comment are difficult to capture in English. "Saben convivir" implies enjoyment in being with people who are different.

Convivir is often used to describe people who are different but who get along well, whether in a conversation, a neighborhood, a job, or a community. *Convivir* also carries the implication of an ideal way of living, a mature and morally sound way of life. In the Midwest, we find a series of instances in which Anglos "saben convivir" with Latinos as well as contrasting examples of rural insularity and inertia among Anglos in dealing with social and economic problems.

In Rubén's neighborhood, Anglos and Latinos are drawn together through their pride in their modest new homes, which are all maintained beautifully, regardless of ethnicity, and their interconnections through relying on one another for child care, support for their children's soccer team, and neighborly advice on various homeowners' issues. Although their communication is limited because the Latino parents tend to speak little English, the two ethnic groups have much in common in their upward mobility into the middle class and little pulling them apart; hence, the absence of tension between Anglos and Latinos in the neighborhood.

An instance of a food processing plant in western Illinois also provides an example of ameliorated conditions. The town has a meatpacking plant, a type of factory notorious for low-wage, physically demanding, dangerous jobs (Gouveia and Stull 1995; Hackenberg and Kukulka 1995; Stull, Broadway, and Griffith 1995). In this case, though, a few faculty, staff, and students from a small college in a nearby town have succeeded in putting some enlightened policies into place. They have assisted Latino newcomers to learn English, adjust to the schools, and otherwise have greater comfort and acceptance as they settle than they would find in many other meatpacking towns (Kuthy and Delany-Barmann 2000). The college as a whole is not any more accepting of Latinos than other Midwestern higher educational institutions, but a few faculty, staff, and students, including some Spanish teachers, scholars from Mexico, and former migrant workers, have succeeded in modifying the local context to make it more tolerant of cultural and other differences with recognition of the history of Latino immigration. The influence of a few people at a small college can thus improve the well-being of Latino newcomers entirely independently of the Latinos' employers.

Economic Differences and Latino Standards of Living

A crucial dimension of variation among rural Midwestern communities is the local economy. Latino newcomers are recruited to specific jobs, and

JOBS IN THE RURAL MIDWEST

		Food processing and agricultural	Light industrial factories
PREVIOUS JOBS	Farmwork in the U.S. and Mexico	Low Pay* Poor to no benefits Working poor Families	Higher pay* Better benefits Lower middle class Families
	Nonagricultural work in Mexico	Very few workers, if any*	Higher pay* Better benefits Solo males, some followed by family members

*Undocumented workers may appear in any of the categories. Although the lack of documents is a tremendous source of psychological stress and a reason to stay in hiding, it is not clear that it is a reason for lower pay on an individual level.

Figure 1.1. Typology of the pathways of Latino newcomers to jobs in the rural Midwest

those jobs determine their standards of living. As noted above, food processing jobs generally provide the lowest pay and benefits; as a result, communities with food processing plants tend to face some of the most difficult problems associated with Latino poverty (see Figure 1.1).

Food Processing: Low Wages and Poor Benefits
In Johnstown, Ohio, northeast of Columbus, we visited Buckeye Egg Farm, an employer of Latinos who commuted from the city.

> The farm is a huge industrial complex of long, low, windowless, gray cement buildings, grouped in sets of six to ten, regimented at right

angles. The farm's 125 barns, each as large as two football fields, harbor altogether 15.5 million chickens (*Poultry Times* 2002), six birds to a cage, stacked four high (Ludlow 1998). The employees, many of whom are recent arrivals from Mexico, are forced to keep their mouths shut all the time at work because the air is thick with flies inside the buildings. Huge fans pierce the building walls and expel air with a sickening stench. The putrid odor is a bitter issue among townspeople living in a radius of three miles; some display protest signs in their front yards. Local restaurants proudly refuse to serve eggs from the farm. The town has a new, upper-middle-class development half a mile from the closest part of the egg farm. Under certain wind conditions, the stench smothers the new homes and they disappear under a blanket of insects.

Millard and Chapa, field notes

This mega-size egg farm, one of several in the Columbus region, had the worst working conditions in our research. It was raided for having "unauthorized workers" (*RMN* 2001) in its workforce of about 600 people (Bischoff and Dempsey 2002). The farm owner, Anton Pohlmann, came from Germany, where he had been convicted twice for cruelty to animals; he reestablished his business as the Croton Egg Farm in Ohio in 1982, near a small village (*Columbus Dispatch* 2002). Later, he bought other farms and expanded operations under the names of AgriGeneral and then Buckeye Egg Farm. By the late 1990s, Ohio was the leading U.S. egg producer, with Buckeye producing 4 percent of the national total, that is, 2.6 billion eggs annually (WKYC 2002).

After a 1983 chicken manure spill that killed 150,000 fish in a nearby creek, the company's repeated violations of water and air pollution laws and sanitation laws led to fines totaling more than $1 million (*Cincinnati Enquirer* 2001). In the late 1990s, the company had a succession of four presidents in 28 months (*Columbus Dispatch* 1998), apparently in an effort to claim that changes in policy were being made. One of the presidents, Doucas "Duke" Groanites, had operated DeCoster Egg Farms in Maine, which had been assessed federal fines of $3.6 million for unsafe, unhealthy working and living conditions of migrant workers (*Columbus Dispatch* 1998).

Following actions by the state against Buckeye for illegal treatment of workers and infestations of flies, beetles, and other insects in the areas surrounding the farms, neighboring residents won a judgment of over $19 million for negligence (*Cincinnati Enquirer* 2001; MSNBC 2002). In the summer of 2002, Judge Gregory Frost of the Licking County Common Pleas Court ordered the company to close all of its 40 barns in two counties (72 more barns in a third county were not affected) (*Times Leader* 2002). These problems are an example of the kinds of changes the rural Midwest has undergone with the consolidation of farming into megafarms, which have legal and lobbying forces that far outweigh those of local communities. As the problems unfolded, Buckeye Egg Farm's owner resorted to the judicial system, seemingly to slow down actions against the company, and he continually threatened to go bankrupt or close the farm and move away. At last report, he had put his farm in Licking County, Ohio, up for sale and returned to Germany (*Business First* 2002). In our study, the egg farm exemplifies an unfortunate Midwestern transition to megafarms and an associated widespread pattern of employing Latinos wherever working conditions are the most difficult and wages the lowest.[1] The egg farm example also links poor farming practices (crowding animals under abhorrent conditions), pollution, and worker exploitation, all controversial issues through much of the Midwest.

Light Industry: Better Pay and Benefits

In contrast to communities where Latinos worked mainly in food processing, those where Latinos had jobs mainly in light industry were building lower-middle-class suburban communities. Working in such jobs, as did Alicia and Rubén, a couple may achieve an annual household income of about $44,000/year (reported in the year 2000) and medical benefits. Having two parents working different shifts results in a stressful family life with a fractured daily routine, but Alicia, Rubén, and similar couples tended to be optimistic about the future. Latinos in these circumstances were achieving the American dream—joining the middle class—as were their Anglo neighbors, through both parents working full-time on different shifts at a factory. Their suburban communities integrated Latinos with Anglos in residential neighborhoods with an air of contentment.

Most Latino workers in light industry are Spanish speakers who know a few phrases in English. Some whom we interviewed were born in Texas; some came from Mexico and became U.S. residents through the Immigration Reform and Control Act of 1986; others had arrived in the United

States more recently. Their teenage children, fluent in English and Spanish, felt they did not fit in with either "Mexicans" or Anglos, and their alienation seemed to hold them back from pursuing the aspirations of their parents.

Absence of Upper-Middle-Class Latinos

In this study, we did not deal with Latinos in the upper middle class and the professions, because there were practically none in rural Midwestern communities. We did meet a Latino psychiatrist who had immigrated from South America and was living temporarily in rural western Michigan. We also learned of a Latino physician living in the country in Indiana and commuting to a nearby city for work. Otherwise, there were no Latinos in our study with more than a lower-middle-class standard of living, achieved on the basis of a dual-income household. Upward class mobility is part of the history of Latinos who have settled in the rural Midwest, but it has come largely through a few of their children gaining a college education and taking professional jobs in the cities as teachers, social workers, and the like.

Latinos and Anglos: Terminology

The matter of what to call the populations in this book was not easily resolved, and the use of different terms by the various stakeholders could fill a book itself. Furthermore, during presentations on this study, we found that we needed to clarify our terminology for every audience, ranging from fellow researchers to agency staff and laypeople, Latino and Anglo alike. We take this as a mark of the complexity of the situation and its variations across the United States and throughout the New World.

The Latinos in this study nearly all belonged to a transnational population living in the United States and Mexico, generally united by a common history and social identity (see Table 1.1). In our study, the main Latino groups were Mexican Americans and Mexican immigrants, and they tended to refer to themselves as "Mexicano," paralleling the Anglo designation of "Mexican." (Some Midwestern Anglos also referred to the group as "Spanish.") For the purpose of this research, we use the term "Latinos" to include the various Mexican American and Mexican people comprising nearly all of those in the influx into the rural Midwest.

We use the term "Anglos" to designate U.S. citizens of European de-

Table 1.1 Nationality and Legal Status
of Latinos Settling in the Rural Midwest

Transnational Mexico-U.S. population, including most Latinos in the
rural Midwest

Mexican Americans (i.e., U.S. citizens)
- Descendants of original inhabitants of the Southwest, ceded by Mexico to
  the United States in 1848
- U.S.-born descendants of immigrants from Mexico to the Southwest
  (children, grandchildren, etc., of immigrants)
- Naturalized immigrants

Mexican nationals
- New immigrants and those living in the U.S. for a long time
  Legal residents
  Undocumented workers
- Temporary workers with U.S. government permits to work exclusively and
  temporarily for a specific employer in the Midwest

Those from the Caribbean and Central and South America
- Puerto Ricans (U.S. citizens, can move about the U.S. at will)
- Other skilled professionals (doctors, nurses, pastors, etc.), often hired to
  deliver services to low-income Latino newcomers
- Other unskilled workers

scent who are not Latinos, and we take this term from common usage in
the southwestern United States. "Anglo" thus includes most "non-Latinos,"
more commonly referred to as "whites." (In this usage, "Anglo" does not refer to England specifically; we do not know the derivation of the southwestern term.) The Latinos in this study called them "Americanos" (Americans),
a term never used by any participant in this study to refer to any Latino,
regardless of nationality. "Anglos" did not generally have a term for their
own group but if pushed, would probably have said "white." They included
typical mainstream rural residents of the Midwest, mostly descendants of
German, Belgian, Dutch, British, Scandinavian, and Slavic immigrants.[2]
The terms "Mexican" and "American" are confusing because of their conflation of ethnicity, nationality, and legal status; thus, we find it clearer to use
the terms "Latino" and "Anglo." The twists and turns of history and ethnic

relations have become oversimplified in rural Midwestern public perception, and this book provides a more complex analysis by examining the history and the economic and social dimensions of the new rural Midwestern Latino population.

People, Places, and Authors

Throughout this book, we use pseudonyms for people and their towns when conveying information provided to us confidentially, and in some cases we have created a composite person or town to guard people's privacy. We do accurately identify people, however, in a few instances, when we use publicly available information such as newspaper articles.

We intersperse chapters with short passages that we call "En Pocas Palabras" ("In a Few Words") to provide readers with different modes of engagement with the materials. These pieces exemplify general rural Midwestern patterns that we found over the course of our study, and they are concrete examples rather than self-contained analyses.

As noted in the preface, this book is the product of a research team begun by Rochín and Saenz and later headed by Chapa and Millard. All of the ethnographic researchers had previous research experience in the rural Midwest, and most were fluent in Spanish as well as English. We could not have carried out this study without researchers fluent in Spanish. Easy access to Latino and Anglo community members, plus the inclusion of both Latino and Anglo members in the research team, led us to question many assumptions about rural Midwestern people and their communities. In the ethnographic chapters, the first author is the researcher who collected most of the data and wrote the first draft of the chapter, and she or he occasionally writes in the first person in referring to experiences in the field.

Dynamics of Change in Ethnicity and Class in the Rural Midwest

This study finds that Latinos are doing extraordinarily well in some circumstances, but generally Latino newcomers are struggling at the bottom of the income scale, holding the most dangerous jobs and living in the worst housing in rural communities. Their reason for settling in the rural Midwest is to work in food processing plants or light industry; however, the communities that employ them are often reluctant to meet their needs as human beings—decent working conditions, housing, health care, social services, and educational opportunities for their children.

As a result, shortages of housing, lack of Spanish-speaking staff at vital points of contact for Latino newcomers, and outright discrimination are common in the rural Midwest. These new problems tend to be caught up in conflicts and lack of communication among factions in the Anglo community, resulting in a lack of local will to find solutions to enhance the future of the rural Midwest.

Ironically, many of the communities in this study would be losing population and facing a dearth of unskilled workers if Latinos had not settled there in significant numbers. Throughout the rural Midwest, the people who are currently supporting the growth of light industry and food processing by taking factory jobs are Latinos. Despite the many problems arising in ethnic relations, local government budgets, and the like, Anglos and Latinos in many communities are devising means of living together, cooperating, and appreciating one another. With this volume, we suggest that, despite their tendency toward internal conflict, rural communities can develop the capacity to appreciate not only apple pie and enchiladas but also the Anglo and Latino people who go with them.

En Pocas Palabras [In a Few Words] I

Ten Myths about Latinos

Ann V. Millard, Jorge Chapa, and Eileen Diaz McConnell

Ten myths about Latinos, widely held and strongly believed by Anglos, shape interactions in daily life in Midwestern small towns.

Ten Myths Held by Many Rural Midwestern Anglos about Latino Newcomers

1. Latino newcomers to Midwestern towns have just arrived from Mexico and are "illegal."
2. Migration from Mexico to the Midwest started in recent years.
3. Latino newcomers do not speak English and do not want to learn it.
4. They are the poorest of the poor; their living conditions at home are worse than those in the Midwest.
5. They want to stay separate from Anglos.
6. They love hard physical labor.
7. They love moving from place to place, producing high rates of turnover at factories.
8. They come to live on welfare and are a drain on the economy.
9. They do not experience racism because Midwesterners are not racist, and certainly not against "Mexicans."
10. They are grateful for whatever they get and uncritical of their conditions and treatment.

These stereotypes are widespread among Anglos in many parts of the United States, though not subscribed to by all. In the rural Midwest, they enter into most decisions that affect Latinos, as we found in our study.

1. Latino newcomers to Midwestern towns have just arrived from Mexico and are "illegal."

Some Latinos come directly from Mexico to the Midwest, but many were born in the United States or have spent many years in south Texas, Florida, and other states while working on farms and in other physically taxing labor.

For example, in meatpacking plants in Nebraska, Gouveia and Stull (1997) found that 41 percent of people came from California. Of all Latinos in the United States, according to the Current Population Survey in 2000, 61 percent had been born in this country and 74 percent of those born abroad had become naturalized citizens (Therrien and Ramirez 2001; see also Rosenbaum 1997 on Latinos in Michigan).

The Midwestern use of the term "Mexican" to apply to all Latinos reinforces the stereotype that all Latinos are immigrants, all of whom come from Mexico. The notion that they have no government authorization to work in the United States is closely tied to the assumption about their nationality. These notions form a basis for Anglo exploitation and denial of rights to Latinos.

2. Migration from Mexico to the Midwest started in recent years.

To the contrary, at the end of World War I, Midwestern beet sugar factories and other industries recruited workers in large numbers from Mexico (Valdés 1991:8, 2000a,b; see also García 1996 and Vargas 1993 on Latino migration to the Midwest). The sugar beet migration to the Midwest occurred from 1917 to 1929, with a brief hiatus during this period, and was followed by an anti–Mexican immigrant era throughout the 1930s, when immigrants were actually deported to Mexico, in many cases illegally. The Bracero Program followed, recruiting workers from Mexico for agricultural work throughout the United States (1943–1964); then another era began in which unskilled workers from Mexico could not obtain official permission to enter the country. Most recently, the Immigration Reform and Control Act of 1986 offered legal residency to some of those workers living and working in the United States without official permission. During part of the 1990s, the U.S. Immigration and Naturalization Service was commanded not to deport Latinos who lacked authorization as long as they held jobs. Mexican migration to the Midwest thus has continued for over a century, has usually occurred as a result of vigorous recruitment by employers, and has often contributed to economic growth in the region.

3. Latino newcomers do not speak English and do not want to learn it.

Most Anglos think that all Latinos speak only Spanish; some, however, speak no Spanish and many are bilingual. The view that Spanish monolinguals do not want to learn English is part of the ideology of some organizations, such as U.S. English, Inc., that have great credibility among the Anglo public. On the other hand, research shows that with more exposure to the United States, immigrants from Mexico improve English skills (Espinosa and Massey 1997), implying their willingness to learn the language.

Cole notes that the accusation that "aliens refuse to assimilate" has been made about "every new group of immigrants to arrive on U.S. shores" (1998:14). We have found consistently that Latino immigrants all want to learn English; however, they usually lack an effective way to do so. Latino immigrants all see learning English as a way to obtain better jobs and to deal more effectively with various situations in daily life.

4. They are the poorest of the poor; their living conditions at home are worse than those in the Midwest.

Those who arrive in the Midwest are not the poorest of the poor; the poorest cannot afford to travel (see Massey 1998 and Massey and Espinosa 1997 on those from Mexico). The newcomers tend to be members of the working poor if they are from south Texas, and some from Mexico are from better-off families who can afford to send them north. In some cases, their parents' homes in Mexico are considerably nicer and safer than the run-down Midwestern trailer parks catering to Latino newcomers. Latinos come to the rural Midwest with some resources and a strategy for survival; they usually have jobs waiting and a place to stay with relatives. To get to the Midwest, most Mexican Americans have to obtain a car that runs well enough to travel 1,700 miles and enough money to provide for some days without pay. Workers who come directly from Mexico usually pay their passage to travel directly to the town where they will work.

5. They want to stay separate from Anglos.

Anglo organizations do not invite Latinos to join (see Vargas 1993 on discrimination against Latino religious and social participation in community organizations by Midwestern Anglos). The exceptions are the few churches that have established separate Latino congregations. The language of Latino congregations is usually Spanish, making language a symbol and rationale for separation. Some Anglos have commented that they would not refuse Latinos membership in their organizations; however, they recruit new members through their social networks, which always exclude Latinos. Latinos thus have few ways of entering the Anglo social universe.

6. They love hard physical labor.

The Latinos in this study work hard and take pride in supporting themselves; however, they do not regard hard physical labor as ideal. Historically, they are known as very hard workers (Vargas 1993). The current high turnover in meatpacking plants (Gouveia and Stull 1997; Gouveia, Sanchez, and Saenz 2001) suggests that they move out of the most physically difficult and dangerous jobs when they can. They regard their jobs as backbreaking ("Se acaba uno" [You get worn out]), and they want their children to have less arduous jobs.

7. They love moving from place to place, producing high rates of turnover in factories.

Although Latino newcomers speak of the benefits of getting to know new places and people, many miss faraway family and home communities, whether in the United States or Mexico. They prefer not to live on the move; when they have an opportunity to work in one place year-round for decent wages, most tend to settle down, as seen in this study.

8. They come to live on welfare and are a drain on the economy.

In this study, we did not find people moving to the Midwest to live on welfare. Many Latino newcomers do not apply for all the services for which they are eligible. Recent analyses show that undocumented immigrants from Mexico pay more in taxes than they gain in benefits at the federal level, but the reverse is true for local government budgets (see Chapter 3; on southern California, see Chavez 1992:143, who reports that over half of the workers from Mexico and Central America interviewed in 1986 had taxes withheld, did not file federal tax forms, and thus forfeited refunds). Historically, immigrants from Mexico were the last to receive aid during the Great Depression (Vargas 1993).

9. They do not experience racism because Midwesterners are not racist, and certainly not against "Mexicans."

In this study, we found that many rural Midwesterners are people of goodwill, but some are not. We did not find one Latino who had not experienced racism in the Midwest, whether it was having "beans" yelled at them on the street (seen as silly by study participants) or being told, "Go back to Mexico." (See Burke and Goudy 1999; Vargas 1993.)

10. They are grateful for whatever they get and uncritical of their conditions and treatment.

The statements from Latinos in this study show that many have sophisticated, sociologically sound criticisms of the way the local society and economy work in their new communities. They are quite critical of power structures in the Midwest, south Texas, Florida, and Mexico.

CHAPTER TWO

Latinos in the Rural Midwest: The Twentieth-Century Historical Context Leading to Contemporary Challenges

Eileen Diaz McConnell

In the past, Latino immigrants tended to move to specific regions of the United States, and Mexicans tended to settle in the Southwest with the Mexican Americans who were already present in large numbers. In addition, the overwhelming majority of Latinos have tended to reside in urban areas; in 1990, more than 90 percent of the nation's Hispanics lived in metropolitan areas (Fuguitt 1995). Thus, researchers studying Mexican immigrants and Mexican Americans tended to focus their attention predominantly on the Southwest and on urban areas.[1]

Census 2000 data confirm, however, that Latino settlement in the United States has become diffuse in recent years. The movement of Latinos to the Midwest is one example. During the 1980s, the Latino population in the region grew by 800,000, accounting for the bulk of overall population growth in the Midwest (Aponte and Siles 1994; see also Guzmán 2001). This trend continued throughout the 1990s. The majority of Latinos in the Midwest, like those in other areas of the United States, continue to be urban dwellers, with large populations living in Chicago, Cleveland, Detroit, Gary, and Milwaukee (Santiago 1990). In recent years, however, scholars have noted the movement of Latinos to rural areas of the United States (Cromartie and Kandel 2002, 2003; Kandel and Cromartie 2003). Rochín (1995) notes that the nonmetropolitan Latino population grew 30 percent between 1980 and 1990.[2] This phenomenon has also been noted in the rural Midwest, where the rural Latino population increased from 3.1 percent to 3.9 percent during the 1980s (Fuguitt 1995). Indeed, 18 percent of Latinos in Nebraska and 15 percent in Iowa lived in rural areas in 1990 (Aponte and Siles 1994).[3] Rapid Latino growth continued in rural Midwestern areas during the 1990s, as discussed in Chapter 3 (Aponte 1999; Aponte and Siles 1997; Burke and Goudy 1999; Flora and Flora 1999; Gouveia and Stull, 1997; *Migration News*, January 2000). Consequently, many areas of the rural Midwest have more ethnic diversity than ever before.

This chapter reviews the historical context of the Latino experience in the rural Midwest. People of Mexican ethnicity will be the focus, because Mexicans and Mexican Americans comprise the majority of Midwestern Latinos (Aponte and Siles 1994; García 1996; Guzmán 2001; Guzmán and McConnell 2002). As Valdés (2000b) has noted, past studies describing the unfolding of Latino migration to the Midwestern United States tended to focus on the period between 1900 and the Great Depression (García 1996; Vargas 1993), though some span longer time periods (e.g., Cardenas 1976; Valdés 1991, 2000a). The journey that led to the migration of Latinos to the Midwest began before 1900 and continues to the present; thus, this chapter traces the history of Latinos in the rural Midwest beginning with the signing of the Treaty of Guadalupe Hidalgo (1848) and continues through the Legal Immigration and Family Equity Act of 2000 (LIFE Act). This chapter provides a historical context for examining the challenges confronting contemporary Latinos and the rural communities in which they reside.

Exploring the history of Latinos in the rural Midwest is important for several reasons. First, non-Latinos have numerous misperceptions about Latinos in the region. One such misperception is that the presence of Latinos in the Midwest is a new phenomenon. In fact, as described in "En Pocas Palabras I," Mexican immigrants and Mexican Americans first arrived before World War I. Since the very beginning, they have been visible contributors to the development of the Midwest. Another stereotype is that all rural Latinos are "field hands" (Rochín 1995); however, history shows that employment opportunities for Latinos in the rural Midwest have never been limited to agriculture. The recent influx of Latinos into the Midwest is related to these earlier periods of Latino migration and settlement in the region. Thus, tracing this history contextualizes the current phenomenon. Indeed, as this review will show, the historical experiences of Midwestern Latinos at the beginning of the twentieth century are strikingly similar to the situation faced by their counterparts today. Second, the experience of Latinos in the Midwest has been very different from that of their counterparts in other areas of the United States. Third, as Latinos begin to move into southeastern states such as Georgia and North Carolina (Camarota 2001; Guzmán 2001; Therrien and Ramirez 2001, table 8.1), research on the Midwestern experience may shed some light on what can be expected in these newer areas of settlement.

The Historical Context of Latino Migration to the Midwest

In 1821 the Spanish governor granted permission to three hundred families to settle in Texas; the families were led by Moses Austin, the father of Stephen F. Austin (Foley 1997:17–18). In the same year, the Mexican government, newly independent from Spain, continued providing land in Texas to Anglo immigrant settlers (ibid.). By 1836, 20,000 non-Latino settlers were living in the state, and some of them joined forces with the local people to defeat the Mexican Army and to declare Texas a republic (Foley 1997). The United States annexed Texas in 1845 (Foley 1997). (At that point, Texas occupied a small part of its current territory.) Not surprisingly, Mexico and the United States disagreed over the national boundaries (whether they followed the Nueces River or the Rio Grande in Texas) (Gutiérrez 1995). This disagreement became a pretext for the U.S.-Mexican War, which ended when the two governments signed the Treaty of Guadalupe Hidalgo in 1848. This treaty signed northern Mexico over to the United States and was the final step in the extraction of territory from Mexico by U.S. forces. The treaty proclaimed that the approximately 75,000 to 100,000 Mexicans living in the region could move south and remain Mexicans or remain in the area, in which case they would be considered full U.S. citizens (Gutiérrez 1995). Most remained in the United States, and their homelands, in Texas and elsewhere, became places in which they soon began to experience a great deal of discrimination (Foley 1997).

In the mid-1800s, there were no physical border markers separating the two countries, and international movement was common. Within a few decades, railroads linked central Mexico to the United States, facilitating the immigration of additional Mexicans to the United States (Gutiérrez 1995). The Mexican Revolution, from 1910 to 1917, impelled large numbers of Mexican citizens to migrate northward to escape the terrible political and economic conditions in their home country (Massey et al. 1987; Gutiérrez 1995). People of Mexican ethnicity tended to remain in the U.S. Southwest; however, eventually some were drawn to the Midwest because of changes in federal immigration policies, the northward reach of railroads, and growing employment opportunities in the region.

In the Midwest, after the 1840s, large forests were logged, and Anglos and Europeans established farms that prevented forest regrowth. Toward the end of the nineteenth century, with the increase in sugar consumption and the growing U.S. population, sugar beet farming became important in the Midwest, particularly in the Great Lakes states (Valdés 1991). Farmers found the physical labor required in their sugar beet fields difficult and refused to work close to the ground, stooping, squatting, or crawling on their knees. The companies that owned sugar refineries took up the work of recruiting workers for the sugar beet fields, and they often hired employment companies and others to bring workers to the Midwest (Valdés 1991).

Successive waves of immigrants from Europe worked on sugar beet "gangs" in the Midwest at the end of the nineteenth and in the early twentieth centuries (Valdés 1991). They included European-born women and children, followed by single Belgian men recruited from Midwestern cities, followed by eastern European immigrant families. Eastern European immigrants dominated the Midwestern agricultural labor force in the 1910s and 1920s. They included Europeans of German descent who had lived in Russia for several generations and were recruited by sugar-processing factories to work in the beet fields in the northern Midwest. Hungarian, Polish, Serbian, and other Slavic immigrants were also recruited from Midwestern cities to work in the fields (Valdés 1991).

European immigrants were thus the dominant labor force in Midwestern agriculture for many years. Two factors began to decrease their dominance in Midwestern agriculture. First, many had experienced upward mobility by the beginning of the twentieth century and no longer desired the low-paying jobs available in Midwestern agriculture (Vargas 1993). Second, the 1917 Immigration Act limited the number of Europeans entering the United States and thus further decreased the available European labor supply (Gutiérrez 1995). This act also ended the ability of immigrants to freely enter the United States.

Mexicans were exempt from the 1917 act (Alarcón 2000); therefore, employers began to turn to Mexican nationals to meet the increasing demand for labor across the United States (Vargas 1993), including the Midwest (García 1996; Rosenbaum 1997). Companies such as Michigan Sugar, Continental Sugar, and Columbia Sugar required large labor forces to harvest sugar beets (Valdés 1992). Other widespread agricultural employment options included harvesting cherries, peaches, and apples in Michigan and other Midwestern states (Rochín et al. 1989). In sum, agriculture played a key role in attracting Mexican immigrants to the rural Midwest in the early part of the twentieth century.

The overall U.S. economy was expanding during this time, as World War I required a large labor force to work in the industrial sector. Not surprisingly, industrial employment also drew Mexican immigrants to the Midwest. For example, by 1914 railroads linked Mexico with cities such as Kansas City, St. Louis, and Chicago, encouraging migration by Mexicans and Mexican Americans to the northern United States (García 1996). Mexican migration to these areas was encouraged, as the U.S. government did not yet consider Mexico-U.S. migration to be a problem.[4] Manufacturing employers also began to recruit Mexican immigrants and Mexican Americans to work in factories in the Midwest (Vargas 1993). Thus, employment opportunities for Latinos during this era included both agricultural jobs and employment in manufacturing firms such as Ford Motor Company, Inland Steel, and other companies in Michigan, Indiana, and Ohio (García 1996). In fact, by 1920 an industrial community in East Chicago had the densest concentration of Mexican-origin individuals in the country (García 1996).

Neither industrial nor agricultural sectors provided year-round work, as automobile companies stopped the assembly lines each year when they changed to the new models (Vargas 1993) and agricultural employment wound down with the end of the harvest season. Some Mexican Americans and Mexican immigrants returned to the Southwest seasonally in search of other employment. Others remained in the Midwest, especially entire families who had migrated to the Midwest together. The agricultural sector had encouraged this phenomenon, because families were considered stable yet inexpensive economic investments (García 1996). In the industrial sectors, while the majority of workers were male, their female partners often ran boardinghouses or other businesses (García 1996; Vargas 1993). Thus, many Latinos settled permanently in the Midwest during this period.

Mexican American and Mexican immigrant communities left their mark on the Midwest during the period leading up to the Great Depression. Indeed, many operated Latino-oriented restaurants, markets, boardinghouses, and barbershops (Vargas 1993). In addition, Mexicans participated in the religious life of Midwestern communities, especially in Detroit, by establishing Mexican Catholic societies in local Catholic churches. Eventually, Latinos raised money to build their own Catholic churches in the Midwest, partly because of ostracism by "white ethnic Catholics" (Vargas 1993:71). Such churches often were built in honor of the popular patron saint of Mexico, the Virgin of Guadalupe. Latinos also instituted mutual aid societies and civic organizations and celebrated Mexican holidays (García 1996; Vargas 1993). All such businesses, organizations, churches, and social events enhanced their visibility, contributed to the character of the area, and assisted the newcomers in their quest to remain connected with others. Many of these aspects of Latino settlement in the 1920s describe the current phenomena in the rural Midwest.

Building ethnic communities in the Midwest was essential in helping Latinos cope with the difficult conditions of the region. Latinos tended to receive the worst industrial jobs available: the work was noisy, the machinery and chemicals were dangerous, and accidents were common (Shapiro 1996). In addition, throughout the 1920s, companies increasingly sped up the assembly lines, which made the work even more repetitive and difficult (Vargas 1993). Further, Mexican immigrants and Mexican Americans were often brought in to serve as strikebreakers during events such as the 1919 steel strike in East Chicago (Shapiro 1996). Although many Latinos worked as strikebreakers unknowingly or refused to work as scabs once they learned of the strike, the situation fostered conflict with Midwestern natives (Vargas 1993). Additionally, housing was high in cost and poor in quality because of the demand for accommodation near the factories. Thus, establishing ethnic communities helped Mexican Americans and Mexican immigrants deal with the many hardships of this period.

Latinos experienced heightened discrimination during poor economic times despite the fact that they had been recruited to the region and many had lived in the area for years. Indeed, during the depression of 1920–1921, sugar beet farmers and factory employers fired many Mexicans. Immigration officials began sweeping areas such as Chicago and deporting all Mexicans who were unable to prove legal residence before 1921 (Vargas 1993). Mexicans were compelled to leave the Midwest again after the Great Depression began in 1929, because they were blamed for the terrible economic conditions and rampant unemployment. There were nationwide calls for Mexicans to be returned to Mexico, since many Anglos believed that government assistance and the few remaining jobs should go to Anglos (Vargas 1993). Consequently, there was intense pressure on employers to fire people of Mexican origin first and for local governments to withhold relief from Mexican citizens and Mexican Americans. Eventually, even Catholic pastors and Mexican consuls in areas such as Detroit became convinced of the need for Mexican immigrants to return to Mexico (Vargas 1993).

Local governments dealt with anti-Mexican sentiment by instituting repatriation programs that provided rail transportation to Mexico at reduced rates (Vargas 1993). These programs were intended to provide Mexican nationals with the opportunity to return home voluntarily. Some Mexican citizens returned to their home country as a strategy to deal with the high cost of living in Midwestern urban areas and to be closer to their extended families during the difficult period. Some enforcers of repatriation programs were overzealous, however, and began to round up individuals forcibly and send them south in boxcars. They often did not differentiate between Mexican nationals and Mexican Americans (Griswold del Castillo and De León 1996; Vargas 1993); thus, some U.S. citizens and U.S.-born children of Mexican immigrants were sent to Mexico, some going to the country for the first time (Valdés 1992). Approximately half a million people, one-third of those of Mexican ethnicity living in the United States, were deported to Mexico during this period (Shapiro 1996). In sum, the 1920–1921 depression, the Great Depression of 1929, and repatriation programs instituted during these periods greatly decreased the Mexican population in the Midwest, as in the rest of the country (García 1979). Nevertheless, some stayed in the region to ride out the economic downturns.

Labor shortages during World War II brought many Mexicans and Mexican Americans to the Midwest once again (Bustamante 1973; García 1979). For example, many Latinos worked in defense factories during the war era (Rosenbaum 1997). Agricultural workers were desperately needed because many native-born individuals left the fields for urban areas during the early 1940s (Gutiérrez 1995). Consequently, the United States established a guest-worker program during the war (Alarcón 2000). The Mexican and U.S. governments signed a bilateral agreement for the Emergency Farm Labor Program in 1942, which provided six-month contracts for Mexican laborers to work in U.S. agriculture (Gutiérrez 1995). Later called the Bracero Program, the agreement called for standardized wages and required the employer to provide transportation between Mexico and the U.S. destination and housing and food at a reasonable cost (González 1993; Gutiérrez 1995). While the program was planned as an emergency measure, pressure from the agricultural sector after World War II led to various extensions of the program through 1964.

As a result of the Bracero Program, many Mexican immigrants continued to work seasonally in agriculture, as their six-month contracts were renewed year after year (Valdés 1992). The passage of amendments to the Immigration and Nationality Act (INA) in 1965 allowed many former braceros and their families to apply for citizenship under the legal provisions of entry for family members (Massey et al. 1987; Mines and Massey 1985). In fact, over the next 15 years, more than 1 million Mexican immigrants gained documents giving them permanent residence in the United States (Alarcón 2000; Passel and Woodrow 1987). Documentation undoubtedly allowed more freedom of movement and greater efficiency in the use of binational networks. Thus, as a result of earlier migration from the Southwest and immigration from Mexico, Latinos in the late twentieth century were able to establish social networks that linked the traditional areas where Mexican Americans lived in the Southwest with the rural Midwest.[5] The existence of these social networks stimulated Latino population growth in later decades.

Early agricultural and industrial employment opportunities, the Bracero Program, and the 1965 Immigration and Nationality Act amendments thus greatly increased the number of foreign-born Latinos in the United States, including the rural Midwest.[6] Indeed, by the 1960s, Mexicans had acquired relatively lengthy experience with the Midwest through traveling back and forth or settling in the region with their families. Puerto Ricans and Cubans were also firmly established in the Midwest by this time. Many Latinos went on to have Midwestern-born children, whom Valdés (1992) calls the "third generation" of Latinos in the Midwest.

Employment in agriculture, political resettlement, and social networks were not the only explanations for Latino population growth in the Midwest. Indeed, the role of manufacturing in attracting Latinos to the Midwest should not be underestimated. The Midwest has long been a core area in the economy of the United States, offering well-paid positions to those with few skills (Frey 1987). In fact, one-third of all manufacturing jobs from 1950 to 1970 were located in the Midwest (Saenz and Cready 1996). As they had in agriculture, American employers aggressively recruited Mexican immigrants and Mexican Americans to work in the steel and auto industries of Indiana, Michigan, and Illinois during and after World War II (Griswold Del Castillo and De León 1996). Moreover, corporate canneries—for example, Green Giant, Campbell's Soup, and Del Monte—had opened in the Midwest by this time and required more workers than the available labor supply in the area could provide (Rochín et al. 1989).

All in all, the largest flows of Latinos to the Midwest before the 1980s occurred between 1916–1928 and 1942–1964 (Betancur 1996). Though fewer migrants arrived after 1965, many continued to live in the Midwest because they did not have money to return to their places of origin, were encouraged to stay by their employers, and had formed tight-knit Midwestern communities (Rosenbaum 1997).[7] At that point, then, they had become integral members of communities in the United States.

The economic situation in the Midwest took a sharp turn in the following decades. Indeed, the region lost approximately 17 percent of all manufacturing jobs between 1970 and 1988 (Santiago 1990). Latinos were particularly affected, and they averaged unemployment rates of 12 percent during the 1970s and 1980s (Santiago 1990). Despite the high unemployment rate overall, Latinos continued to arrive in the region during this period. The expansion of service employment in the Midwest may be one factor underlying this migration of Latinos. Indeed, the number of jobs in the service sector in the region doubled during the 1970s and 1980s (Santiago 1990). As in the past, the most common jobs for Latinos included domestic service, commercial janitorial services, and positions in the restaurant industry (Binational Study 1997; Bustamante 1990; Massey et al. 1987).

Legislation passed during the 1980s also influenced Latinos in the Midwest. The most significant was the Immigration Reform and Control Act (IRCA) passed in 1986. IRCA was called an "amnesty" program because it was set up to confer legal status on a large number of undocumented workers in the United States; however, extensive evidence was required to obtain documentation (e.g., rent receipts proving residence in the United States for a five-year period).[8] One particularly significant program stipulated by IRCA was the Special Agricultural Workers (SAW) program, which provided undocumented individuals working in agriculture with legal residency (Chavez 1992; Martin 1996). Once formerly undocumented individuals were granted amnesty, they were able to sponsor additional family members to become legal residents of the country under the 1965 amendments of INA. Indeed, because of IRCA, at least 3 million Mexican immigrants became legal residents (Alarcón 2000). IRCA's legalization of many formerly undocumented individuals in the United States contributed to the growth of the Latino population in the Midwest (U.S. Commission on Agricultural Workers 1992) and elsewhere.

IRCA has had numerous unintended consequences for the United States and, consequently, the rural Midwest. Although IRCA temporarily decreased undocumented Mexican immigration (Donato et al. 1992), in 1989 undocumented migration increased once again (Bean et al. 1990). Thus, IRCA did not stop future undocumented immigration as intended. Instead, IRCA led to the diffusion of migrants to new areas of the United States because undocumented agricultural workers left for the Midwest and other areas to avoid detection (U.S. Commission on Agricultural Workers 1992). In addition, the density of Mexican immigrants and other Latinos in the Southwest resulting from widespread legalization under IRCA saturated the labor market and drove down wages (Binational Study 1997). This drop in wages also encouraged migration of Latinos to the Midwest. Similarly, because IRCA increased the supply of documented agricultural workers, the wages of all agricultural workers shrank (Gutiérrez 1995). Indeed, IRCA contributed to the sharp increase in rural poverty in the United States after 1986 (Martin 1996).[9] Thus, IRCA increased undocumented immigration, influenced the dispersion of undocumented immigrants and other Latinos to places such as the rural Midwest, and increased poverty in such areas.

Additional Latinos arrived in the Midwest during the 1980s independently of IRCA. As in earlier decades, agricultural employers continued to aggressively recruit Latinos from Texas and the South to work in seasonal agriculture (Rosenbaum 1997). In fact, one survey of Michigan service providers conducted in 1989 documents that most migrant farmworkers in Michigan were of Mexican origin (Rochín et al. 1989). Moreover, continuous migration to the area expanded social networks even further, which linked "older" migrants with native residents and also drew "new" migrants to the area. Indeed, direct contacts between growers and migrant workers established after many years of agricultural specialization continue to exert a significant "pull" force attracting migrant workers from border areas to the Midwest (Rochín et al. 1989). This combination of factors may explain why farms in the Midwest remained a stepping-stone to settlement during the 1980s and 1990s, despite the seasonality of agriculture and decreasing wages.

The 1990s saw additional changes in the landscape of the Midwest. Most significantly, employment opportunities in the meatpacking industry expanded dramatically in the rural Midwest as part of the industry's rural industrialization strategy (Broadway 1995). Growth in this industry in the Midwest mirrored changes occurring in the nonmetropolitan United States as a whole, as manufacturing jobs in nonmetropolitan areas increased by 5.4 percent nationwide between 1990 and 1997 (U.S. Department of Agriculture 2000). This strategy involves the decision by companies to relocate their urban meatpacking plants to rural counties in Kansas, Nebraska, and Iowa (Broadway 1995). Several factors explain the relocation of meatpacking operations to rural areas. Most importantly, rural areas have cheaper land for building factories and rural workers are less likely to be unionized and more willing to accept lower wages than their urban peers (Stanley 1992). In addition, technological improvements, such as vacuum packing and refrigerated trucks, make it possible for meatpacking operations to be located far from metropolitan markets (Martin et al. 1996). Consequently, many plants have relocated to areas closer to the source of feed for animals (Broadway 1995). At the same time, increased mechanization has limited the need for highly skilled workers. Therefore, plants can draw from locals or recruit low-skilled persons from elsewhere to fill the plant floor.

The economic situation in many Midwestern communities improved during the decade, leading to a report published by the U.S. Census Bureau, *Rust Belt Rebounds* (U.S. Census Bureau 1998). Indeed, much of the rural Midwest continued to boast very low unemployment rates (under 4 percent) at the end of the 1990s, increasing the likelihood that Latinos would secure employment in the region (Martin et al. 1996). A low unemployment rate requires that employers offer incentives to increase their workforce. Employers in the manufacturing sector have responded by providing incentives such as starting bonuses (Gouveia and Saenz 1999; Martin et al. 1996), on-site day care (Gouveia and Stull 1997), and bonuses to workers for recruiting friends and family as employees (Fink 1998; Griffith 1995).

During the 1990s, many rural communities believed that the relocation of new meatpacking and other food processing plants would further improve local economies (Gouveia and Stull 1995). Some companies, however, insisted on tax subsidies from state and local communities before relocating. Communities agreed because they believed locals would receive jobs that paid well and the local economy would improve. Consequently, communities often provided special incentives such as suspended property taxes and the creation of tax-dollar-supported infrastructure to benefit new plants (Broadway 1995). At first, locals did work in the plants, but meatpacking jobs are typically poorly paid, physically demanding, and in some cases physically dangerous, leading to high turnover in the local workforce. As a result, there was a continuing need for new employees for the plants, and companies looked beyond the local workforce.

Following the strategies employed 50 years earlier, many companies recruited workers from Mexico and the border states to fill the plant floors in rural areas of the Midwest (Broadway 1995). Employers offered incentives to draw more workers, a strategy that is especially effective for attracting Latinos, who often are members of extensive social networks composed of relatives and friends (Green et al. 1999). These social ties span large geographic areas. A substantial proportion of the Latinos in rural Midwestern plants had previously worked in California (Gouveia and Stull 1997), though others arrived in the rural Midwest directly from the U.S. border areas or by slowly moving northward for jobs (García 1979, 1996).

Employer preferences also played into the shift to a heavily Latino workforce (Stull et al. 1992). Gouveia and Stull (1997) report that the first new beef plant to be built in the United States in many years opened in Lexington, Nebraska, in 1990. While many of the first employees were non-Hispanic, within a few months the majority of new hires were Latino. Latinos are relatively cheap sources of labor who potentially can provide employers with access to dozens of additional workers; thus, employers may be especially interested in hiring them. Latino immigrants generally work in nonsupervisory positions; many employers still prefer Anglo or bilingual individuals for higher level positions (Gouveia and Stull 1995).

Agricultural employment continued to draw native and foreign-born Latinos to Midwestern states, such as Michigan, during the 1990s (Heiderson and Leon 1996). Furthermore, manufacturing employment opportunities, direct recruitment by employers, and employer preferences for Mexican immigrants also attracted Latinos to rural communities in Iowa (Martin et al. 1996) and Indiana (Aponte 1999) during the decade (Gouveia and Stull 1995; Martin et al. 1996).

The increase in Latinos in the rural Midwest also may be fueled by the affordability of the region compared to the Southwest. The rural Midwest has remained relatively inexpensive, and this, coupled with somewhat better pay and more stable jobs than other regions, makes the Midwest relatively attractive. In general, the cost of living in nonmetropolitan areas is approximately 16 percent less than that in urban areas (Nord 2003). Moreover, Bureau of Labor Statistics data indicate that the consumer price index was lower in the nonmetropolitan Midwest than in other regions and the nation as a whole during the 1990s.[10]

As in earlier periods, legislation shaped the development of Latino migration to the Midwest during the 1990s. The passage of Proposition 187 in California in 1994, a law intended to restrict health care and education for undocumented immigrants, also may have contributed to Latino population growth in the Midwest, perceived as having a less hostile political climate (Guzmán and McConnell 2002). In addition, rigorous border enforcement programs were established in many southwestern states over the decade, such as Operation Gatekeeper in San Diego in 1996, which may have also encouraged both native and foreign-born Latinos to move to regions with less surveillance (Bustamante et al. 1997; Martin 1997).

Federal legislation passed during the 1990s has had additional effects on Latinos. One example is the Illegal Immigration Reform and Immigrant Responsibility Act (IIRIRA) passed in 1996. IIRIRA became law partly due to political pressure related to the amnesty of many undocumented immigrants through IRCA. The primary focus of IIRIRA was to tighten controls at the border and to increase funding for border enforcement activities (Binational Study 1997). Under IIRIRA, undocumented immigrants were eligible to apply for legal permanent residence if they had entered the United States before December 1988 and submitted their application by January 1998. The conditions imposed by IIRIRA encourage migrants to stay in the United States rather than migrate between the United States and Mexico (Binational Study 1997).

Other recent federal legislation has also encouraged undocumented immigrants to stay in the country, including the rural Midwest. For instance, the Legal Immigration and Family Equity Act of 2000 (LIFE Act) extended the deadline of Section 245(i), a provision of the Immigrant and Nationality Act of 1952 that allowed some undocumented immigrants to get Green Cards if certain criteria were met. The LIFE Act extended the IIRIRA deadline for application for legal permanent residence from January 1998 to April 2001. Eligible individuals had to be physically present in the United States in December 2000 and at the time of filing (INS 2001b). The LIFE Act created new visas that provide legal status and work authorization to some relatives of legal permanent residents while the applicants are in the United States. Thus, legislation such as Proposition 187, IIRIRA, and the LIFE Act, as well as INS surveillance activities, have influenced the flow of foreign-born Latinos into the United States (Massey 1998), their dispersion across the country, and their plans to remain in the United States.

In response to the growth of Latinos in the Midwest during the 1990s, recent Immigration and Naturalization Service (INS) efforts have begun to focus specifically on undocumented Latino immigrants in the region. For instance, between 1992 and 1997, the INS raided 15 Iowa and Nebraska plants and arrested 1,000 undocumented employees (Aponte and Siles

1997). Moreover, the INS established an ambitious project called Operation Vanguard in Nebraska in 1998. The project compared the employee records of Nebraska meatpacking plants with Social Security Administration records and then requested interviews with those employees with inconsistent records (*RMN* 2000). As of June 1999, the INS had subpoenaed the records of 20,000 meatpacking employees, identified approximately 3,500 discrepancies, and arrested 30 individuals (Gouveia and Saenz 1999). Plans to expand the operation to other states are currently on hold because of privacy objections made by the Social Security Administration and complaints by meatpacking plants (*RMN* 2000).

Recent legislation has made life more difficult for Latinos in other ways. For example, IIRIRA restricted the ability of undocumented immigrants to get drivers' licenses and obtain Social Security benefits and other cash assistance. Further, the passage of Proposition 187 in California in 1994 deterred many undocumented people from seeking medical care or education for their children (Martin 1995), though others applied for citizenship to ensure access to these resources (Massey 1998). While there is an injunction against most terms of Proposition 187, the combination of increasingly restrictive immigration policies and state laws seems to be related to a growing anti-Latino immigrant sentiment in recent years (Alvarez and Butterfield 2000; Wilson 2000). Because many Anglos do not differentiate between Latino citizens and noncitizens, the situation affects all Latinos. Anti-Latino sentiment has grown in all areas of the United States, and it may be especially prevalent in places where long-term residents have had limited personal exposure to Latinos, such as the rural Midwest.

Despite recent legislation leading to the deportation of immigrants, the denial of services to the undocumented, and deteriorating working conditions and wages in the agricultural, service, and manufacturing sectors, the native and foreign-born Latino population increased rapidly in the rural Midwest at the turn of the twenty-first century. Undoubtedly, factors such as growing employment opportunities, a relatively affordable standard of living, and existing social networks contributed to this phenomenon.

In sum, the growing Latino population in the rural Midwest produces particular challenges for both Latino newcomers and long-term residents. These challenges include healthcare, education, housing, and social relations between Latinos and others (Benson 1996b; Burke and Goudy 1999; Flora and Flora 1999; Grey 2001; Hackenberg and Kukulka 1995; Stanley 1992; Stull and Broadway 1995). Factors such as community preparation for

Latino population growth, employer policies, the composition of the labor force, employee turnover, the permanence of the newcomers, and stereotypes of Latinos all influence the extent to which they can be successfully incorporated into the community.

Summary

As this historical review demonstrates, Latinos had a rural presence in the Midwest for most of the twentieth century. At the beginning of the twentieth century, auto companies, steel plants, and the sugar beet industry recruited Mexican immigrants and Mexican Americans to the Midwest. Discrimination against newcomers is historically linked to the strength of the economy and access to jobs, and indeed, during times of economic hardship, many Latinos were voluntarily and involuntarily deported to Mexico (Vargas 1993). Further, subtle and not-so-subtle discrimination led Latinos to create social institutions parallel to those of Anglos, with their own businesses, organizations, and churches. This strategy served to set Latino culture apart from that of the Anglo mainstream and to create a situation in which anti-Latino sentiment could easily grow.

Latinos are even more visible in the contemporary Midwestern landscape. Although many continue seasonal residence because of employment in agriculture, others have moved into stable, year-round manufacturing employment in rural communities. As in the past, recent anti-Latino sentiment and overt discrimination against Latinos may wax and wane with the strength of the economy and the availability of well-paid jobs for the Anglo majority.

The challenges that contemporary Latinos face in the rural Midwest are strikingly similar to the experiences of Midwestern Latinos at the beginning of the twentieth century. It is clear, however, that Latinos are in the region to stay, even after accounting for the high turnover of Latinos in some nonmetropolitan locales. Indeed, Latinos will continue to be attracted to the rural Midwest by employment opportunities, direct recruitment by employers, and social networks, even as government surveillance and deportation activities increase in the region. Nevertheless, widespread recognition of the historical and contemporary contributions of Latinos to the region would do much to decrease hostility and aid the political, social, and economic incorporation of Latinos into the rural Midwest.

The Battle for Chapita Hills
Catalina Burillo and Ann V. Millard

Among the farms and rolling hills of Oceana County, not far from the
broad, sandy beaches of Lake Michigan, near the small town of Shelby,
a winding road leads to a set of neat, two-story apartments. With well-
kept lawns and neatly placed sidewalks, the apartments fit in with local
architecture. They are surrounded by children playing. Teenagers come
home from high school and afternoon jobs; adults return from work
and grocery shopping. It is hard to believe that this tranquil place was
the subject of a community battle two decades ago.
Burillo, field notes

The fight over Chapita Hills Apartments exemplifies one of the explosive
issues in the rural Midwest: low-income housing for Latinos. Chapita Hills
Apartments were built in Shelby, Michigan, as transitional housing for agricultural workers who were moving to the area to live year-round. The farmworkers were nearly all Mexicans and Mexican Americans, and local Anglos
misconstrued the apartments as reserved for Hispanics. This Anglo perception, common in many Midwestern towns regarding government programs
to assist farmworkers, tended to play into local political struggles, as in the
case of Chapita Hills.

We assembled this account from newspaper reports, editorials, letters to
the editor, and interviews about the proposal to build the apartments. Those
eligible for housing as "agricultural laborers" were to be people moving to
the area to work in fields, orchards, vegetable and fruit packing houses, and
food processing factories. Throughout the Midwest, nearly all of these jobs
are filled by Latinos—Mexican Americans and Mexicans. Although many
are factory workers, they are classified as agricultural workers under some
government programs, as long as their factory is on a farm that produces
crops.

Controversy over Chapita Hills began in the early spring of 1981, when
a nonprofit organization, Michigan Economics for Human Development
(MEHD), produced plans to build the apartments. MEHD applied for

$900,000 in federal grants and loans to build the housing. Opposing residents formed the Shelby Concerned Citizens Committee ("the committee" or "CCC"). These organizations led the opposing factions in the battle over the project.

A Shelby farm owner, William Field, began the opposition with a letter to the editor saying, "The data presented by the MEHD [to justify building the apartments] was one-sided and obtained from sources that they knew would be beneficial to their application" (*Oceana Herald Journal,* March 5, 1981). Field invited farmers to contact him and express their opinions of the housing plan.

The committee soon conducted a survey of farmers and farm laborers who lived year-round in the county. Field tried to disprove the need for the housing with the survey results. Also, the committee's lawyer sent a letter to the village council that pointed out various discrepancies in zoning procedures. In addition, the committee questioned the tax status of the housing complex. They argued that Chapita Hills was a waste of taxpayers' dollars because there would not be enough tenants. Furthermore, they argued that Shelby already had sufficient housing for farm laborers and their families.

At a meeting held February 13, 1981, in the Shelby Village Hall, some residents objected to the Chapita Hills plan, claiming there was a high local unemployment rate and a decreasing need for farm help due to mechanization. They argued that it was illogical to encourage people to stay in an area where there was no work (*Oceana Herald Journal,* March 17, 1981). The Shelby Concerned Citizens Committee also stated that the duplexes were not consistent with the single-family dwellings in the neighborhood, and they expressed concern that property values might drop. Whether the storm-water holding ponds at the project would be safe and reliable was another concern of the Chapita Hills opponents.

Grover Merrill, a Shelby business manager, claimed that a housing complex only for farm laborers would be discriminatory and stated, "There are low income people working in small local factories who too should be considered" (*Oceana Herald Journal,* March 12, 1981).

During the 16-month battle between the Shelby Concerned Citizens Committee and MEHD, funds for the housing project were halted several times. The Oceana County Board of Commissioners asked for a temporary halt of the federal funds in response to two resolutions. Those attempting to halt the project also claimed that the rezoning for the duplexes was improper; however, the village attorney said, "It's up to the landowner to insure the zoning procedure and not the village [of Shelby]" (*Muskegon Chronicle,* March 18, 1981). State Congressman Vander Jagt stated that the funding would be delayed, however, "until a full review of the application, zoning requirements, and other concerns have been completed" (*Oceana Herald Journal,* April 9, 1981). The Farmers' Home Administration (FmHA) also stopped the funding until MEHD met "the requirement of having a membership with a variety of interests in the Shelby area" (*Oceana Herald Journal,* March 25, 1982). Processing of the funding resumed two months later, when MEHD added new members from the Shelby area. Names of these new members have been protected from public disclosure.

Field, speaking for the Concerned Citizens Committee, reported that 38 farmers were against the project and that no one who had called him was in favor of it. The CCC requested that FmHA conduct an impartial survey on a "housing need that doesn't exist" (*Muskegon Chronicle,* March 18, 1981). Then, the CCC was given four weeks to "disprove the statistics used by MEHD to obtain their grant" (*Oceana Herald Journal,* March 17, 1981). The CCC was apparently unable to provide convincing evidence that the project was not needed, but the committee continued to argue that the property zoning did not allow for multiple-family housing units.

Phillip Roberts, state director for the U.S. Department of Agriculture, refused to stop FmHA funds for the project. He stated that the CCC had not supported their argument factually, that it was "obviously an emotional issue, and that the CCC doesn't understand the problem or is unwilling to accept the facts" (*Oceana Herald Journal,* May 6, 1981).

The project continued, with a firm in Ludington, Michigan, winning the contract for construction. The village gave final approval for a zoning permit, and the contractor applied for building permits. Meanwhile, the CCC continued to fight to halt the project. Ed Spiech, attorney for MEHD, warned, "The first amendment provides for the right of free speech, but persons cannot interfere with contractual relations unless they have an interest in it. They should be aware we may take the offensive" (*Oceana Herald Journal,* October 15, 1981).

A federal district court judge cleared the way for financing Chapita Hills when he denied a request for a preliminary injunction filed by the CCC. The judge's decision followed a 10-hour hearing over two days in Kalamazoo, Michigan. Judge Enslen also stated that the five MEHD members from the

Shelby area, out of the total membership of 26, did reflect a "variety of interests" (*Oceana Herald Journal,* June 21, 1982).

After a battle lasting almost two years, construction was completed. The complex consists of 12 duplexes with a total of 24 units. Each unit has two, three, or four bedrooms. The original plan called for six townhouse buildings, but they were redesigned as duplexes because the property had been zoned for two-family, not multiple-family, dwellings.

The apartments are attractively designed in two-story buildings constructed to blend with local architecture. In early 1983, Chapita Hills was ready for occupancy, and the first tenants were expected to move in within a few weeks (*Oceana Herald Journal,* January 27, 1983). According to the *Muskegon Chronicle,* however, on August 2, 1983, six months after completion, Chapita Hills was still empty. Petra Villa, manager of the Hart office of MEHD, stated that everything was in order, but the application process for tenants was very lengthy. Ms. Villa commented that "applications for the housing can be as long as 18 pages" (*Muskegon Chronicle,* August 2, 1983).

According to another article, some vandalism had occurred at the complex sometime after construction; however, according to Mike Uriegas, director of MEHD, the damages were slight. In the article, Uriegas wrapped up his interview about Chapita Hills by saying, "It's there to help people in the community and so I think it's for the whole community" (*Muskegon Chronicle,* September 6, 1983).

Nowadays at Chapita Hills, there is a one-year waiting list for an apartment. According to Olga Herrera, resident manager, in 2000 the waiting list included 27 families. "That's a low number," she said, "basically because we've had such a huge turnover this year; usually we have 40 to 50 families on the waiting list." Herrera, who had been resident manager for nearly 12 years, stated in an interview (with Burillo) that Chapita Hills stayed full consistently. "Currently we have five empty units, which is a first. However, these units will be filled just as soon as the fix-up and cleanup of the vacated apartments is complete. I'm very proud of the families, because all but one [who vacated apartments] this year have bought their own homes. That's about 20 families who did so in 1998 and 1999. In the 12 years I've been here, every year more families apply."

A survey in 1991, eight years after the completion of Chapita Hills, showed that the shortage of housing for farmworkers persisted in the state. As one respondent remarked, "There is work, but no place to live" (Rochín et al. 1989:61). As noted by Ehrenreich, the national low-income housing market has worsened, as "expenditures on public housing have fallen since the 1980s, and the expansion of public rental subsidies came to a halt in the mid-1990s" (2001:201).

Latino newcomers are often blamed for living in substandard housing, ruining the appearance of Midwestern towns. When new low-income housing is proposed, however, some local residents go to great lengths to prevent construction. Typically, in our community studies we found that Anglos do not criticize the employers and landlords who create the conditions under which Latinos work and live in their communities.

Chapita Hills has a subsidized housing formula that bases a family's rent on 30 percent of their income. Income is defined to include the earnings of adults in the household but not the wages of any minors who are employed. Also, according to Herrera, "Government assistance, or 'disability income,' for a disabled minor or adult is considered part of the family income for calculating the rent they will owe."

Qualifying for a lease at Chapita Hills requires a "substantial" amount of earnings from agricultural work. The initial lease period is for one year; thereafter tenants can rent on a monthly basis. "I always ask the families if they're planning on staying year-round. Out of 79 families this past year, only 2 planned to return [to south Texas]. However, many families on the waiting list have already returned [to south Texas] because they can't find housing," adds Herrera.

"Basically, the first year most families who move in can afford to pay the rent. Having a place to stay year-round helps the families move out of the fields, in some cases, and into [food] processing plants, for example. Usually after the first year, families living in Chapita Hills can afford to save money for a down payment on a house," adds Herrera.

"I recently was talking with a local realtor to see if houses for sale on the market could be rented to families needing housing, and the realtor commented to me that nine out of ten houses sold in the area are being bought by Hispanics. That's great," she added.

When Herrera was asked about the current general opinion of the townspeople of Shelby, she replied, "Once in a great while, you still hear something negative. But on the whole, the businesspeople of Shelby have said that Chapita Hills has helped the Shelby community a lot. Opinions have changed since the early days of Chapita Hills."

In other rural Midwestern communities, the controversy over housing for Latino newcomers continues, often resulting in rejection. In 2000, for example, a rural newspaper in Ohio published, "Ulery Gives Up Plan for Migrant Housing: Proposal Creates Uproar in Limecrest" (Cover 2000). A flier had circulated through the community to marshal protest at a meeting about the proposed housing on January 24 (flier collected by our research team). Headed "Attention," the flier stated:

> To all Clark Shawnee Residents,
> You need to be aware that Ulery's Greenhouse is planning the building of a migrant work camp at the corner of Highview and York (ball field). Our concerns are these:
>   1. Exploitation, slave labor.
>   2. Over crowding of our school.
>   3. Property value.
>   4. Crime rate.
>   5. Loss of jobs.
> There will be a meeting held on January 24, 2000 at 2681 May Street. 7:00 PM. Please try to attend.

For all those considering the issues of housing and low-income Latino workers, this list has elements of truth. The focus of rural people on the housing as the battleground, however, implies a "not in my backyard" approach.

In this case, the greenhouse company had planned to build a one-story apartment building on company land to house ten migrant workers and their families. Community members had not been consulted about the plan for the housing, and when they found out about it they protested, and the company agreed not to proceed with the construction. This situation was somewhat different from that in Oceana County, as the Ulery Greenhouse Company wanted to bring in workers for eight months of the year, not year-round. This case, nonetheless, illustrates the contentiousness of the issue of housing, as it highlights one of the human sides of the recruitment of low-income Latino workers to rural communities.

CHAPTER THREE

Latinos and the Changing Demographic Fabric of the Rural Midwest

Jorge Chapa, Rogelio Saenz, Refugio I. Rochín,

and Eileen Diaz McConnell

Latinos and Rural Economic Change

While policy makers, advocates, and analysts today recognize that farming is no longer the dominant source of economic activity in rural America, relatively little emphasis is placed on the "new agents" of agriculture: the thousands of workers, primarily Latino workers, laboring in large, recently built agro-industrial plants. Despite popular views to the contrary, many of the newly arrived Latino employees are settling in rural communities of the Midwest.

Latinos are becoming a major part of rural America. The growth of the Latino population in rural localities is intimately linked with the restructuring of agriculture and food processing. The farm crisis of the 1980s, resulting from farmers' high levels of debt, poor markets, and bankruptcies of many family farms, produced a loss of rural population in many regions. Small towns such as Waterloo, Marshalltown, and Columbus Junction in Iowa; Lexington, Nebraska; and Garden City, Kansas, located in the midst of hog and cattle country, have seen their Latino population grow from about 4 percent to upwards of 50 percent in less than ten years. These communities developed dependence on large meat processing plants for their survival after the 1980s farm crisis, and the plants have, in turn, become dependent on a labor force of Latino newcomers—primarily from Mexico, and also from Central America and the United States. Today, Latino population growth is singled out as the most important factor behind the first net population gains since the farm crisis in states such as Nebraska. Similar shifts are observed in poultry processing communities in Willmar and Marshall, Minnesota, where Latino newcomers are becoming the majority labor force. In Adrian and Holland, Michigan, and Toledo, Ohio, Latinos have established their presence over decades. Recently, however, these locales have also drawn Latino newcomers, increasing their Latino concentration. Latino growth results not only from natural increase (i.e., births in excess of deaths) but also from in-migration of people who find employment in labor-intensive businesses, such as food processing and plant nurseries.

Researchers in California have focused on rural towns of California's major agricultural areas that have become "Mexicanized"; that is, through a combination of immigration, high Latino fertility, and the continued decline of the white rural population through out-migration and deaths, a number of towns now have populations that are preponderantly Mexican-origin Latinos. These agricultural towns of California are harboring major social problems in progress or waiting to happen. The high poverty rates, low levels of education, low levels of government resources, and the concentration of agricultural workers who earn low incomes and face seasonal unemployment all point to difficult futures for the residents and their children. The low property values and incomes of the residents lead to low budgets for local governments. In contrast to Texas colonias that were built without drinking water and wastewater systems, electric power, or adequate roads, these California colonias once had a standard infrastructure but are losing the tax base to maintain it (Allensworth and Rochín 1999).

One of the major questions addressed by this study is whether this process of "Mexicanization" is occurring in the rural Midwest. Numerous rural towns in this region have experienced a sudden influx of Mexican Americans and Mexican immigrants, usually caused by expanding food processing facilities or light industry. The new residents can strain available housing and also place demands on schools and social services that are completely unprepared to effectively meet the needs of new Spanish-speaking residents and their children. This study carefully documents these trends; however, whether they are leading to Mexicanization is another issue.

Case studies since 1990 have documented the dramatic impacts of immigration and changing ethnicity in specific rural places, brought about by changes in the meatpacking industry (e.g., Amato 1996; Benson 1996b; Gouveia and Stull 1995; on demographic changes before 1990, see also Aponte 1995 and Huang and Orazem 1996). These studies agree that communities experiencing increased Latino settlement have not been prepared for the consequent demands for housing, schooling, translators, and community specialists and services. Furthermore, many local, state, and federal government policy responses to these changes have been reactive or have brought about reactionary consequences, such as the growing presence of U.S. immigration agents in places such as Cedar Rapids, Iowa. Newspapers often suggest that the economic consequences of rapid demographic change from new ethnic groups are negative, despite some economic benefits brought by increased employment, agro-industrial development, and local population growth. Places such as Marshall, Minnesota, and Lexington, Nebraska, have held community awareness programs to create a dialogue between Latinos and local leaders. In their own ways, they want to welcome Latinos but are questioning the best way to do so (Amato 1996; Martin et al. 1996).

Global trends include increasing mobility and migration of people and industry. Immigration to the United States is at its highest point ever in terms of absolute numbers, and is increasingly from Latin America and Asia, rather than Europe (Rumbaut 1996). At least 10 percent of the growth of the U.S. labor supply in recent years has come from Mexican immigrants, producing a greater impact on the U.S. economy than U.S.-Mexico trade or direct Mexican investment (Bustamante et al. 1992).

At the same time, rural America is going through a period of economic restructuring, resulting in greater economic polarization of both people and places. Pockets of poverty and extreme wealth are emerging, reducing regional homogeneity and the size of the middle class. Local policies are being developed in line with these trends. Many policies related to Latino newcomers, however, appear to be reactionary and destructive.

Since the 1980s, the Midwest has received substantial migration of Mexican Americans from the Southwest, as well as increasing immigration directly from Mexico (Saenz and Cready 1996). Census data show that the rate of immigration to the Midwest is increasing. At the time of the 2000 census, 47 percent of immigrants in the Midwest had arrived in the United States in the past 10 years (SF3 tabulation from American Factfinder, www.census. gov, accessed 12/12/03). This growth consists both of people coming directly from Mexico (legally and illegally) and other Latinos who come primarily from California and south Texas. Among the immigrants are small numbers of Guatemalans, Salvadorans, and Cubans (Amato 1996; Aponte 1995).

While Midwestern Latinos work in many different industrial sectors (Huffman and Miranowski 1996), and many still work on farms (Amato 1996), a major magnet is now the restructured meatpacking industry. Factories for butchering and packaging meat offer year-round jobs that pay at least $6 an hour—much higher and more stable earnings than those available to most seasonal farmworkers (Martin et al. 1996). Jobs at meatpacking plants are attractive to immigrants because they do not require English skills or previous experience, because there are few alternative opportunities for immigrants, and because there is not much competition from locals for these dangerous and unpleasant jobs (Grey 1995).

Since 1980, the food processing industry (poultry and egg processing and meatpacking, i.e., butchering and packaging beef and pork) has expanded substantially in rural areas of the Midwest, while transforming itself through increased levels of competition and concentration of ownership, plant closings and relocations, and substantial decreases in workers' wages (Friedberger 1989; Stanley 1992). This transformation can be seen as part of the larger economic trends of industrial and agricultural restructuring occurring nationally, brought about by increasing global competition, technological innovations, and pursuit of higher profits. Industrial restructuring is characterized by a decrease in manufacturing and increase in service sector jobs, the geographic redistribution of manufacturing jobs, and an increase in low-wage, low-skill jobs as well as in high-level professional jobs (Sassen 1990). Agricultural restructuring includes greater integration of farms into the control of large agribusiness corporations and a shift from owner-operated farms to hired-labor contractors.

In the 1970s, agribusiness expanded its markets to become an industry of multinational corporations, integrating the Midwest increasingly into the global market (Cantú 1995). With the farm crisis of the 1980s, meatpacking expansion and relocation in rural areas was encouraged to make up for devastating economic losses. These areas were attractive to meatpacking companies because of the reduced costs in transportation and spoilage achieved by locating closer to sources of animal feed and rural areas' lower labor costs, weaker unions, cheap land, and government economic incentives (Broadway 1991; Stanley 1992). Labor recruitment, especially of immigrants and minorities, was initiated in response to labor shortages and increasing competition (Cantú 1995; Stanley 1992). By de-skilling operations (i.e., simplifying tasks to require less training), plant reorganization, and hiring low-wage labor (i.e., immigrants, minorities, and women), the industry has been minimizing labor costs (Benson 1996b; Stanley 1992).

Population growth resulting from the installation of new meatpacking plants has had positive economic effects on rural places, such as a stable market for farmers, growth in local business, strengthening of community organizations, revitalization of local schools, and tax base expansion (Amato 1996; Benson 1996a,b; Eggerstrom 1994; Gouveia and Stull 1995). It has also brought new problems, however. Meatpacking creates unusually high population mobility. The work is difficult, unpleasant, and dangerous, and the job hierarchy is relatively flat. Some plants encourage workers to leave to avoid paying health benefits, which are usually only offered after the first six months of employment. Turnover is therefore very high, as workers have a hard time staying on the job because of illness, injury, problems with (and harassment from) management, economic insecurity, and dislike of difficult working conditions (Amato 1996; Martin et al. 1996; Gouveia and Stull 1995; Stanley 1992). Plants constantly hire new workers to fill vacancies, so there is a continuous stream of newcomers to the host communities. Because poultry and meatpacking jobs pay relatively low wages, and because they attract the most financially needy workers, poverty and correlates of poverty increase.

Places undergoing this rapid growth have had to confront sudden demands for housing, education, health care, social services, and crime prevention (Gouveia and Stull 1997; Grey 1995; Martin et al. 1996). Often, available housing has been inadequate, overcrowded, and dangerous (Benson 1996a,b; Gouveia and Stull 1996). Lack of health insurance and, among the insured, difficulties in making copayments have led to inadequate prenatal care, weak identification and treatment of tuberculosis, gaps in child immunization, and deficient dental care (Benson 1996a,b). Rapid increases in school enrollments have brought about the need for bilingual and English-as-a-second-language instruction. It is difficult, however, to attract qualified bilingual teachers to most rural areas. Teenagers find it especially difficult to gain enough English skills or social confidence to be successful in high school, which leads to problems with truancy, pregnancy, dropouts, and gang development (Benson 1996a,b), implying worsening conditions for future generations. School turnover is high in meatpacking towns, paralleling the turnover in the plants (Gouveia and Stull 1995). Language has become an expensive issue for courts, schools, and social service providers (Amato 1996).

Changing ethnicity can also bring about ethnic tensions and negative feelings in established residents. The Worthington, Minnesota, *Daily Globe* reported that an overwhelming majority of residents surveyed felt that the influx of minority groups had not been good for their community and many made shockingly racist comments about the newcomers. Changes in local culture due to immigration can be seen as threatening the traditional culture of the community, or as positive—adding diversity and international flavor (Amato 1996; Benson 1996a,b).

For the most part, neither the industries that are attracting Latinos to the Midwest nor the communities that host the plants have planned sufficiently for the integration of the new workforce (Amato 1996; Martin et al. 1996). Some communities have tried to prepare for changes prior to the installation of a new processing plant. In Garden City, Kansas, for example, a ministerial alliance began a public education program when negative rumors started circulating about refugees who began arriving in the 1980s. Because of these efforts, newcomers were at least tolerated by most established residents, although it is less certain whether they have been integrated into the community (Benson 1996a,b). Lexington, Nebraska, hired consultants to estimate housing needs for the new population expected from the installation of a new meatpacking plant. The need was drastically underestimated, however, because of the plant's low projections of worker turnover and nonlocal hirings (Gouveia and Stull 1997). In general, policy making by local communities has mostly consisted of saying yes or no to industries proposing new plant construction.

Obviously, the meatpacking industry and the growing employment of Latino workers are affecting certain towns and states in the Midwest. Other small towns seek ways to invite industries to their communities and to reduce the social and infrastructure costs of new plants. Such attempts present several dilemmas. Where will the workers come from if the local population is not large enough or interested in the new jobs that are created? Where will the money come from to equip the towns with the services and other resources needed for large numbers of newcomers? Also, what alternatives are available for sustaining the economic viability of most Midwestern towns that have lost population in recent years?

Observers of these population changes generally agree that, in this new context of globalization and "flexible" production strategies, communities cannot rely solely on highly mobile industries, such as meatpacking, when developing strategic plans for their economic future. As the director of a rural development commission recently told us, "The biggest challenge facing us today, and I am speaking for the commission, is how to create an environment for the Latino population so that they stay even after meatpacking is gone; they are the only future these communities have." The same is true for more established Latino communities in rural settings where opportunities for skill development and employment for young Latinos have not been forthcoming.

Contemporary Challenges

The relocation of industrial plants to rural communities in the Midwest and the resulting influx of Latinos have increased the ethnic diversity in the region. Observers have noted new Spanish radio stations, Latino-owned businesses, and celebrations of Mexican patron saints in small towns across the Midwest (Burke and Goudy 1999; Flora and Flora 1999; Wherritt and González 1989). As they did in the past, Latino newcomers are creating their own communities in the region. Researchers have noted, however, that Latinos and other residents in rural areas are experiencing many challenges related to rapid population growth (Flora and Flora 1999; Burke and Goudy 1999). Not surprisingly, those who move to rural areas to work in food processing plants bring their families, who require medical care, schooling, housing, and social services (Martin et al. 1996). Long-term residents are noticing rapid population changes in their communities. The following discussion describes some of the most significant challenges.[1]

Health care is an issue for Latino newcomers and the rural Midwestern communities in which they reside for several reasons. First, access to health care is problematic because the ratio of physicians to population in rural communities is much lower than in metropolitan hubs and has declined drastically in rural communities since the 1970s (Hackenberg and Kukulka 1995). Second, meatpacking and other food processing industries have extremely high injury rates (Stanley 1992; Stull and Broadway 1995), yet many employers do not provide health insurance during the first few months of employment (Stanley 1992; Gouveia and Stull 1997), the time when inexperienced workers are most likely to be injured on the job. The high monthly fees and large deductibles discourage many employees from acquiring health insurance and from using routine and preventive medical care (Rochín et al. 1989). Finally, in many Midwestern communities, medical care tends to be provided by non-Latinos who do not speak Spanish and who have no interpreters on staff (see other chapters in this volume; Martin et al. 1996). This language barrier makes it even more difficult for Spanish-speaking newcomers to meet their health care needs.

Meeting the educational needs of the changing rural population poses another challenge. Some rural areas with rapidly growing manufacturing employment, such as Lexington, Nebraska, have experienced large increases in the school-age Latino population (Benson 1996a,b; Gouveia and Stull 1997). This growth, irrespective of ethnicity and national origin, is problematic because even small increases in the student population in rural areas can lead to overcrowded schools. Moreover, English-as-a-Second-Language (ESL) classes will be required in schools with rapidly growing populations of children with limited English proficiency (LEP).

Midwestern states are grappling with how to provide such services. For example, Iowa schools experienced a 177 percent increase in LEP students during the 1990s (Krantz and Santiago 2000, cited in Grey 2001).[2] Many rural schools do not have personnel certified to teach Spanish-speaking students or bilingual staff capable of communicating with Spanish-speaking parents. Even if staff is available, when ESL students are isolated from the mainstream student population, they have few opportunities to interact with others and may feel marginalized (Grey 2001). In addition, many manufacturing plants in rural areas experience high levels of employee turnover, which is, of course, accompanied by high student turnover (Gouveia and Stull 1997). It is difficult for educational systems to address the needs of a constantly changing student population.

Latino newcomers also require affordable and safe housing, as do all other residents. In rural areas, rental housing fills up quickly because of limited rental stock. Consequently, although housing may initially be relatively inexpensive in a town, as the supply dwindles some Latinos are forced to live in expensive, overcrowded, and dangerous housing (Rochín 1995). Trailer parks are frequently hastily established on the edge of town for Latino newcomers (Gouveia and Stull 1995), but their stock is often used house trailers, which are subject to rapid deterioration. Residential concentration on the periphery of towns may tax the infrastructure with requirements for water, electricity, and sewer services. Some newcomers must live outside the community to find suitable housing and commute an hour or more to their employment (Grey 2001).

Immigration—the National Context

Immigration has long been at the forefront of the nation's attention, and most of the vociferously expressed sentiments have been against it. The number, variety, and visibility of immigrant groups in general and immigrant Latinos in particular have been increasing. There is an additional reason to expect immigration to be a significant factor in shaping the future composition of Latino communities in the United States. Immigration rates are up and expected to stay high. Current laws and programs are currently admitting about 800,000 to 1,000,000 new documented immigrants a year. The Census 2000 Supplementary Survey (C2SS) reported an estimate of 13.3 million foreign-born people residing in the United States who had immigrated since 1990 (U.S. Census 2001c).

Although the Latinos who informed this study had various backgrounds and legal statuses, many were undocumented immigrants. For many years, undocumented immigrants have provided the United States with a "de facto guest worker program" (Massey et al. 2002). U.S. employers have benefited from the widespread availability of reliable workers who will do onerous work for low wages. In addition, the employers have not had to bear any costs associated with administering this "program," including those due to the rapid increase in immigrants in their community. The immigrants have benefited from wages higher than in their home countries, but they also have borne many of the costs and risks associated with immigration, including the actual financial cost of migrating, the risk of dying in the process, the inability to obtain drivers' licenses, and all of the other problems associated with living in the United States without legal authorization. Moreover, the communities to which they have migrated also have incurred costs, many associated with providing services to a Spanish-speaking population.

The population of undocumented Latino immigrants grew throughout the 1990s and at a very high rate during the economic boom between 1997 and 2000. The midpoint of one set of estimates of the undocumented Mexican population in the United States as of mid-2001 was 4.5 million (Bean et al. 2001).[3] This estimate is consistent with an independent analysis by the Census Bureau (see Robinson 2001).

The proportion of the U.S. population comprised of immigrants is now approaching the historic high level of 15 percent that the United States experienced as the wave of European immigrants crested in 1890. There is one major difference, however; the majority of immigrants to the United States before the 1960s were Europeans. Immigration laws passed in the 1920s institutionalized a strong preference for northern and western Europeans by making the number of immigrants permitted from any country proportional to the group's size among existing U.S. citizens. As a result, a large proportion of immigrants from the 1920s to the 1960s came from England, Germany, and Ireland, since those were the nationalities most commonly found in the United States. Of course, this system made it difficult for people from countries with small or negligible numbers already in the United States to get through the door.

It is important to note, however, that Mexicans were not covered by these quotas. Instead, they were seen as agricultural workers who could easily be sent back to Mexico when they were no longer needed (Tichenor 2002, chap. 6). The immigration law reforms of the 1960s opened the door to other groups. The decrease in the proportion of documented immigrants who were European and the large increase in Latin American and Asian immigrants are direct consequences of this change.

Half of all immigrants in the United States are from Latin America, and the largest group by far is from Mexico (U.S. Census 2001c). Furthermore, increased international economic integration in the near future will likely increase Latino, especially Mexican, immigration to the United States for several reasons. First, in Mexico, U.S. imports have undermined broad sectors of the economy, dislocated millions of workers and their dependents, and increased the motivation for emigration. The sector in which the demographic magnitude of these impacts will likely be the greatest is agriculture. NAFTA (the North American Free Trade Agreement) has increased migration from Mexico to the United States. Perhaps in the decades ahead, migration from Mexico may decrease as a consequence of economic and political reform, but the immediate question is how many millions of Mexicans will immigrate to the United States over the next decade.

There is an overwhelming consensus among researchers that the major reason undocumented immigrants come to the United States from Mexico is for relatively well paid jobs. An immigrant can make about ten times as much in the United States as in Mexico. The remittances that immigrants send back to Mexico amount to several billion dollars every year. In Mexico, these "migradollars" have a major positive impact on the Mexican economy (Durand et al. 1996).

In addition to the wage differential, another important driver of the immigration process is previous migration. It is generally agreed that the start of large-scale undocumented migration from Mexico to the United States was the termination of the Bracero Program in 1964. Since the Immigration Reform and Control Act of 1986 (IRCA) was enacted, nearly 2.7 million people "adjusted from unauthorized to temporary lawful residence in 1987 and 1988 under IRCA. In the years 1989–1992, most of them were granted lawful permanent residence" (USCIS 2003:2, n. 1). Many of them aided additional immigrants. Likewise, the rapid increase of undocumented Mexican immigrants in areas where there is no settled Mexican or Latino community has, in some cases, been tied to the hiring of documented temporary migrant workers under the H-2A labor contracting program. The pattern whereby temporary labor migration or guest worker programs lead to permanent settlements has been observed in many other countries around the world.

Efforts to decrease undocumented immigration may have prevented its further expansion, but they have not actually reduced it. For example, IRCA did not result in a decrease in undocumented immigration, because the sanctions for employing undocumented immigrants were very rarely enforced. Likewise, the 1996 reforms to U.S. immigration law did not decrease the number of undocumented immigrants. The number of Border Patrol agents was increased substantially, and the increased level of surveillance at the border, unfortunately, greatly increased the death rate of border crossers (Eschbach et al. 1999). Before the increase in border surveillance, many undocumented immigrants were sojourners who worked in the United States for short periods and then returned to Mexico and other countries of origin. The strict border enforcement, however, ironically increased the number of Mexican and Central American immigrants staying in the United States for longer periods. The increased risk and difficulty of border crossing has turned them into long-term, undocumented residents.

First, there is an immediate large net economic benefit to the United States as a whole from undocumented Mexican immigration. Second, the immigrants generally work very hard in low-wage, undesirable jobs. Third, at the national level, undocumented immigrants pay far more in taxes than they consume in social services (Fix and Passel 1994). Access to government benefits, especially welfare, has never been shown to be a motive for undocumented migration. Also at the national level, numerous research efforts have shown that undocumented immigrants have not had a negative effect on the employment or earnings of U.S.-born minorities. The exception to this generalization seems to be in areas where Mexicans and Central Americans are found in large concentrations. In locales such as these, wages are substantially lower even after controlling key variables (Catanzarite and Aguilera 2002).

In times of economic growth such as the 1990s, immigrants can help sustain a boom that might otherwise be forced to stop because of a shortage of workers. During economic recessions, however, undocumented immigrants are typically unwelcome. The costs of undocumented immigration are greatest at the state and local levels. The government services needed by undocumented immigrants, especially education, are financed with state and local taxes. An influx of Latinos into low-wage jobs thus is an asset to the federal budget and to local employers but a cost to local entities providing education, health care, and human services. Moreover, low-wage immigrants may have constrained the growth of wages and employment opportunities for U.S. minority workers.

Employers in the United States play a major role in sustaining high levels of undocumented Latino immigration. Employers typically perceive that Latino immigrants have the following traits: (1) they are willing to do low-pay work that is boring, dirty, and dangerous, with no prospects for upward mobility; (2) they are reliable, flexible, punctual, and willing to work overtime; and (3) they utilize transnational labor recruitment networks, which are a powerful means for "delivering eager new recruits to the employer's doorstep with little or no effort on his part" (Cornelius 1998:119). One example in which the transnational recruitment network operates is richly detailed by Suro (1999:31–56).

To summarize, large-scale undocumented immigration to the United States would not exist without a strong demand by employers during times of rapid economic growth. The superheated economic growth of the 1990s U.S. economy, the resulting extremely tight labor market, the changes in immigration law, and the challenges facing the Mexican economy all resulted in extremely high levels of Mexican immigration to the United States. The ubiquitous penetration of the transnational labor recruitment network drew Latino immigrants to areas with small Latino populations. Economic and demographic changes ensured that some of these areas would be found in the rural Midwest. While international immigration was the major source of Latino population growth in the United States in the 1990s, secondary migration of U.S.-born Latinos to new states was also important, as was natural increase.

Latino Growth and Characteristics by States and Regions

The data from the 2000 U.S. census have revealed two new and striking aspects of Latino population growth. One is a noticeable number of Latinos in metropolitan areas that previously had very few Latinos. For example, the Mexican American Legal Defense and Education Fund (MALDEF), a leading advocacy group long established in Texas and California, recently opened an office in Atlanta, Georgia. The 2000 census shows that the Latino population of Georgia increased by almost 300 percent (Table 3.1). Also, the amnesty provisions of the Immigration Reform and Control Act of 1986 (IRCA) facilitated the creation of new immigrant destinations (see Hernández-León and Zúñiga 2000).

The 2000 census also revealed a very large nationwide increase in the proportion of Latinos in small towns typically associated with agricultural and food

Table 3.1. U.S. Total and Latino Population in Modified Census Divisions, 1990–2000

	1990 Total Population	2000 Total Population	% Increase	1990 Latino Population	2000 Latino Population	% Increase
UNITED STATES	248,790,938	281,421,906	13.1	22,378,541	35,305,818	57.8
NEW ENGLAND						
Maine	1,227,928	1,274,923	3.8	6,829	9,360	37.1
New Hampshire	1,109,252	1,235,786	11.4	11,333	20,489	80.8
Vermont	562,758	608,827	8.2	3,661	5,504	50.3
Massachusetts	6,016,425	6,349,097	5.5	287,561	428,729	49.1
Rhode Island	1,003,464	1,048,319	4.5	45,755	90,820	98.5
Connecticut	3,287,116	3,405,565	3.6	213,116	320,323	50.3
MIDDLE ATLANTIC						
New York	17,990,778	18,976,457	5.5	2,213,943	2,867,583	29.5
New Jersey	7,747,750	8,414,350	8.6	747,737	1,117,191	49.4
Pennsylvania	11,882,842	12,281,054	3.4	232,286	394,088	69.7
MIDWEST						
Ohio	10,847,115	11,353,140	4.7	139,695	217,123	55.4
Indiana	5,544,156	6,080,485	9.7	98,789	214,536	117.2
Illinois	11,430,602	12,419,293	8.6	904,449	1,530,262	69.2
Michigan	9,295,287	9,938,444	6.9	201,597	323,877	60.7
Wisconsin	4,891,954	5,363,675	9.6	93,232	192,921	106.9
Minnesota	4,375,665	4,919,479	12.4	53,888	143,382	166.1
Iowa	2,776,831	2,926,324	5.4	32,643	82,473	152.7
Kansas	2,477,588	2,688,418	8.5	93,671	188,252	101.0
Nebraska	1,578,417	1,711,263	8.4	36,969	94,425	155.4

(continued)

Table 3.1. U.S. Total and Latino Population in Modified Census Divisions, 1990–2000, continued

	1990 Total Population	2000 Total Population	% Increase	1990 Latino Population	2000 Latino Population	% Increase
MO, ND, SD						
Missouri	5,116,901	5,595,211	9.3	61,698	118,592	92.2
North Dakota	638,800	642,200	0.5	4,665	7,786	66.9
South Dakota	696,004	754,844	8.5	5,252	10,903	107.6
SOUTH ATLANTIC						
Delaware	666,168	783,600	17.6	15,824	37,277	135.6
Maryland	4,780,753	5,296,486	10.8	125,093	227,916	82.2
District of Columbia	606,900	572,059	-5.7	32,713	44,953	37.4
Virginia	6,189,197	7,078,515	14.4	160,403	329,540	105.4
West Virginia	1,793,477	1,808,344	0.8	8,487	12,279	44.7
North Carolina	6,632,448	8,049,313	21.4	76,745	378,963	393.8
South Carolina	3,486,310	4,012,012	15.1	30,500	95,076	211.7
Georgia	6,478,149	8,186,453	26.4	108,933	435,227	299.5
Florida	12,938,071	15,982,378	23.5	1,574,148	2,682,715	70.4
EAST SOUTH CENTRAL						
Kentucky	3,686,892	4,041,769	9.6	22,005	59,939	172.4
Tennessee	4,877,203	5,689,283	16.7	32,742	123,838	278.2
Alabama	4,040,389	4,447,100	10.1	24,629	75,830	207.9
Mississippi	2,575,475	2,844,658	10.5	15,998	39,569	147.3
WEST SOUTH CENTRAL						
Arkansas	2,350,624	2,673,400	13.7	19,876	86,866	337.0
Louisiana	4,221,839	4,468,976	5.9	93,067	107,738	15.8

(continued)

	1990 Total Population	2000 Total Population	% Increase	1990 Latino Population	2000 Latino Population	% Increase
Oklahoma	3,145,576	3,450,654	9.7	86,162	179,304	108.1
Texas	16,986,335	20,851,820	22.8	4,339,874	6,669,666	53.7
MOUNTAIN						
Montana	799,065	902,195	12.9	12,175	18,081	48.5
Idaho	1,006,734	1,293,953	28.5	52,927	101,690	92.1
Wyoming	453,589	493,782	8.9	25,752	31,669	23.0
Colorado	3,294,473	4,301,261	30.6	424,309	735,601	73.4
New Mexico	1,515,069	1,819,046	20.1	579,227	765,386	32.1
Arizona	3,665,339	5,130,632	40.0	688,355	1,295,617	88.2
Utah	1,722,850	2,233,169	29.6	84,597	201,559	138.3
Nevada	1,201,675	1,998,257	66.3	124,408	393,970	216.7
PACIFIC						
Washington	4,866,669	5,894,121	21.1	214,568	441,509	105.8
Oregon	2,842,337	3,421,399	20.4	112,708	275,314	144.3
California	29,811,427	33,871,648	13.6	7,704,348	10,966,556	42.3
Alaska	550,043	626,932	14.0	17,803	25,852	45.2
Hawaii	1,108,229	1,211,537	9.3	81,396	87,699	7.7

Source: U.S. Census Bureau 2001a,b.

processing operations. In Siler City, North Carolina, 184 Latinos comprised 4 percent of the town's population in 1990. In 1999, after a rapid increase in hog farming, Latinos made up half of the total. This chapter will examine both types of Latino population growth in the Midwest (Chapa 2000).

Despite the trend toward geographic dispersion throughout much of the United States, a large part of the Latino population is concentrated in just a few states. California and Texas are home to more than half of the national Latino population. In spite of this concentration, however, for the nation as a whole and for every state except Hawaii, the Latino population grew much more rapidly than the total population (see Table 3.1). Even in states where this growth occurred on top of a small base population, the magnitude of the growth was such that Latinos became noticeable, and their rapid growth was remarked upon. As outlined in the previous chapter, Latinos have a long history in the Midwest, but as seen in Table 3.2, the Latino population of the Midwest experienced significant growth from 1990 to 2000 in both numeric and percentage terms. Moreover, as will be shown later in this chapter and throughout this book, there are many towns in the rural Midwest where Latino population growth is mostly from immigrants.

The Rural Midwest—Mexicanization or Polarization?

In the California experience, "Mexicanized" towns generally had populations that were largely Latino (Allensworth and Rochín 1999). We did not find much evidence in the Midwest of Mexicanization as defined in the California case, however. The Latino population of the rural Midwest would have to continue growing at a rapid rate before the pattern of "Mexicanization" found in California could occur. Note that while the term "Mexicanized" refers to a process and not necessarily a specific Latino national origin, almost all of the Latinos we encountered in the rural Midwest were of Mexican ancestry. It is also noteworthy that we found many examples of xenophobia and hostility directed at Latino immigrants by some of the Anglo long-term residents.

For the purpose of this analysis, we have identified rural counties as those not in Metropolitan Statistical Areas (MSAs). The U.S. Department of Agriculture's system of Urban Influence Codes (UIC) identifies seven types of nonmetropolitan counties, ranging from those adjacent to a large metro area and having a city of at least 10,000 (UIC 3) to very sparsely populated counties (UIC 9). Nationally, the Latino population of all nine levels of

Table 3.2. Regional Total and Latino Population in Modified Census Divisions, 1990–2000

	1990 Total Population	2000 Total Population	Total Increase	% Total Increase	1990 Latino Population	2000 Latino Population	Latino Increase	% Latino Increase
UNITED STATES	248,790,938	281,421,906	32,630,968	13.1	22,378,541	35,305,818	12,927,277	57.8
NEW ENGLAND	13,206,943	13,922,517	715,574	5.4	568,255	875,225	306,970	54.0
MIDDLE ATLANTIC	37,621,370	39,671,861	2,050,491	5.5	3,193,966	4,378,862	1,184,896	37.1
MIDWEST	53,217,615	57,400,521	4,182,906	7.9	1,654,933	2,987,251	1,332,318	80.5
MO, ND, SD	6,451,705	6,992,255	540,550	8.4	71,615	137,281	65,666	91.7
SOUTH ATLANTIC	43,571,473	51,769,160	8,197,687	18.8	2,132,846	4,243,946	2,111,100	99.0
EAST SOUTH CENTRAL	15,179,959	17,022,810	1,842,851	12.1	95,374	299,176	203,802	213.7
WEST SOUTH CENTRAL	26,704,374	31,444,850	4,740,476	17.8	4,538,979	7,043,574	2,504,595	55.2
MOUNTAIN	13,658,794	18,172,295	4,513,501	33.0	1,991,750	3,543,573	1,551,823	77.9
PACIFIC	39,178,705	45,025,637	5,846,932	14.9	8,130,823	11,796,930	3,666,107	45.1

Source: U.S. Census Bureau 2001a,b.

urban influence experienced a high proportion of Latino population growth (Table 3.3). Latino growth rates in the Midwest were substantially higher than the national rates (Table 3.4). Further examination shows that the Midwest Latino growth rates were particularly high for the counties with the least amount of urban influence. Table 3.4 compares the Latino population growth for each level of urban influence with the total population growth. It shows that while the Latino population grew at a very rapid rate, the numerical growth of the total population was far greater. This finding also leads to a main focus of this book; that is, observing the relationship between the long-term, largely Anglo residents and the Latino immigrants in towns where the proportion of Latinos increases quickly.

Counties are convenient units for demographic analysis, but their boundaries often differ from those within which many people, especially rural residents, live and work. In our ethnographic studies, we found that workers in agricultural processing often commuted to work in neighboring towns, and they sometimes crossed county lines to do so. Thus a county-level analysis can only approximate a description of rural Latinos' daily routines.

One of our analyses focused on counties in the Midwest where at least one-eighth of the workforce was employed in agriculture. We found that all such counties but one had experienced a substantial growth of Latinos. This one county actually contained a number of immigrant Latinos seasonally employed on farms, but the county was small and had few farms, and the Latinos commuted from a much larger town that was just over the county line, only a few miles away.

We also noted in our fieldwork that in comparison to other rural areas of the United States, the roads in the rural Midwest are often better and the distances between towns are shorter, making rural commuting convenient. In another field site, we found an advertisement in a local newspaper for a grocery store that featured Mexican food, but it was across the state line and outside the bounds of our study. An interview with the shopkeeper revealed that many immigrants from the area in our study did indeed drive at least 35 miles each way to shop at this store. The Latino population we are studying thus is highly mobile and engages in rural commuting to work, school, and shopping (see Chapter 4).

Table 3.5 presents the distribution of places in the nonmetropolitan Midwest by the concentration of Latinos counted as residents by the 2000 census. A place is defined by the Census Bureau as "a concentration of population either legally bound as an incorporated place or identified by

Table 3.3. Increase in the U.S. Total and Latino Population by Rural-Urban Status, 1990–2000

Urban Influence Code[a]	1990 Total Population	2000 Total Population	Total Increase	% Total Increase	1990 Latino Population	2000 Latino Population	Latino Increase	% Latino Increase
1	62,115,597	70,452,459	8,336,862	13.4	15,565,503	23,726,787	8,161,284	52.4
2	55,480,773	61,974,335	6,493,562	11.7	4,656,709	7,992,799	3,336,090	71.6
3	4,531,610	5,038,993	507,383	11.2	248,026	470,945	222,919	89.9
4	6,884,057	8,142,635	1,258,578	18.3	124,560	215,416	90,856	72.9
5	14,246,834	16,188,109	1,941,275	13.6	446,503	717,155	270,652	60.6
6	38,640,024	44,718,487	6,078,463	15.7	390,551	700,381	309,830	79.3
7	18,695,211	20,663,722	1,968,511	10.5	420,212	673,233	253,021	60.2
8	24,202,675	27,576,697	3,374,022	13.9	354,987	555,299	200,312	56.4
9	20,438,816	23,206,199	2,767,383	13.5	78,653	133,598	54,945	69.9
Total[b]	245,235,597	277,961,636	32,726,039	13.3	22,285,704	35,185,613	12,899,909	57.9

Source: U.S. Census Bureau 2001a,b.

[a]Urban Influence Codes (UIC):

Metro (urban)

1 Large—Central and fringe counties of metro areas with a population of at least 1 million.

2 Small—Counties in metro areas with a population of less than 1 million.

Nonmetro (rural)

3 Adjacent to a large metro area and with a city of 10,000 or more.

4 Adjacent to a large metro area and without a city of at least 10,000.

5 Adjacent to a small metro area and with a city of 10,000 or more.

6 Adjacent to a small metro area and without a city of at least 10,000.

7 Not adjacent to a metro area and with a city of 10,000 or more.

8 Not adjacent to a metro area and with a city of 2,500 to 9,999 population.

9 Not adjacent to a metro area and with no city or a city with a population of less than 2,500.

[b]This analysis excludes the few census-designated cities that are not considered to be in counties.

Table 3.4. Increase in the Midwestern Total and Latino Population by Rural-Urban Status, 1990–2000

Urban Influence Code	1990 Total Population	2000 Total Population	Total Increase	% Total Increase	1990 Latino Population	2000 Latino Population	Latino Increase	% Latino Increase
1	6,079,566	6,356,813	277,247	4.6	1,138,586	1,927,339	788,753	69.3
2	7,956,763	8,451,091	494,328	6.2	281,015	545,736	264,721	94.2
3	1,929,348	2,121,496	192,148	10.0	50,137	120,705	70,568	140.8
4	1,693,969	1,830,076	136,107	8.0	5,385	10,321	4,936	91.7
5	4,130,299	4,661,552	531,253	12.9	38,656	66,882	28,226	73.0
6	8,301,287	8,953,435	652,148	7.9	48,578	107,770	59,192	121.8
7	8,389,847	8,980,857	591,010	7.0	54,810	119,282	64,472	117.6
8	7,327,057	8,005,599	678,542	9.3	27,921	68,107	40,186	143.9
9	7,327,057	8,011,100	684,043	9.3	9,802	21,109	11,307	115.4
Total[a]	53,135,193	57,372,019	4,236,826	8.0	1,654,890	2,987,251	1,332,361	80.5

Source: U.S. Census Bureau 2001a,b.
[a]This analysis excludes the few census-designated cities that are not considered to be in counties.

Table 3.5. Percentage of Latinos in Nonmetro Midwestern Places, 2000

Range of Latino Percentages	Number of Places	Average Size	Total Population	Latino Population	% Latino	% Latino under 18	% Latino 18 and Older
Zero % Latinos	1,036	195	201,665	0	0	0	0
Up to but not including 5% Latino	3,285	1,917	6,297,502	103,996	1.7	2.6	1.3
At least 5% and less than 10% Latino	251	3,108	780,185	53,629	6.9	11.0	5.5
At least 10% and less than 15% Latino	65	3,686	239,583	30,158	12.6	19.1	10.3
At least 15% and less than 20% Latino	35	3,962	138,660	23,638	17.0	25.4	14.1
At least 20% and less than 25% Latino	25	3,552	88,793	19,635	22.1	33.3	18.0
At least 25% and less than 35% Latino	23	916	21,079	6,348	30.1	40.8	25.2
At least 35% and less than 45% Latino	8	10,821	86,569	36,916	42.6	55.3	36.7
At least 45% and less than 59% Latino	6	3,159	18,956	9,343	49.3	62.1	43.3
Overall	4,734	1,663	7,872,992	283,663	3.6	3.6	2.9

Source: U.S. Census Bureau 2001a,b.

the Census Bureau as a census designated place" (U.S. Census 2003). The examination of Table 3.5 shows that more than a thousand inhabited places have no Latino residents at all. By far, most of the towns and places had relatively small Latino populations that accounted for less than 5 percent of the total population. Only a few had a majority Latino population. Mexicanization is thus extremely rare in the Midwest, in contrast to rural California. While the rural places that have high concentrations of Latinos merit close examination, we will have to wait at least until the results of the 2010 census before we can see whether Mexicanization is a widespread phenomenon in the Midwest.

Age Distribution

Latinos are a relatively young population. This is true internationally, nationally, and in the rural Midwest. For example, Table 3.6 shows that more than a third of Latinos in both the metropolitan and nonmetropolitan Midwest are under age 16, compared to less than a quarter of the non-Latino population. Any analysis of Latino population growth thus must consider the large percentage who will reach reproductive age over the next decade. The current age distribution results in high proportions of Latinos among the preschool and school-age population. The strong potential for future population growth and the concentration of Latinos in the younger age groups underscore the importance of policies pertaining to Latino youth.

Table 3.6 also shows the large difference in the median ages of Latinos (23) and non-Latinos (36) in the nonmetropolitan Midwest, as well as the large differences in their age distributions. Much larger proportions of non-Latinos are concentrated in the two older age groups, 36–64 and 65 and older. The fact that a large proportion of the non-Latino population, which is overwhelmingly Anglo, is nearing retirement age will also shape the future of these towns and their ethnic composition.

Industry and Occupation

Because the major reason that Latinos have migrated to the United States is to take jobs, we focus on employment of Latinos in the rural Midwest. In

Table 3.6. Age Distribution in the Metro and Nonmetro Midwest by Ethnicity, 2000

	Metro		Nonmetro	
Age Group	% Latino	% Non-Latino	% Latino	% Non-Latino
0–15	33.8	24.1	37.7	23.6
16–35	38.2	28.1	35.5	25.2
36–64	25.3	36.8	24.9	36.8
65+	2.7	11.1	1.9	14.5
Total	100	100	100	100
Median Age	24	34	23	36

Source: U.S. Census Bureau 2000.

2000 half of the rural Latinos had jobs in manufacturing and almost one-third (32.6 percent) of the Latino workers were employed in industries that manufactured nondurable goods (including the manufacture of food products; see Table 3.7). Moreover, the proportion of Latinos was more than three times the proportion of non-Latinos (9.3 percent) working in this same industry category in the rural Midwest. The concentration of Latinos in food processing is a striking confirmation of the ethnographic studies and the literature on rural economic restructuring.[4]

In the nonmetro Midwest, a high proportion of Latinos (16.0 percent) also work in the retail trade industry. Note that this is less than the 25.0 percent concentration of Latinos employed in retail trades in MSAs (Table 3.7). This category includes not only typical stores but also lumberyards, retail plant nurseries, and gas stations; thus, a number of the jobs involve heavy labor. In many areas, Anglo residents often see Latino immigrants working in such jobs, sights that reinforce a concept that Latinos belong at the bottom of the occupational scale.

A number of tables in this chapter present analyses of the March Annual Demographic File of the Current Population Survey (CPS). The low proportion of Latinos listed in Table 3.7 as working in agriculture may indicate a weakness of the CPS in general and of the March file in particular. The CPS does not collect data from people living in group quarters, particularly farm labor camps, and in many parts of the Midwest a survey conducted in March would miss most migrant farmworkers, who tend to arrive from late April to July. Note that according to these data, the non-Latino proportion of

Table 3.7. Industrial Employment in the Metro
and Nonmetro Midwest by Ethnicity, 2000

Industrial	Metro		Nonmetro	
Group	% Latino	% Non-Latino	% Latino	% Non-Latino
Agriculture	3.6	1.7	5.4	8.5
Construction	7.5	8.0	8.1	8.9
Manufacturing— durable goods	16.5	17.1	18.8	22.2
Manufacturing— nondurable goods	14.5	8.6	32.6	9.3
Transportation	3.1	6.6	6.4	5.1
Wholesale trade	6.4	5.9	2.3	5.3
Retail trade	25.0	24.1	16.0	22.5
Finance, insurance, and real estate	6.0	10.2	1.9	4.7
Private household and miscellaneous	0.7	0.7	0.5	0.7
Business and repair	9.9	10.0	6.5	6.4
Personal services	5.0	3.4	1.4	3.4
Other	1.9	3.8	0.0	3.0
Total	100	100	100	100

Source: U.S. Census Bureau 2000.

rural Midwesterners who do work in agriculture, 8.5 percent, is greater than the Latino proportion of 5.4 percent (Table 3.7). Nonetheless, because our analysis deals with Latinos who live year-round in the Midwest, not migrant farmworkers, the March CPS is by far the best for our purposes. It provides detailed questions about immigration and oversamples Latinos.

The distribution of Latinos in the Midwest is concentrated in a few occupational groups (Table 3.8). More than half of the rural Latinos are employed in the following three occupational groups, listed in descending order: (1) machine operators, assemblers, and inspectors; (2) people working in precision production, craft and repair; and (3) handlers, equipment cleaners, helpers, and laborers. These occupations are common in manufacturing industries. (An analysis of the data used to construct Tables 3.7 and 3.8, not presented here, further supports this finding.) Typical jobs of Latinos in the rural Midwest seem to be working on the line in agricultural processing plants or in factories.

Table 3.8. Occupational Distribution in the Metro
and Nonmetro Midwest by Ethnicity, 2000

Occupational Group	Metro		Nonmetro	
	% Latino	% Non-Latino	% Latino	% Non-Latino
Executive, administrative, and managerial	7.6	15.2	3.8	10.1
Professional specialty	5.5	16.0	2.1	10.8
Technicians and related support	1.2	3.2	2.0	2.7
Sales	8.4	12.7	5.4	9.6
Administrative support, including clerical	11.7	14.2	8.4	12.7
Private household	0.6	0.5	0.4	0.5
Protective service	1.0	1.6	4.1	1.0
Other service	18.4	11.5	10.4	13.7
Precision production, craft, and repair	12.5	10.3	17.5	13.3
Machine operators, assemblers, and inspectors	16.3	6.0	21.2	9.1
Transportation and material-moving equipment	4.5	3.5	5.9	5.7
Handlers, equipment cleaners, helpers, and laborers	9.1	4.1	12.8	4.8
Farming, forestry, and fishing	3.3	1.2	6.0	6.0
Total	100	100	100	100

Source: U.S. Census Bureau 2000.

Educational Attainment

Table 3.9 shows that the educational attainment of Latinos living in metro areas is characteristically skewed to the lower attainment levels, and nonmetro Latinos have even lower levels. The fact that a larger proportion of rural Latinos are recent immigrants probably accounts for this. (In Mexico, the norm is a lower level of education than in the United States.) Note that the proportion of non-Latinos outside of metro areas who had a B.A. or more is substantially lower than that in the metro areas.

Table 3.9. Educational Levels in the Metro and
Nonmetro Midwest by Ethnicity, 2000

Educational	Metro		Nonmetro	
Level	% Latino	% Non-Latino	% Latino	% Non-Latino
Eighth grade or less	23.9	4.5	28.6	6.4
Some high school	20.7	13.1	24.2	13.8
High school graduate	29.0	30.9	26.8	40.1
Some college	17.5	26.8	15.6	26.3
B.A. or more	9.0	24.6	4.8	13.3
Total	100	100	100	100

Source: U.S. Census Bureau 2000.

Summary and Conclusions

The Latino population across the United States, including the rural Midwest, has grown rapidly between 1990 and 2000. In some parts of the rural Midwest the Latino population has grown at very high rates, but the total percentage of Latinos is still small. Much of this growth has occurred in areas where there were relatively few Latinos in the past. This growth has affected all categories of population density, ranging from big cities to sparsely populated rural areas. The distribution of Latinos is quite uneven and has responded to opportunities for jobs. While most places in the rural Midwest have Latino residents, typically Latinos were less than 5 percent of the residents in 2000. The "Mexicanization" seen in rural California is not occurring yet in the Midwest, and it is too early to tell whether it will happen.

The distribution of Latinos is quite uneven and reflects Latinos' responses to opportunities for jobs. There are only about 500 towns in the Midwest where more than 5 percent of the population was Latino in 2000 (Table 3.5). Those rural places tended to have employers who recruited Latino workers, according to this and other studies. Our demographic analyses show that it is a general Midwestern pattern that rural Latinos are employed in blue-collar occupations and in manufacturing and food processing industries. The fact that a third of rural Latinos are employees in nondurable goods manufacturing (Table 3.7) shows that food processing plants have been central to Latino migration to the rural Midwest.

The rural Latino population has grown because of the widespread reliance on Latino labor in rural areas, the restructuring of rural economies since the

1980s farm crisis, and U.S. policy established through various laws on the federal and state levels in the 1980s and 1990s. Rural economic restructuring has depended partly on an influx of laborers to work for low wages in difficult conditions, and the laborers who have been recruited are frequently Latinos, both from other parts of the United States and from Mexico.

The Latinos who are settling in the rural Midwest tend to be low-paid and poorly educated, placing them in the lowest socioeconomic strata in rural communities. On the basis of their ethnicity, therefore, rural Latinos are often assumed, by Anglos, to belong to the working poor, an assumption that plays into Anglos' negative stereotypes of Latinos, as will be seen in later chapters in this book. The young age structure and the lower levels of educational attainment typically found in the Latino population suggest that the towns and villages where they are concentrated will face social and political challenges familiar in California (see Hayes-Bautista et al. 1988). That is, the aging Anglo population may need to depend on younger, less skilled, low-paid Latinos to pay taxes to support social services in the future and to provide much of the next generation to keep the towns alive. Moreover, the industrial concentration of Latinos might make an entire community vulnerable to economic crisis when a key industry collapses or moves away.

There is no sign that the flow of Latinos to the rural Midwest will slow. Furthermore, Latino demographic characteristics of a young age structure and relatively high fertility suggest that the Latino population will grow even without further immigration. Therefore, policy discussions addressing Latino issues are an urgent priority.

Emergency Medicine and Latino Newcomers

Lansing State Journal · **Sunday, February 25, 2001·9A**

Boy, 11, saves brother by translating CPR instructions
Associated Press

HAMMOND, Ind.—Police say a bilingual 11-year-old helped save his young brother's live when he calmly listened to an emergency dispatcher's instructions for performing CPR, then translated for his Spanish-speaking mother. Daniel Tinajero said he knew it was important to stay calm and listen to the dispatcher.

"If I didn't remain calm, I couldn't translate everything," Daniel said. "I learned how to use 911 in school.... They told us that in cases of emergency to stay calm."

Jose Tinajero Jr. had been sick with a fever the night of Feb. 14. Shortly after 5 p.m., Theresa Tinajero noticed he had stopped breathing and she began to panic. She speaks little English and had to rely on Daniel for help.

Daniel dialed 911, told the dispatcher what was wrong, and then talked his mother through CPR with the dispatcher's help. The 20-month-old brother began breathing shortly before paramedics arrived.

Officer Chris Matonovich, a Hammond police spokesman, said the department plans to honor Daniel.

Reprinted with permission of The Associated Press.

CHAPTER FOUR

Research Overview: The Rural Midwestern Context and Qualitative Methods

Ann V. Millard, Maríaelena D. Jefferds, Ken R. Crane, and Isidore Flores

The Midwestern Context

Many small Midwestern towns have the familiar presence of red brick, two-story buildings lining the main street, typical from the late 1800s. On first impression, their appearance suggests a timeless, seamless homogeneity and solidity of the community. In some towns, however, about half of the first-story businesses have signs in Spanish.

> Venturing a walk along the main street of Ligonier, Indiana, you will notice that many customers are Latino. Wandering into the rear of El Milagro Supermarket (once a Kroger's), you can sit at the old soda-fountain-style counter. The store is reminiscent of Woolworth's, except norteño music is playing loudly and the cook is frying *lengua* [tongue] for a *torta* [Mexican sandwich].
>
> Beyond the back door and parking lot, run-down housing is crowded with Latinos who have arrived to work in the local factories. It is a short distance to the town park, and if you sit there long enough, you will observe at least one, probably several, Amish buggies pulling up. Families will unload; the men, in white shirts and black trousers or overalls, will tie up the horses. The women, in blue dresses and bonnets, will fill water buckets for the horses from the fire station before they walk to the dentist, bank, or dollar store. The family is running errands during the men's days off from factory work.
>
> Run-down housing lines the foot of a street that rises up a small hill. Up the street, as the housing begins to improve, a small but imposing portico with Greek columns leads into a tiny jewel of a Carnegie library. Still further along the street are magnificent Victorian homes, some well preserved. One enormous pink house is now a bed and breakfast inn. Its dining room ceiling was painted in Europe and shipped here. The sliding doors have Honduran mahogany on one side, oak on the other, to match the wood in the adjoining rooms.

Across the street, a turreted house has an elevator. Ligonier has seen
splendorous times.
Crane, field notes

Waves of people of different ethnic groups and religions have populated
Ligonier over the nineteenth and twentieth centuries. Most of the newcomers would have been considered "outsiders" in the region when they first
arrived. The earliest were western Pennsylvanians who founded the town,
then Jewish refugees, next "hillbillies" from Appalachia, and most recently,
Latinos of Mexican descent. Other refugee populations, including Mennonites and Amish, settled in surrounding towns. All the later arrivals were
subjected to attitudes of exclusion from those who consider themselves descendants of the original settlers of European ancestry.

Arriving in the small, northern Indiana town from the west, you first
pass a large automotive parts plant on the left, and immediately on
your right is a run-down trailer park with large puddles in the unpaved
driveway. A shiny, twin-prop aircraft in good working order is parked at
the end of the trailer park's dirt track, imparting a feeling of contradic-
tion to the scene. That is only the beginning of a series of surprises to
the visitor who has time to look around.

As you window-shop along the main street, you will come to one
sizable shop full of exotic carvings. On closer inspection, they are
African carvings of human figures, some as tall as eight feet; there are
many baskets of dried palm fronds and several masks. There is no
sign on the door or name. (It turns out that these are the remnants of
a failed import business begun by a local man who had traveled exten-
sively in Africa and who now is the main landlord of Latino tenants in
the town.)

Up the street and over one block is a former synagogue built in 1889
to serve the 60 Jewish families in town. A distinctive characteristic of
town history is its Jewish heritage; the town seal has the Star of David
among its other images. That history is now a historical footnote, as
the earlier families left, and the town synagogue was turned into a
museum.

There you will learn that Ligonier was founded by a man who happened to come from a town of the same name in western Pennsylva-

nia. In 1835, he chartered the county of Wayne, Indiana, and platted the town of Ligonier. Ligonier, Pennsylvania, continues to be a sister city, and one of the mayoral responsibilities is to attend the sister town's parades. (One year, the mayor drove Ligonier's fire truck from Indiana to the parade in Pennsylvania.)

Tourism is down. The Marshmallow Festival used to attract more interest, but since the marshmallow factory closed the town can no longer make the claim of being the world's largest producer. The economic base, fortunately, does not rely on tourism. The town has always had an industrial base, as evident in the museum's "cold boxes" (refrigerators) and photographs of the buggies made locally. Industry now attracts people from near and far. A large industrial park on the northern side of town employs around 3,500 workers (only about 4,000 people live in Ligonier). Products vary from exhaust systems to plastic bottles.

Crane, field notes

Although Ligonier has a unique history with regard to its founding and later settlement by various ethnic groups, it now resembles other Midwestern towns in that its apparent Anglo homogeneity has given way to the recent, sudden arrival of "Mexican" newcomers.

Other Midwestern towns have also experienced recent, dramatic ethnic shifts in population. Postville, Iowa, recently underwent economic change by attracting new ethnic groups. A New York businessman bought a defunct meatpacking plant in the town to produce kosher products, attracting Hassidic Jews and a Mexican immigrant workforce (Bloom 2000).

This is a town where on one side of the street an Israeli can get halvah, while on the other a Mexican can wire money back home. A town where you can hear both the Norwegian *uff da* and the Yiddish *oy vey* in a single office. A town of just 2,300 residents, but more than 20 ethnic groups. Welcome to the United Nations of Iowa. (Marbella 2001)

Many small towns of the Midwest were populated by successive waves of different peoples, including Native Americans pushed from their original lands, European immigrants of various nationalities and religions, and U.S. citizens moving from the East and South. In many cases, their descendants still define themselves as ethnically distinct; however, they tend to see the current Latino influx as a new kind of phenomenon and a threatening one.

In 1998, for example, the Indiana Association of Cities and Towns began meeting with mayors to deal with the "dramatic surge in the growth of Spanish-speaking residents" in "Indiana cities and towns of all sizes" (Quinn 2001:9).

> Hot topic discussions at the monthly Mayor's Roundtable meetings focused on the challenges of accommodating the large [Latino population] increases in communities across the state. Such issues as coping with language barriers for non-English-speaking persons, a lack of adequate housing, and defusing cultural conflicts with non-Hispanic neighbors dominated discussions among mayors. (Quinn 2001:9)

These issues were significant in all the communities in our study that had large Latino influxes. In some cases, political office seekers used these issues in their campaigns, contributing to ethnic polarization in their communities (see "En Pocas Palabras VI: The 'Mexican Situation' and the Mayor's Race").

Migration History in Ligonier

Ligonier's Jewish phase began in the 1850s with the arrival of Jewish refugees fleeing persecution in Prussia.[1] Two Jewish peddlers found the town attractive, partly due to the atmosphere of religious tolerance among the German Mennonites and local Amish settling in the region (Crane interview with two volunteers, Chamber of Commerce). The peddlers decided to settle where the railroad had been planned because of the potential for shipping products to Chicago and the East. They went into business, prospered, and later became commercial rivals as they expanded their economic ventures into banking, manufacturing, a network of electric railways, and the largest real estate agency in the United States.

According to most town historians and old-timers, the era from the late 1800s to the late 1920s was the town's "golden age." It was a vibrant "Jewish town," in its early days and rapidly expanding, with beautiful streets, three banks, and a booming economy. A favorite pastime of locals during this era of affluence was to go to the train station and watch wealthy families return from Chicago decked out in their latest acquisitions. During the high holidays, "Everybody in Ligonier dressed very elegant and were very somber and sedate during the Jewish New Year festival of Rosh Hashanah. And everybody always wore hats, and also gloves for the women—you didn't go to temple without them" (*Ligonier Advance Leader,* September 22, 1994). The descendants of the wealthy families eventually moved away from the town, and the last local Jewish resident died in 1981.

Other groups who settled locally in the 1800s included the Amish, descendants of Anabaptists and Mennonites who, like the Jews, were fleeing religious persecution in Europe. Their farms and communities have a distinctive appearance and economic profile; nowadays, many work side by side in factories with Latinos.

In the 1950s a great migration of people from the economically depressed coal-mining regions of Appalachia began. Coming from states such as Kentucky, West Virginia, and Tennessee, they migrated to northern industrial cities. During the early 1960s, some of these so-called hillbillies found their way to Ligonier. Little has been written about these people. Residents of the region characterized them as outsiders—poor, uneducated, and generally an undesirable element that occupied the lowest rung on the socioeconomic ladder. A generation later, it is difficult to find anyone who claims descent from this group or knows very much about them.

Latino Migration

In the 1960s another group was settling in rural northern Indiana: migrant farmworkers who sought factory jobs so that they could stay through the winter. In the past, migrant farmworkers came from Texas to northern Indiana seasonally in great numbers to work on the region's tomato farms.

The journey of Alicia and Rubén, described in Chapter 1, exemplifies this pathway to settlement in the Midwest. Alicia and Rubén saw settlement as a way to improve their living condition and to provide their children with a good place to grow up. They had several reasons to be hesitant about spending the winter there, however. They wondered whether they and their family could physically survive the cold. Various families had reported that some family members could not, whereupon they moved southward and continued migrant farmwork. Alicia and Rubén also wondered whether the chemical fumes at the factory would sicken them, as was the case with some workers they knew. They found that they could survive these problems but reported that they found their existence in the Wheelerton area "lonely." Alicia's brothers and their families had already moved to the area; however, they missed the larger Mexican American cultural and social sphere of south Texas and parts of Florida where they used to winter. For Alicia and Rubén, and other former migrant workers as well, a mixture of structural and personal constraints played into the decision about settling in the rural Midwest.

The trickle of families who joined the earlier group of Latinos in the Midwest became a wave in the late 1980s and early 1990s, and began to include people moving directly from Mexico. In the 1990s, the people of Mexican descent really began to make their presence felt. The economic context in a nutshell is that during the early 1990s, north central Indiana (Elkhart, South Bend, Fort Wayne), which earlier had been hit hard by deindustrialization, began to ride the economic boom and reemerge with a dynamic manufacturing base. Smaller communities such as Ligonier and Wheelerton attracted auto component companies, which relocated from Detroit to outmaneuver unions and take advantage of other lower production costs. In Ligonier, employment in manufacturing nearly tripled during the decade of the 1980s (DUP 1994). Soon the demand for production workers outstripped the local supply. Turnover was high, especially in the more demanding second and third shifts.

This study thus had a historical context of in-migrating refugees and low-income people looking for a safe place where they could better themselves. The local non-Latinos, however, tended not to understand the history of ethnic diversity in the region. Their perspective made it possible for political campaigns to portray the newcomers as a threat to the local way of life.

Qualitative Research Questions and Methods

We began our qualitative studies of rural communities in a deliberate and well-planned manner. The community study phase of this research focused on the following questions:

1. What is the social, economic, and cultural place of Latinos in rural Midwestern communities?

2. Why and how are Latinos settling in specific communities?
3. How do Anglo communities respond, and what are the relationships between Latinos and Anglos at work, school, and church, and in other daily activities?

Unlike its general image as a staid and deliberate process, research often becomes an adventure because of the unpredictability of the real world compared with the assumptions of the research design. Unanticipated situations in fieldwork require flexibility, intuition, and knowledge of a wide array of methods. The unpredictability of research often takes investigators by surprise; if all the issues were understood, however, the research would not be worth doing. We found a number of surprises in our fieldwork, discussed in this and subsequent chapters.

On the basis of previous research, we had expected that many of the Latino newcomers would be former migrant farmworkers settling in areas familiar to them from previous seasonal employment. This study thus deals with migrant farmworkers as part of the rural Midwestern context. We include in this study only former migrants who have become year-round inhabitants (see Chapter 1). This was not the only pathway to settlement, however, as shown by other Latinos who arrived in the Midwest with factory jobs awaiting them, often after a journey of 1,500 miles from central Mexico.

Recognizing that rural villages and towns are intertwined socially, economically, educationally, and religiously, we did not study a single community alone but focused on clusters of communities, as discussed below. The current and past ethnic diversity in rural communities also required attention as part of the context of the study. We found that prejudice against Latino newcomers permeated our qualitative data (see Chapter 5; "En Pocas Palabras I: Ten Myths"; and "En Pocas Palabras VI: The 'Mexican Situation'"). It is not the purpose of this study to analyze ethnicity and class separately, but our research found that many rural Anglos view the combination of "Mexican" identity and low income as particularly unacceptable. We were surprised at the extent to which prejudice against Latino newcomers shaped social relations ranging from daily interaction to public policy, whether or not Anglos had had previous experience with "Mexicans."

Despite the pervasive prejudice, we met many Anglos and Latinos who cooperated enthusiastically with our project, and without their willingness to cross ethnic and class divides in doing so, our qualitative research could not have been carried out. We knew, as we began the qualitative research, that fluency in Spanish would be important to the success of our data collection; however, we had not expected that it would be crucial in challenging stereotypes about Latino newcomers. These were several of the surprises we encountered during this study.

In this study, we used a mixture of qualitative methods. Crane and Jefferds carried out participant observation and semistructured interviews in several communities. Two other members of the research team (Millard and Flores) assisted them in carrying out focus group discussions with three separate types of inhabitants: Latino newcomers, long-term Latino residents, and long-term Anglo inhabitants. In addition, we (Chapa, Crane, Jefferds, Flores, and Millard) visited other rural communities to learn about Latino newcomers (see Appendix A on methods, Appendix B on interview questions, and Appendix C on focus group questions).

In writing this book, we want to convey the sense of adventure and discovery that we experienced during this project. Although we found numerous brewing crises in rural areas that call for immediate policy change, we also encountered vibrancy in rural people as they sought ways to move on with their lives despite many obstacles. A number of the study participants impressed us with their willingness to consider new pathways of development for their communities. For example, an Anglo farmer said she would rather sell her place to "Mexicans" for farming than to a developer for vacation homesites. We were also impressed with the humor of many rural people, as in the case of the same farmer, who said that every fall she puts out a "For Sale" sign at her farm because the fall work is so hard, and the sign stays there until her husband notices it and takes it down.

Dynamics of Contemporary Latino Migration to the Rural Midwest

Five out of the six longest highways in the United States run within 20 miles of Ligonier. (Wall sign, Ligonier Radio Museum)

With a population of about 4,000, Ligonier in Noble County appears to be one of the cities and towns in northeast Indiana most affected by the growth of the Hispanic population. (*Ligonier Advance Leader*, March 5, 2000)

By the mid-1980s, Latino workers in many Midwestern towns had proved themselves model workers. Some of these long-term employees were asked by companies to recruit additional workers and they did, bringing friends and relatives from Mexico, the border region, and other parts of the United States. In the early 1990s, larger numbers of workers of Mexican descent came to the industrial parks in the regions of Ligonier, Wheelerton, and Logansport in northern Indiana and similar communities.

Reporting on Postville, Iowa, Marbella (2001) wrote:

How this community in the northeast corner of the state became the United Nations in miniature is in some ways the story of America, circa 21st century, writ small.

It is the story of immigrants flocking to take jobs that too few native-born Americans want. It is the story of refugees—whether from poverty in Guatemala or crime in New York or joblessness in Ukraine—seeking somewhere better to live and raise a family. And it is the story of a small town uneasily coming to terms with its newfound diversity, a task made all the more difficult by the very fact that it is a small town.

Aponte and Siles (1995) predicted that the most dramatic impacts of immigration would befall the small towns of the Midwest, not the expected urban entry points such as Miami, New York, or Los Angeles. The succeeding chapters in this book provide a detailed look at the ways in which the Latino influx is reshaping life and town economies in the rural Midwest. The success of the original Latino families in gaining a foothold in the economic life of small Midwestern towns, combined with their strong family networks and religious organizations, has given Latinos a presence that cannot be ignored. The ongoing supply of new immigrants from Mexico and the U.S. Southwest will sustain the Latino communities in these towns for decades to come.

If current estimates of the population of Wheelerton are accurate, the growth in the Latino population has been dramatic, from around 300 in 1990 (8.5 percent), to 1,500 (or 37.5 percent of the town population) in the year 2000. A survey in the mid-1990s identified some characteristics of the burgeoning Latino population: 70 percent of adults were employed; 85 percent considered themselves permanent residents of Wheelerton; and 95 percent were interested in becoming U.S. citizens.

A Mexican American minister who helped organize the survey believed that of those interviewed, 98 percent were of Mexican descent and 25 percent were born in the United States, many of whom had lived previously in Texas, Florida, or California. He also believed that many who originally had planned to return to Mexico or the southern United States now wanted to stay in the area. He said that 99 percent want to learn English. Those who know the Mexican population believe that most of those who immigrated from Mexico come from the Mexican states of Durango, Aguascalientes, and Zacatecas. These families reportedly maintain frequent contact with relatives and friends there.[2] (*Ligonier Advance Leader,* March 23, 1995)

Although the in-migration of Latinos to Wheelerton began to pick up in the 1980s, many residents identify the period from 1993 on as the time of the major Latino influx. For example, in the early 1990s, school officials began to report much larger numbers of "Spanish language minority" students; by the mid-1990s, Spanish-speaking students added up to about 15 percent of the high school population.

The economic stagnation of the Mexican economy plus the family sponsorship of those who became residents under the Immigration Control and Reform Act (IRCA) provision added momentum to the social networks linking Ligonier and Wheelerton with states in Mexico. Several of those interviewed in the Latino community identified IRCA as a catalyst for new migration to the region.

The Mexican presence is highly visible in the old downtown Wheelerton area. A large *tienda* [store], whose owner hails from Durango via Chicago, has a full line of produce, as well as a *taquería* [lunch counter selling tacos] and *carnicería* [butcher shop]. In addition, there are the restaurants, clothing stores, Oficina de Servicios [Western Union, CartMex, and Uniteller money transfer services], Servicio de Impuestos [assistance with income taxes], and several other Mexican shops with video libraries, Paula's Floral Shop with a sign saying "Se habla español" [Spanish spoken], the pool hall with a sign, "Billar," and the landmark Tito's Tacos. The nearby Harwood Bank has a large Mexican clientele.
Crane, field notes

The Latino community in Wheelerton includes two groups. The first is comprised of those who arrived in the 1960s, their children, and grandchildren. Theirs is a community bound by kinship (many have common grandparents), class (they are middle-class professionals—teachers, police officers, business owners), and religion (most belong to Templo Cristo Rey or one of the other Pentecostal churches). Many of the businesses they operate (shops, translation services, real estate) have been created to serve the new immigrant population. The second group includes those who moved to the town in the 1990s. They are largely unskilled production or service workers who are monolingual Spanish speakers, and most live in crowded apartments downtown.

The second stories of the buildings lining the main street have largely been converted into weekly rentals to house newly arrived Mexican tenants. Other newcomers live in three run-down trailer parks outside the city limits. Some of the more upwardly mobile are buying or building houses in better residential parts of the city. The longtime Latino residents have lived in the better parts of town for several decades.

These two groups of Latinos, the old-timers and the newcomers, are present in all the communities in our study that have had a recent Latino influx. Latinos themselves discuss their membership in one group or the other and the relations between them. They are also recognized as distinct groups by many Anglos.

Midwestern Villages and Towns in This Study

The communities in this study range in size from less than 100 to about 4,000 people. Most of them have existed for decades, many for at least 75 years, and some for over a century. We had planned originally to study several rural communities separately, to characterize the various types of small towns in the rural Midwest. We found it best to study clusters of communities, however, because town boundaries do not circumscribe spheres of social interaction, and the sense of community identity is thus somewhat blurred.

We focus mainly on communities where Latino newcomers were settling rapidly. It is interesting to note that typically the community clusters doubled their percentages of Latinos in the ten years since 1990; however, in most cases the total percentage of Latinos in the year 2000 was only 10 to 15 percent. Nonetheless, we found that when the percentage of Latinos rose to that level in the public schools, many community members responded with surprise and dismay, and teachers and authorities complained that they were overwhelmed with a large Latino influx. We were surprised that these low percentages created such a strong reaction among local people.

The seasonal influx of migrant farmworkers often increases the local population by 30 percent or so, and some new settlers arrive by this route as well. The areas employing migrant farmworkers are those growing fruit, vegetables, bedding plants, and Christmas trees, and nearly all the migrant workers are Mexican and Mexican American.

From World War II to the 1990s, relatively small numbers of Latinos settled in the rural Midwest. During the 1990s, though, a large number took jobs in rural areas and stopped migrating. Newly settled Latinos tend to be economically precarious, most speak very little English (even if they have lived for years in the United States), their children generally are not doing well in school, and many live in substandard rental housing. They are relatively isolated as a group and socially separated from Anglos by the language barrier. Among year-round Latino residents, those who have lived in the community for many years tend to be much better off than the newcomers. They tend to own their own homes, speak English well, and have children who are upwardly mobile. Among both groups of Latinos, many still do farmwork as a second job during the harvest season or, in a few cases, they hold jobs through the spring, summer, and fall in more skilled farm jobs such as driving a tractor.

The towns and villages in this study with 1,000 or more residents all have at least one restaurant, several public schools, a post office, and a few stores, but none have a large commercial complex or megastore such as Wal-Mart. They all have a Mexican restaurant or a "Mexican store" selling merchandise from Mexico and Latino businesses in Chicago. The bulk of the population is Anglo, including large Amish communities, and there may also be a few Native Americans, African Americans, or Asian Americans.

Most towns and villages in this study were established to deal with the local farming population; however, some also had food processing and manufacturing plants early in the twentieth century. Typically, a town in our study lies near a crossroads with a main road leading to the commercial center, which is usually about three blocks long and includes about half of the storefronts in the community. In some cases, the center bespeaks a former grandeur, with three-story brick buildings and nearby stately houses with impressive facades. Spreading out from the center of town, neighborhoods shade off into farms and fields in about a quarter of a mile. The neighborhoods typically have unimposing one- and two-story frame houses surrounded by grass and trees and close enough to the road to make digging out of the snow manageable in the winter. The neighborhoods may have schools and often have a small park with playground equipment, and each town has a trailer park or two and businesses scattered along the roads leading through the neighborhoods to the center of town. Usually the town and neighborhoods are kept clean, neat, and mowed and have a simple, unadorned appearance.

Dimensions of Separation of Anglos and Latinos

The communities have little visible evidence of ethnic diversity other than the contrast between Anglos and Latinos. Their apparent homogeneity is an overlay on a more heterogeneous past, as noted above in the history of Ligionier. Anglos themselves, however, perceive that they are currently quite diverse because of their memberships in different churches and descent from different European nationalities. The region has a surprising number of churches in the various small towns. For example, the town of Fox, Michigan, with only 2,000 people, has churches belonging to Roman Catholics, Jehovah's Witnesses, Baptists, and various other Protestant denominations. The Anglo split between Catholics and Protestants has been quite pronounced for many decades and still presents a barrier to some marriages.

In any region, one Catholic church will usually offer mass in Spanish. Latinos sometimes travel many miles to participate in such a mass, even when they are fluent in English. Latinos also belong to churches other than the Catholic Church, and in this respect, they fit into rural Midwestern communities, which may have surprisingly large numbers and varieties of churches for their size.

Commerce: Separation in Employment and Business Ownership

Latinos and Anglos are separated in many ways in small Midwestern towns. To research team members, the separation was familiar; however, we had not realized before this study how cleanly divided the ethnic groups are

Table 4.1. Ethnic Distribution of Owners, Managers, Workers, and Patrons in the Rural Midwest

Type of Organization	Nearly All Anglos	Nearly All Latinos	Both
"Mexican" store			
Owners (family)		X	
Managers (family)		X	
Workers (family)		X	
Patrons		X	
Other stores[a]			
Owners	X		
Managers	X		
Workers	X		
Patrons	X		
Restaurants (not "Mexican")[b]			
Owners	X		
Managers	X		
Workers	X		
Patrons	X		
Local government			
Elected officials	X		
Other officials	X		
Police and jails	X		
Driver's license bureau	X		

in regard to access to jobs and commercial opportunities. As employees and business owners, Latinos fill low-income niches in the local economy. Throughout our study, we found a pattern of Anglo ownership of larger restaurants, bigger stores, and all factories.

> A Latino with a store near Ciderville asserted that Latinos cannot get business loans. (He commented that he could file the papers with the Small Business Administration, but the papers would never be processed; there would always be more questions to answer and forms to change or fill out; thus no deliberations on the loan would ever take place.)[3] (Millard, field notes)

The proliferation of small, family-run Latino restaurants and stores that provide only marginal incomes suggests that Latinos do not have access to

Table 4.1. (Continued)

Type of Organization	Nearly All Anglos	Nearly All Latinos	Both
Library	X		
Social services			
Management	X		
Service workers[c]	X		
Clerical staff	X		
Health services			
Health professionals[d]	X		
Staff	X		
Courts	X		
Most staff	X		
Professional interpreters[e]			X

[a] The study found one store owned by a Latino, the grocery in Ligonier, Indiana.
[b] Mexican-owned restaurants have little capital and are family-run. See Chapter 1 for an example.
[c] Bilingual Latinos are hired seasonally to deal with migrant farmworkers. For example, community health clinics and migrant clinics have bilingual staff, but they are not professionally trained as interpreters.
[d] One exception was a Latino psychiatrist who had moved from South America to Michigan and was working as a mental health specialist.
[e] The only professional interpreters worked for the court system in larger cities. Some rural organizations had bilingual staff who served as interpreters.

the better-paying jobs in the communities (Table 4.1). The typical Mexican store does not seem to do enough business to support anyone, but it does provide a small amount of additional income to families with members who have other jobs or attend school for part of the day and staff the store on a rotating basis. Some stores are important resources for Latino newcomers and migrant farmworkers, who come in to cash checks, send telegrams, buy state lottery tickets, find out about local work opportunities, and get assistance with any paperwork or telephone calls that require assistance in English.

Factories
The factories we have studied in the rural Midwest are owned by Anglos or by corporations traded on the New York Stock Exchange. We have not heard of any factories owned by Latinos (Table 4.2). The management tends

Table 4.2. Ethnic Distribution of Occupations as Owners, Managers, and Laborers in Factories in This Study

Type of Factory and Job	Anglos Only	Latinos Only	Both[a]
Food processing and meat packing			
Ownership	X		
Management except lowest rung[b]	X		
Work force		X	X
Light industry			
Ownership	X		
Management except lowest rung	X		
Work force	X		X
Separate shifts at the same factory	X	X	X

[a]Some organizations had occupational categories including both Latinos and Anglos.
[b]The lowest rung tends to have a bilingual Latino in a plant where Latinos work on the floor.

to be Anglo, although if a plant has a Latino workforce, a bilingual Latino supervisor will often occupy the lowest managerial rung, and he or she will interpret for upper-level managers.

One of the companies well documented in this regard is IBP, Iowa Beef Processing Company (formerly under other names). The company opened a factory in 1996 in Logansport, Indiana, and became the town's primary employer of Latinos (Peck 2001:10–11). By 2001, 65 percent of IBP's work-force of 1,800 at the plant was Latino; the company expressed surprise at the high percentage, although it has relied on immigrants from Latin America to work in many IBP plants in the Midwest. (In 2003 IBP had a recruit-ment office on 10th Street in McAllen, Texas, a mere eight miles from the Mexican border, and was advertising jobs in Spanish in Reynosa, the neigh-boring city in Mexico, which suggests that the company plans to continue importing workers from Mexico to the Midwest.)

In Logansport, IBP worked with local government, the Chamber of Com-merce, and United Way to direct services to plant workers, including but not limited to Latinos. The services included programs dealing with free trans-portation for local people (including IBP employees) and for those with poor English skills, instruction about buying local housing and about police and fire matters, especially what to do in emergencies, and free classes in Eng-lish as a second language funded by IBP and the local school system. (The school system needed assistance because by 2001 10 percent of its students did not speak English.) IBP also funded classes in Spanish for its non-Latino employees, and worked with local organizations on diversity training and related efforts for community members (Peck 2001:10–11).

The workforces of the plants in this study tended to be separated by ethnicity. Some plants had all-Anglo workforces; others had one or two shifts that were virtually entirely Anglo and another that was all-Latino, the night shift. In some cases, there was an Amish shift or two. These plants tended to pay relatively good wages for rural employees, for example, $10.50 an hour in the year 2000; however, in some cases this wage level was paid only to plant managers. The only plants we learned of that had all-Latino workforces paid near the minimum wage (around $5.25 to $6.00 an hour). In nationwide perspective, wages for the poorest 10 percent of workers rose from 1996 to 1999, but they still did not reach the levels of 1973 (Ehrenreich 2001:202, drawing partly from Bernstein et al. 2000). Generally, Latino newcomers work under the most difficult and dangerous conditions in plants that do food processing, including meatpacking. They move in to take jobs under working conditions refused by local residents.

Farms

In general, Midwestern farms are owned by Anglos (Table 4.3). The children of many Anglo farmers express no interest in farming, and their parents anticipate that their children will leave for the cities. As noted earlier in

Table 4.3. Ethnic Distribution of Positions as Owners and Laborers on Farms in This Study

Type of Farm and Job	Anglos Only	Latinos Only	Workforces of Both Anglos and Latinos
Fruit and vegetable production			
Ownership[a]	X		
Workforce (hand laborers)		X	X
Grain production			
Ownership	X		
Workforce (machine drivers)	X		

[a]The exceptions are a handful of small farms (about ten acres) owned by Latinos in Southwestern Michigan; these owners hire Latino migrant farmworkers to work in their fields.

this chapter, a woman farmer said that it would make sense for Latinos to take up such farms; she does not want hers to turn into a housing development. If Latinos cannot obtain loans, however, they will not be able to take advantage of such opportunities. Currently, a few farms in southwestern Michigan are owned by Latinos who purchased small parcels of land, about ten acres each, from farmers who employ them seasonally and thus gain better access to their labor. We learned of only one Latino farmer in our community studies, and Latino farmers generally were not mentioned by study participants.

Government-Provided Services: Employment of and Service for Latinos

In rural Midwestern governmental and nonprofit organizations, the staff is nearly all Anglo and has no Spanish speakers, even if the organization has a substantial Latino clientele. The exception is organizations that have responsibility for extending limited services to Latino migrant farmworkers. The result is that, at all other agencies, Latinos who are monolingual Spanish speakers receive fewer services, and services of lower quality, than do other clients (see Chapter 7, on education).

The funneling of government services away from monolingual Spanish speakers also occurs in hospitals, employment agencies, libraries, police stations, and other organizations. It is also true for many nongovernmental services, including those offered by churches, county foundations, and clubs. This phenomenon occurs nationwide, not just in the Midwest, as documented in reports on the U.S. Department of Labor and its poor protection of workers with limited English proficiency related to occupational safety, minimum wage, and other policies (National Employment Law Project 2001).

A rural Midwestern area that has a migrant clinic or a community health clinic funded by the federal government will usually have Spanish-speaking staff available and, in some cases, Spanish-speaking doctors. Other medical and dental services, however, generally do not have anyone on staff who can interpret. That includes emergency rooms in hospitals, even in hospitals that have Spanish-speaking social services workers.

The result has been the turning away of patients with emergencies or their relegation to the back of the line regardless of their health problem. Above all, it has meant frightening and dangerous experiences for Latino patients receiving treatment from people who cannot communicate with them. Furthermore, hospital staff assume that a Spanish monolingual patient will not be able to pay for services, whereas Latinos frequently want to make arrangements to pay off bills in small payments over a long period.

In employment agencies, libraries, police stations, churches, county foundations, and charitable clubs, few if any of the staff are bilingual, resulting in no or few services to those who cannot speak English. It is true that Spanish-speaking parents often have children who can speak English, and that they take them out of school to serve as interpreters at appointments. Depending on an eight-year-old child to deal with emergencies and complex concepts, however, is highly problematic. Clients who communicate in Spanish, then, have less access to services and receive services of inferior quality compared with others.

The few middle-class Latinos in rural areas tend to be bilingual social service workers, a few clergy, occasionally community clinic staff, and a few others in the service sector. Also, some organizations are undergoing change in regard to bilingual capacity. For employment in social services in the fall of 1999 in Michigan, for example, all positions advertised in western Michigan required that candidates be able to speak Spanish. We have not heard of this occurring in other organizations and other states, but this instance is a sharp break from the practices of the past. The language problems found in this study are forms of institutional discrimination in the sense that, because they lack interpreters, many organizations direct resources away from Spanish monolingual Latinos, as discussed in a later chapter.

Political Representation

Latinos in the communities in this study have not yet directly engaged in politics by voting in any discernable block. Of the Latino immigrants who received residency under the Immigration Reform and Control Act of 1986, some are moving toward citizenship, although it is uncertain whether they will vote. Large numbers of Latinos from south Texas have settled in some parts of the Midwest, and many already have the right to vote. In a case where Latinos work for a food processing plant in Michigan eight to ten months out of the year, however, the workers are categorized as migrant farm laborers and they do not vote in Michigan. If they did, they would be able to assert political power, because they are relatively numerous.

Rather than working directly through politics, Latinos tend to exert political pressure indirectly, through churches. Latino pastors sometimes use moral suasion to try to improve policies toward their congregants, and at other times they encourage laypeople to organize a response to a problematic situation. As shown in Chapter 8, at times these efforts can make a significant improvement in community relations. Some churches have youth groups that keep teenagers busy and out of trouble, and they also provide sites for participation in music, dance, and charitable works, thus contributing to local Latino identity and culture.

Comparisons of Midwestern Rural Communities

In this study, we made an effort to identify communities that offer contrasts in how Latino newcomers are faring. We hypothesized that differences among communities regarding the quality of life of Latinos would be clear; however, the picture is more complex than we had expected.

Rising Sun, Indiana: A Community with No Latinos

We found one community with about 13 percent of the population engaged in agricultural work but with no Latino residents—Rising Sun, Indiana. Rising Sun is a small community on the Ohio River. It depends economically on farming and commerce from the river. River commerce recently was revived by the mooring of a casino boat there, leading to the construction of a tourist hotel and other facilities. Latino migrant farmworkers likely visit the area seasonally to work in the fields; hence, the area probably has at least some Latino population for part of the year, although they would not be recorded in the U.S. Census. There is at least one Mexican restaurant nearby; however, there is no evidence of a Latino influx into Rising Sun or any stimulus to attract one. The hotel is the main employer in the community, and it hires mainly local Anglos. Because of the casino and hotel, the town is unusual compared to many in the rural Midwest; however, it is not apparent why Latinos have not been recruited to work there.

Amish Communities: Labor-Intensive Farming with Very Few Latinos

Amish communities provide a contrast to the typical Anglo farming communities in the Midwest, as they have practically no Latino residents or workers. We were surprised that the number of Amish settlements was growing rapidly. Table 4.4 compares the number of Amish settlements

Table 4.4. Amish Population Growth in the Midwest, 1990–1995

State	Year First Settled[a]	Settlements before 1990	Settlement and Year Founded, 1990–1995	Estimated Population[b]
Illinois	1864	2		4,064
			Ava (1991)	176
			Macomb (1992)	168
			Belle Rive (1993)	200
			Pittsfield (1994)	200
				4,808
Indiana	1839	13		30,696
			Rockville (1991)	184
			Williamsburg (1992)	168
			Worthington (1992)	208
				31,256
Iowa	1846	6		4,752
			Chariton (1992)	176
			Mt. Ayre/Redding (1995)	160
				5,088
Kansas	1883	3		1232
Michigan	1900	21		7,880
			Fremont (1990)	192
			Coral (1991)	176
				8,248
Minnesota	1972	5		1,960
Nebraska		0		
Ohio	1808	26		45,904
			Brinkhaven (1990)	184
			Somerset (1990)	200
			Dorset (1991)	176
			Leesburg (1991)	200
			Loudonville (1991)	176
			Andover (1992)	160
			Barnesville (1993)	176
			McKay (1993)	192
				47,368

(continued on page 96)

Table 4.4. (Continued)

State	Year First Settled[a]	Settlements before 1990	Settlement and Year Founded, 1990–1995	Estimated Population[b]
Wisconsin	1925	19		9,184
			Athens (1990)	184
			Oconto (1990)	144
			Readstown (1990)	368
			Mondovi (1991)	368
			New Holstein (1992)	200
			Owen (1992)	176
			Viroqua (1992)	200
			Bloomington (1993)	208
				11,032
Total population, 27 new Midwestern settlements (1990–1995)				8,512
Total Amish population, 122 Midwestern settlements, 1995				110,992

[a] *Source:* Hostetler 1993:98. *Source for other data:* Garrett 1996:34–40.

[b] Estimated population = (no. families) × 8 (based on Garrett's statement that "family" (i.e., household) size ranges from 6 to 10).

existing before 1990 with the large number of new settlements developed from 1990 to 1995. Amish settlements in the Midwest in 1995 numbered 122, of which 27 had been founded between 1990 and 1995 (Garrett 1996). As noted above, Table 4.4 population estimates result from multiplying the number of families per settlement by the median "family size," as Garrett terms it (in anthropological terms, it would be "household size"). According to these calculations, the total Amish population in the Midwest was 110,992 in 1995. Hostetler states that in 1992 there were 90,400 Old Order Amish in the Midwest, excluding Minnesota (1993:98). Regardless of the exact population size, the point here is that the Amish comprise a sizable rural population in some areas of the Midwest and that they are expanding their number of settlements vigorously. They do not account for a large percentage of rural Midwesterners, but their communities probably account for most of the growth in farms and farmers in the region. They do not farm for the sake of profit but to maintain close family ties and to cultivate the ties to God and nature prescribed by their religion (Hostetler 1993). Their farms are labor-intensive, yet very few Latinos are employed there.

Contrary to the general impression, moreover, many Midwestern Amish farmers also work off their farms, whether in small local factories manufacturing such Amish goods as furniture and buggies or in light manufacturing plants serving the auto industry. Their engagement in factory work was surprising to us, considering that the Amish are forbidden to drive cars; however, factory work has been approved by Amish religious leaders, and Amish factory workers drive their horse-drawn buggies to work or pay for transportation in cars driven by Mennonite drivers.

Latinos do not join Amish religious communities, but the two groups have had increasing contact. Some construction crews include Latino and Amish workers. We also found one Mexican restaurant in Amish country, BJ's Burritos in Topeka, Indiana. The owner's father had worked for an Amish employer. The restaurant opens on weekends, and the clientele are Amish, complete with bonnets and buggies.

Community Variation in Regard to How Latinos Are Faring

The communities in this study that are drawing Latino newcomers do not differ in many aspects from those that are not. As the attraction of Latinos to rural communities depends on job availability, Latino migration operates independently of other community characteristics, such as the orientation of the churches, schools, social service providers, and other organizations. These organizations find themselves in a reactive state, and few have made the effort to reach out to Latino newcomers unless they have been funded to reach out to migrant farmworkers settling locally.

The only dimension of difference that we found between communities that drew Latino newcomers and those that did not was in the types of employment. If a community did not have jobs in food processing or light industry, it did not attract Latinos.

As noted by Mayor Hyman of Postville, Iowa, in 2001:

Like it or not, this is the new face of Postville . . . There are always people who do not want change in their life. But the town was stagnant. It was dying basically before the meatpacking plant got going again. We were an aging community, so it's been a positive thing that we are growing again. (Marbella 2001)

How well Latinos are faring in a given community depends mostly on their type of employment and the number of wage earners in their households. Those working in light industry, particularly if they live in double-earner households (where husband and wife both work full time), belong to the middle class (see Chapters 1 and 6). Those working in food processing plants and living in single-earner households barely make ends meet, and they belong to the working poor.

Local Police, the INS, and "Churning Bad Public Opinion"

Ken R. Crane

Officer Frank of Wheelerton, Indiana, takes a large manila envelope and pours the contents onto his desk in front of me. It is a mass of fake resident alien cards, Social Security cards, and driver's licenses. He shows me which ones are obviously fake; I pick one up and feel where a photo had been cut out and pasted onto a card and then laminated. He tells me, "The alien cards can be purchased in San Bernardino [California] for $200, or in Brownsville [Texas}, they buy a temporary ID used by residents in border towns to cross daily. Here I've noticed people using that kind for the last seven years."

The county prosecutor asks them to keep a file whenever they charge someone suspected of being illegal. Frank goes on to say that once they had seven male suspects held for some misdemeanor charges. They called the INS [U.S. Immigration and Naturalization Service] to report the suspicion that they were "illegal." The INS finally responded and said to call them only to deport a person who had committed a felony, had been convicted as a felon, and had been sentenced to at least one year and a day in jail. Officer Frank concluded, "Otherwise they don't want to hear from us."

Crane, field notes

Officer Frank is chief of police in Wheelerton; he is in his mid-thirties with close-cropped hair. We met in his office, along with a plainclothes police officer.

During this study, confiscation of ID cards from Latinos by various authorities, such as the police and emergency room staff in various communities, was common. There was little evidence that they were concerned about the illegality of confiscating legitimate ID cards. Toward the end of this study, the Mexican consul in South Bend, Indiana, was preparing a visit to some towns in the region to explain that the authorities are breaking the law when they make such confiscations.

Frank, in describing the biggest challenges regarding the Latino population, stated, "They don't understand our ordinances. You try to explain them to people, and you encounter a language problem." According to Officer Frank, this problem worsened about seven or eight years earlier when, in his opinion, large numbers of "Mexicans" coming to Wheelerton were in the country illegally. On warm summer nights, they would gather in the parking lots behind the "slum areas" downtown. He could not approach them to deal with violation of ordinances like public drunkenness or loitering at night without drawing a large and threatening crowd, and he would need backup or dog units.

Once, he and his partner stopped a suspected DUI (someone driving under the influence of alcohol) in the downtown area. They had the suspect out of the car doing a test when young men, many drinking, came into the street to see what was happening. Things then got out of hand; a man actually got into the passenger side of the patrol car; Frank forced him out, and people started throwing things—shoes and beer cans. Frank had to get in his car and leave the area until backup units showed up. Later someone called the state police to complain about civil rights violations; the state police investigated and the local police were cleared.

To overcome the language problem, the police have hired interpreters. There used to be several Latino officers, but they transferred to other departments in bigger neighboring towns. The police also are taking Spanish courses and some have received cultural diversity training.

The previous year, the police had a problem with Paco's Cantina. Paco's was a notorious bar frequented by Latinos until it was shut down. The father and son operators were longtime residents, and the general consensus in the town, among both Latinos and Anglos, was that they were a "bad element." The father was arrested on a cocaine charge and the son narrowly escaped jail.

Paco's was the scene of numerous fights. In June 1998, a man was shot and seriously wounded there. For a while there were nightly raids, and the local police teamed up with the state police to carry out raids for suspected drug dealing. Officer Frank led an effort to block the tavern from renewing its liquor license. Not long after the shooting, it closed down because its liquor license was not renewed.

The problems at Paco's "churned" negative public perceptions about Latinos and downtown Wheelerton. In response to public complaints about a variety of disturbances downtown, the police formed a task force composed of state and municipal police to crack down on even minor violations. Even for infractions such as selling minors cigarettes and loitering, the police would come in and make a high-profile arrest. (Years earlier, police had begun citing young men in the downtown for loitering.)

The crackdown came in response to many downtown merchants, who felt that their part of town had become too lawless; the merchants were ready to take matters into their own hands. I was told that the task force was trying to avert interracial violence. Frank feels that over a two-year period, it made a difference. The police continue to remain visible downtown, but now they work as a bike unit.

Frank says that crime in the Latino community has moved out of the streets into activities such as forgery of Social Security cards to sell to those who need documents. The police are working on a case now in which a person is applying for a tax refund but cannot get it because his Social Security card is being used by someone else. Officer Frank refers to a "Mexican Mafia" of coyotes who use undocumented Mexicans to drive cars carrying drugs north.

When asked about allegations that Mexicans were singled out for a lot of minor violations, he said he believes it is due to their driving "like they are in Mexico." He said that they use forged documents to apply for driver's licenses and that they don't really know the rules.

Reflecting on how the situation had changed since the early 1990s, he said he believes that things have gotten considerably better. "They have adapted, and we have adapted to them as well. We don't have to cite people for as many violations." Education has made the difference, through the schools and through more documents being printed in both languages. Also, he thinks older residents are educating the newcomers. That is important for law enforcement, because of the ongoing arrival, of five to ten Mexican newcomers each week, according to Officer Frank.

He also believes there is a change in the way the Mexican community sees the police. He feels there is a much better relationship. "You don't have the same hostile crowds, and less violence is directed toward police officers. People who are bilingual will offer help in translating on the spot, whereas they didn't before. Now you can go downtown to deal with an incident or complaint and not fear a hostile crowd." One exception is the trailer park, where there are frequent drug arrests, and "you have to get in and out quick, or have plenty of backup; crowds will form quickly." However, Officer Frank feels that "overall, things have improved."

CHAPTER FIVE

"Not Racist like Our Parents": Anti-Latino Prejudice and Institutional Discrimination

Ann V. Millard, Jorge Chapa, and Eileen Diaz McConnell

To oppose racism one must notice race.
Omi and Winant 1994:158

Racism is a familiar topic in social science studies of ethnic relations throughout the United States. In this study, we were surprised to find that "racism" against Latinos is a focus of ordinary conversation among rural Midwesterners, both Anglos and Latinos. Their discussions interrelate prejudice and institutional discrimination, with few attempts to correct it by Anglo leaders of civic and religious organizations. Racism was not the original focus of our study, but we address it here because it came up in every aspect of our research. In this chapter, we explore Anglo and Latino experiences with racism, the process of racialization in the rural Midwest, and forms of discrimination in the communities in our study.

In rural areas, we found a racial hierarchy of privilege and opportunity with whites at the top. Most Anglos in our study denied being prejudiced, while nearly every Latino reported having received clear-cut discriminatory messages, ranging from "Go back to Mexico" to actually getting beaten up by Anglo gangs. In a high school focus group, Anglo students commented on varying levels of everyday prejudice:

> Holly: A lot of times, our student body—like, most of us—will allow the Mexicans to live here and, you know, pretty much do whatever they want, just like a normal person, but I think there are some racists in our school, and I don't see the need to be a racist.
> David: In general, I think the community isn't very accepting, but I think we're more accepting in the student body.
> Emily: With the jocks and the preps and the scares and stuff like that, I mean, the Hispanic people are really their own group, but I'm friends with Hispanic people. They go to my church. It doesn't bother me at all.

I think that might have something to do with growing up in California; there's all kinds of cultural diversity there, but when I came here, I'd hear lots of negative things about the Hispanic people. I was just like, "Why?" I mean, in California, you know, this is pretty much normal, having a lot of Hispanics or Cubans or, you know, whatever you have. I mean, California, it's just normal and then, you move here and there's a lot less Hispanics. I hear a lot of people talking bad about 'em and, you know, stuff like that.

Interviewer: Here in the community?

Emily: In the community, yeah. The school is pretty well accepting, but, I mean, a lot of people in the community don't like 'em, you know, and I just don't understand the need for it. I mean, they're just normal people. They're just like us.

Steve: I think a lot of it stems down from how our parents, I mean, like, I hear sometimes, "They don't pay taxes. All they do is have 40 families in one house, and they don't have to pay taxes, and they're taking our money, and they're taking our jobs." But around school, we don't have to deal with it. We're not competing for jobs — there's none of that because it's just not a big deal.

When the Anglos in this study discussed racism, they equated it with consciously avowed prejudice, that is, with dislike or hatred of someone because of their race or ethnicity. This view of racism is evident in Chapter 7, where Anglo high school students discuss generational differences and assert that "we're not racist like our parents." Generally, Anglos in this study recognized the local presence of racism and saw it as problematic. In fact, Anglo participants in our study regarded racism as a serious character flaw.

Although many disavow racism, however, most Anglos have not considered the issue in any profound way. They have a superficial notion of it as an intentional and highly visible phenomenon equated with conscious prejudice. They therefore continue ingrained social and organizational forms of prejudice and discrimination, as shown in this chapter. Prejudice varies among Anglos by generation, life experience, and to some degree, class. We on the research team, however, are impressed with the continuity of rural Anglo views with those throughout much of the Midwest, including perspectives of Anglo city dwellers and researchers on university campuses, to the detriment of Latinos and other non-Anglos.

This analysis addresses the everyday prejudice of and institutional discrimination by Anglos who think of themselves as enlightened and well meaning in encountering the growing Latino population in their towns. We analyze prejudice and discrimination not in the spirit of uncovering a scandal but to clarify their significance in the lives of Latinos throughout the rural Midwest.

Anti-Latino Sentiment in the Rural Midwest

Evidence from other studies and newspaper accounts reveals the hostility and suspicion toward rural Midwestern Latinos on the part of some local Anglos.[1] Indeed, more than one-third of Latinos in central Iowa stated that one problem with living there is the way they are treated (Greater Des Moines Community Foundation 2000). Many rural Anglos view Latinos as the first "minority" to live in "their" towns, and this misreading of history adds to their sense of alarm.

Not only rapid growth in numbers of Latinos, but also their residential segregation and their need for local health care and education, may influence the perceptions of Anglo residents. Surveys in Nebraska (Burke 2003; Hendee 1997) and Iowa (Johnson et al. 1999) demonstrate that longtime residents often view the influx of Latinos negatively. Common complaints include the claim that newcomers do not assimilate quickly enough and that they do not wish to speak English (Grey 2001).

Rural hostility is related to negative stereotypes about Latinos. For example, rising crime rates in rural communities in Iowa (Grey 1995) and Nebraska (Gouveia and Stull 1995) have been blamed on the Latino influx. The stereotype of Latino newcomers is that they are all foreign-born and lack documentation (Rosenbaum 1997). This misperception is even more damaging to interethnic relations when rapid population growth imposes stresses on local infrastructure. Of course, many Latinos are eligible for a broad array of the same social services that are available to longer-term residents. The interaction of Latinos with medical personnel, schools, and social service agencies, however, increases their visibility as service users and plays into a stereotype that they are dependent. Some longer-term residents react with hostility that poses a serious challenge to the development of meaningful and positive relationships among members of the community.

Researchers have noted a few critical economic and demographic factors that may generate unfavorable impressions of newcomers. One key factor is the lack of planning by local officials before they agree to the relocation of factories to their areas (Stull and Broadway 1995). Local infrastructure is often inadequate for dealing with the increased demand for utilities and the growing waste and pollution, precipitating a local budget crisis that tends to be blamed on Latino newcomers rather than industry. Second, many of the industrial employers seem to mislead local officials into accepting the added financial burden of more workers and their families. Indeed, some factories transfer most of the financial burden of supporting the workers onto local governments, by not offering health insurance and forcing uninsured workers and their families to go to reduced-fee clinics, and by leaving those who have been injured on the job with no alternative except public assistance (Stull and Broadway 1995). Third, as noted above, many communities subsidize plants with the expectation that local residents will be hired. Many factories, however, actively recruit employees from other parts of the United States or abroad. Additionally, many key employers of Latinos structure employment policies and benefits in a way that promotes employee turnover (Gouveia and Stull 1997; Martin et al. 1996), which brings a steady stream of newcomers to an area. Finally, since recent immigration policies have inadvertently encouraged undocumented immigrants to remain in the United States (Binational Study 1997), Latino newcomers may be more likely to settle permanently in the rural Midwest than in the past. This permanence may be threatening to non-Latinos.

Methodological and Ethnological Points and Definitions

Here methodological and analytical clarifications are necessary. To carry out the qualitative phase of this study, we invited townspeople in this study to contribute through interviews and focus groups. We therefore expected that our study would reflect the views of more open-minded Anglos and not those of hard-core white supremacists. Those in our study were the people who were willing to discuss the Latino influx with researchers. We came in contact with many other Anglos but rarely had the chance to see how they stood regarding Latino newcomers. In general, as would be expected, Anglos in our study disavowed racism against Latinos.

In the Anglo focus group, one woman said that she did not realize her neighbors were racist until several years ago when there was a Ku Klux Klan auction at an old farm in the region.

Julie: Um, you know, yes, it's a warm, friendly community, but there are a lot of people here in Fox who moved out of neighboring metropolitan areas. They didn't want to live next to anyone whose skin was not the same color as theirs. So there are prejudiced people here, a shocking number that I ran across a few years ago when they were going to auction off all the Ku Klux Klan stuff. I was just shocked that you could sell hate things for profit. I was just astounded.

They found, in an old farmhouse attic, a trunk, just a treasure trove of KKK stuff . . .

I was stunned to think that people would flock to this, and I spoke with the Anti-Defamation League. I spoke with just, the head of the NAACP called me because I had spoken to the Anti-Defamation League and I also spoke to a rabbi in Detroit. I ended up with this barrage of newspapers calling me, saying, "What is going on?" and I'd say, "I'm sorry, I'm just not about to discuss it." There is a lot of hate in this area, and they knew it. See, these people are my friends and neighbors and I had no idea that in Fox there was all of this prejudice. But it's there.

Tom: But, you know, it is, yeah, I think there are people that are very prejudiced.

Ellen: I think Julie's got a really good point. You know, we talked about all the other reasons why people moved [to the area] and that could very well be, because the farther north you go the whiter it is.

Interviewer: Oh, really? I guess that would kind of make sense.

Bob: Might be redneck, but they're still white.

Ellen: Definitely.

Rural Michigan and Indiana are particularly well known for militia groups and Ku Klux Klan organizations, whose activities intensified in the last two decades of the twentieth century, and these organizations have a much more entrenched anti-Latino and anti-immigrant stance than the participants in our study. Although we researchers did not deal with members of these organizations as far as we know, many Latinos in our study see racism (*racismo*) as an everyday fact of Midwestern life.

Regarding our methods of gathering data from Latinos, although our research team includes Latinos and Anglos, we all look Anglo enough that some Latinos may not have felt free to criticize Anglos as a group. Nonetheless, Latinos did tell us about "racist communities" in the Midwest—communities where Latinos are not welcome. (*Racista* [racist] is a term readily used in Spanish by Latino newcomers in the Midwest.) Perhaps as many as 10 percent of rural communities in Michigan, Indiana, and Illinois are in this category, according to interview data. Some of those communities are associated with organizations such as the Ku Klux Klan; however, others do not have any obvious identity that would suggest to an Anglo outsider that they are racist. Latinos avoid spending any time in such communities.

A visit to a town with a reputation among Latinos as racist, Churubusco, Indiana, found the following: no Mexican restaurants or stores and no common Latino last names such as González and García listed in the phone book. The name of the town is the same as that of a subway stop in Mexico City; hence, its name is in ironic contrast with its reputation. In many ways, the town appeared typical, with buildings for the American Legion and Veterans of Foreign Wars and the familiar main street, churches, and stores, surrounded by neighborhoods. The most popular sit-down restaurant in town had an African American family patronizing it, with obvious acceptance by Anglo patrons and restaurant staff. Regardless of whether such communities really are more racist than others, however, Latinos are convinced that they are and strategize to avoid them.

Although we use the term "racism" in this chapter, it should be noted that the Latinos in our study technically belong to an ethnic group, not a race. As noted by a number of scholars, racism is a complex of viewpoints and actions, in which "race" is in the eye of the beholder. To briefly review the problems with "race" as a system of a few concrete categories (e.g., African American, Asian American, European American, and Native American), copious scholarship in anthropology, biology, and other fields shows that the concept of race is scientifically invalid, a misleading way to understand human biological variation (see Dressler 1993; Leslie 1990; Sauer 1992). As defined by bell hooks (2002), "identity markers" are used in everyday life in the United States to assess racial membership, and they include not only physical features but also clothing, demeanor, and other nonbiological characteristics. Appearance thus provides cues about membership in ethnic groups, and the conflation of a person's biological characteristics with styles of dress and demeanor serves to create impressions of "racial" (i.e., biological) difference. This process is at work in the rural Midwest and sets Latinos apart from Anglos.

For the purpose of this study, we define the Latino ethnic group as a transnational population in the United States, Latin America, and much of the Caribbean, who are united by a common history and social identity, and we define the Anglo ethnic group as "non-Hispanic whites." In the communities in our study, most Anglos called Latinos "Mexicans" or "Spanish people" and themselves "whites"; most Latinos called themselves "Mexicanos" and Anglos "Americanos."

Latinos and Race Formation—The Conflation of Race, National Origin, and Immigration and Legal Status

Latinos do not fit easily into the racial framework as it is socially constructed in most of the United States (especially outside the Southwest and California). Feagin (2000) suggests that most of the country has a primarily bipolar racial structure—black and white. Secondarily, the structure is white and nonwhite (the latter including Asians, Native Americans, and African Americans in that order, from highest to lowest status) (Feagin 2000). The construction of race differs between the United States and Latin America in terms of fluidity, degrees and social recognition of "race mixture," and the mitigation of racial discrimination by social class. In Mexico, most of the population is categorized as mestizos—descendants of the offspring of European colonizers and the indigenous population. Phenotypically, their appearance ranges from light ("white") skin and other features typically ascribed to Europeans to very dark skin with characteristics seen as indigenous (Mexican Indian or Native American) (Rodriguez 2001). The Latinos we studied, however, could typically be distinguished from rural Midwestern Anglos in physical appearance, as well as other identity markers, including language, dress, names, and demeanor.

In their paradigm-changing book, *Racial Formation in the United States* (1986), Omi and Winant define racial formation as "the process by which social, economic, and political forces determine the content and importance of racial categories, and by which they are in turn shaped by racial meanings." For them, race is the "fundamental organizing principle" of the American social order and is evident in "every identity, institution, and social practice in the United States." For them and for us, race is a social and historical construct, not a biological reality.

They define "racialization" to signify "the extension of racial meaning to a previously racially unclassified relationship, social practice, or group" (Omi and Winant 1986:61–69). This process perfectly describes the racial situation of Latinos in the rural Midwest (cf. Naples 2000). Even though they exhibit a range of appearances, birthplaces, and legal statuses, through the process of racialization Latinos are lumped together as "Mexicans"—a subordinate, nonwhite group who, because of their presumed illegal status, have diluted claims to rights and privileges that Anglos take for granted. The label "Mexican" appropriately applies to Mexican citizens, and the fact that all the Latinos we studied—including U.S. citizens, the U.S.-born children of U.S.-born parents, and people from parts of Latin America outside Mexico—had this label applied to them confirms that they were racialized. The social construction given to their distinguishing characteristics was a major factor in determining where they could live, what work they could do, their privileges as citizens, and the educational opportunities available to their children.

Theoretical Aspects of Racism, Prejudice, and Discrimination and Examples from the Rural Midwest

Our analysis in this chapter focuses on Anglo discrimination against Latinos, because Anglos control material resources, politics, and organizations that provide housing, employment, and education to Latinos in the rural Midwest. Chapter 4 provides information on patterns of ownership of businesses and the division of labor in the workforce that forms part of Anglo control. Although members of all groups have the capacity for prejudice against others, we do not give much attention to anti-Anglo prejudice among Latinos because, in the communities that we studied, Latinos lacked control of significant resources and thus had little effect on Anglo life.

Basically, we conceptualize "prejudice" as describing a viewpoint, while discrimination involves behavior. We conceptualize "discrimination" as action carried out knowingly or unknowingly that channels resources away from someone of a less powerful ethnic group. Discrimination includes statements and acts that confront, deprecate, and deprive members of a less powerful ethnic group. In this study, we found discrimination in the form of anti-Latino acts, such as epithets yelled on the street and Anglo teenagers beating up Latino teenagers. Discrimination affects Latinos on the job (Chapter 6), at school (Chapter 7), in church (see "En Pocas Palabras V: The Virgin of Guadalupe"), and in community relations (see "En Pocas Palabras VI: The 'Mexican Situation' and the Mayor's Race").

We enlarge the exploration of racism as discussed by Anglos and Latinos to consider institutional discrimination, defined as routine practices of organizations that direct resources toward a more powerful group and away from the less powerful (Millard 1994b, drawing on Barbee 1993a,b; Harrison 1994; Hine 1989; Kossek and Zonia 1993; Leslie 1990; Littlefield et al. 1982; McIntosh 1992; Page and Thomas 1994; Russell 1992; Sauer 1992; Shanklin 1994). That is, we consider systematic ways in which Latinos are shortchanged in wages, benefits, and services on the job, in school, and in dealing with various community and state organizations.

As pointed out by Ehrenreich, for low-wage workers, regardless of ethnicity, "one job is not enough; you need at least two if you intend to live indoors" (2001:212). The living wage for one adult and two children is $30,000 ($14/hour), according to the Economic Policy Institute, which would include health insurance and child care but no restaurant meals and only the cheapest healthful diet (Ehrenreich 2001:213). In our research, we did not find that Latinos were necessarily worse off economically than poor Anglos in the Midwest, but Latinos have to deal with the added burden of discrimination. Institutional discrimination, structural inequality, and Latino Midwestern history generally do not enter the discussion of racism among rural Anglos, although we were fascinated to find a few exceptions.

Some Anglos discussed relations with Latinos in rural Michigan as having improved recently. Rosemary, a middle-aged Anglo woman, explained that when many Latinos first started settling in the area there was some ethnic tension, but now "ill will has gone by the wayside." She gushed about "our wonderful Spanish families" in the town of Fox.

Mike, an Anglo in his thirties, took a different approach, readily acknowledging that there were Anglo racists in his area. He predicted that as the Latino population increases, the Anglo population will feel more threatened and ethnic tensions will surface more frequently. He described the ethnic tensions as an underlying nervousness that existed in the town. He suggested that in any community, benefits available to only a certain segment of the population (i.e., Latinos) are going to provoke resentment in those excluded. If the majority of Anglos in the area were middle or upper class, he suggested, there probably would not have been as much tension over health care, bilingual education, and housing. As discussed below, we definitely found a discourse of resentment against benefits provided to Latinos, but we do not have evidence that it is distributed as neatly by class as stated by Mike. "En Pocas Palabras II: The Battle for Chapita Hills," for example, shows that farm owners contributed to that discourse, along with various townspeople.

In focus groups and interviews, Latinos by and large did not complain about Anglos as an entire group, although they did criticize specific people and their actions.

Saben convivir. They know how to get along with others.
Rubén, a Latino newcomer in Wheelerton, Indiana, describing Anglos

Rubén made this comment as he discussed relationships of Latinos and Anglos in his town. (Rubén was first introduced in Chapter 1.) He was describing Anglos as people who make good neighbors, and he was responding to comments about problems of racism in the region. Most Latinos and Anglos agreed that most people in the communities in this study are extremely nice, and many were proud of that aspect of their communities. Incidents of violence and verbal abuse between Latinos and Anglos were described as rare.

I would describe this as a county where the people are the kindest I have ever known in my life. I don't make a distinction between Anglos and Mexicans. Here you can see that there's no race, but that we're human beings. [Yo describiría como es un condado donde la gente es la más humana que he conocido en mi vida. No distingo ni Anglos ni Mexicanos. Es donde tú mires que no hay raza, sino que somos humanos.]

It's difficult to believe, right? I have met other people who say, "No, it's been bad for me, you know?" [Es difícil de creer, ¿verdad? Yo tengo experiencia con otra persona que dice que, "No. A mí ha ido mal, ¿verdad?"]

But I would describe the area this way. Those who complain, perhaps they are part of the problem? Some people complain, because you reap what you sow [recoges lo que siembras].

For this reason, I say this is the *kindest* county.
Cristina, a long-term Latina resident of Fall County, Michigan

In addition to Cristina, other Latinos in our study also expressed appreciation for local Anglos in the rural Midwest. Cristina was by far the most enthusiastic, and in her defense of local Anglos, she may have been trying to counter gossip about criticism by an earlier focus group (see Sofía's comments in Chapter 6).

Several scholars have developed analyses that provide a point of departure for our approach to racism, prejudice, and discrimination. We draw on analyses of racism against blacks by Feagin (2000), as noted above, and against Latinos by Menchaca (1995). Feagin and Menchaca agree that since the passing of various civil rights acts in the 1960s, many whites think that "racial oppression no longer seems important" because some aspects of it have been made illegal (Feagin 2000:137). Menchaca notes that "the belief that non-White people should be segregated and treated inhumanely is considered today to be a bigoted position inconsistent with a modern democracy" (1995:171). Menchaca's observation describes the views expressed by most Anglos in our study. Flores (2002) provides a convincing analysis dealing with historical roots of Anglos' negative images of Mexicans and Mexican Americans in history and film.

Feagin, Menchaca, and Flores all point to strong systems of racist oppression in our society. Feagin analyzes racism against blacks as societal and institutional patterns of discrimination manifested by political and legal institutions, lending agencies, and employers (2000:140, 155, 160). For example, research shows that over half of insurance and banking businesses discriminate against blacks by making them pay more or providing them less coverage (Feagin 2000:156). He sees racism against African Americans as the core of white supremacy, white privilege, and the "racist arrangements" that oppress other peoples of color, including Latinos. He holds that racism against Latinos and other people of color is an extension of the "antiblack orientation" (Feagin 2000:267). In the following sections, we draw on analyses of antiblack racism to address prejudice and discrimination against Latinos.

Feagin's Three Types of Racism

Feagin analyzes everyday racist practices of whites against blacks as having different levels—blatant, subtle, and covert (2000:140). All three types of racism were evident in our study.

Blatant Racism

Blatant racism, as defined by Feagin, involves regularly practiced, overtly racist behavior, including lynching and other hate crimes. Feagin sees this type of racism as practiced by a large number of whites. In our study, some Latino teenage boys reported that once when they were driving down a country road, a car of "Americanos" (Anglos) passed them, while another car of Americanos stayed behind them. The lead car slowed, forcing the Latino car to stop; the third car followed close behind to trap the young Latinos. Then the Americanos beat the Latinos up.

Similar incidents have been occurring across the United States, including the attempted murder of Mexican immigrants by young skinheads in 2000 in a rapidly growing Long Island, New York, town (Haughney 2000). In Texas (Foley 1997) and California (Menchaca 1995), Latinos have historically been subjected to Ku Klux Klan lynchings, an obvious extension of white racism against blacks. Latinos thus may not have been surprised to encounter violent racism in the Midwest. In our study, we found that they had a matter-of-fact way of discussing racism; their broad experience with it in the United States may have been part of the reason for their apparent view that it is inevitable.

Subtle Racism

In his analysis of racism against blacks, Feagin defines subtle racism as including less overt discrimination, being practiced by a larger group of whites, and often involving small negative comments, avoidance, and distrust (2000:140). In our focus groups in Fall County, Michigan, Latinos commented that they sometimes heard Anglos making negative generalizations about Latinos. The comments made on the job were especially troublesome to Latinos.

> Julia (a young woman in a Latino focus group): I have not heard any racist comments for a few years now. No one has called me names in the street . . . The Americans have finally realized that we aren't leaving! [Everyone laughs.]
>
> In this area, there is still prejudice against Mexicans. It's probably the hardest prejudice to change. It's a kind of subtle racism. I work with an American [Anglo] woman. One day she said, "Julia, you and your family are different compared to the other Mexicans. You, you're not poor; you

don't take advantage of public assistance. You're not draining society of resources."

I said, "We're not different from other Mexican families." But she didn't believe me. Lots of Americans think this way; they just don't say it in front of Mexicans.

Julia's depiction exemplifies the nuanced concept of racism possessed by some Latinos in our study. It is noteworthy that in her objection to the stereotype of "Mexicans" as poor, taking advantage of public assistance, and draining society of resources, Julia called the discourse "subtle racism," using the same terminology as Feagin.

Another example of subtle racism was reported to us by Latino social service workers. Anglo staff members in various service agencies have a habit of sending all Latino clients to bilingual staff, whether or not the clients speak English. The bilingual staff members are Latinos, and they end up with high caseloads as a result of this practice. Not only are they overworked as a result, but their clients also get less attention because the Latino service workers are always in a rush. This situation exemplifies institutional discrimination, discussed below.

It is noteworthy that some social service agencies are attempting to address this imbalance. According to an Anglo social worker, all positions for social workers in western Michigan in the fall of 1999 required Spanish proficiency on the part of new hires. We were fascinated to learn about this requirement; although western Michigan has a large number of Latino migrant farmworkers and Latino influxes in some communities, the area otherwise tends to be homogeneously white, and it is the home of the most socially and politically conservative legislators in the state. A few black communities exist in the region, which is highly segregated along black-white lines; Native Americans also live in the region but tend to blend in with whites. In the same region, further progress was made in Ottawa County with its Summit on Racism in 2001, largely held to discuss the Anglo-Latino encounter. These reports are typical of the Midwestern struggle over racism in rural areas, with a step forward here, a step backward there.

Covert Racism

In Feagin's analysis, covert racism involves even less direct discrimination but knowing support of those so engaged. Subtle and covert racism are often practiced by people who disavow blatant racism but still maintain racist norms. For example, in our study, some Latino high school students reported finding written on the table where they typically gathered to eat lunch the racist taunts "Mexicans go home" and "Go back to Mexico." (Those Latinos who had never lived in Mexico joked about the ignorance of their Anglo colleagues who wrote the messages.) Although the Anglo high school students in our study disavowed racism in nearly every case, enough students took the stance of unprotesting bystanders for these messages to be written and received. Subtle and covert racism are the categories most often found among Anglos in this study.

Menchaca's Concept of Social Apartness

Menchaca carried out a detailed ethnographic study of a town in California with an analysis of "social apartness," that is, "a system of social control by which Mexican-origin people are expected to interact with Anglo Americans on the terms of the latter group" (1995:173). She sees this system as the successor to segregation, which was formerly enforced in the town through laws and violence against Mexican-origin people. Menchaca states that the problem with social apartness is that "it is a subtle type of oppression, as it serves to humiliate, debase, and marginalize people of Mexican descent. It also leads to unbalanced economic rewards that favor the Anglo American community" (1995:173), which we would analyze as institutional discrimination.

In the Midwest, Anglo farmers in particular tend to assume that "Mexicans" are lesser people, according to a Latino couple in Fox, Michigan:

> They [Anglos] have spent their lives as the bosses of Mexicans. They've always told us where and when to work. In my opinion, farmers see Mexicans as their employees. They see Mexicans as dependents, temporary residents. Many Americans have a hard time understanding that we are here to stay. We are not just their hired help.

The couple who made this statement were long-term residents who were well accepted in the Anglo community, which made their bitterness over the stereotypes particularly poignant.

Local residents report that traditional social groups in the community, such as the Rotary and Optimist Clubs, have at most one or two Latino members. One Anglo explained:

> Most members of these clubs grew up here. Most Mexicans, though, are immigrants or first-generation. The club members choose the new members; they invite people to meetings to see whether they're interested in joining. So it's not surprising that few members are Mexican. Mexicans would be welcome if they were invited to meetings.

> Bob (in a different interview): Whites and Mexicans stay in separate groups. There's not that much mixing or participation in an event sponsored by the other group. Hardly any whites go to those dances every few weekends with the Mexican music—they bring musicians from Chicago, Texas, or even Mexico. The dance hall's always full anyway, so there wouldn't be any room.

Ethnic segregation is evident in other social gatherings as well. Although Anglos are welcome at Latino events, the reverse is not true. As numerous informal political discussions are held over cards and beer at get-togethers of local Anglo clubs, the exclusion of Latinos keeps them from direct participation in determining the economic and political agendas for their towns.

Institutional Discrimination

Anglos in a resource-controlling organization do not need to be knowingly prejudiced to enact institutional discrimination. The participants who belong to the ethnic majority may simply go about their normal routines with the result that resources reach members of an ethnic minority in disproportionately small quantities. Examples in this book include the social service agencies discussed above, with their overworked, bilingual Latino staff and underserved Latino clients; emergency medical services relying on children to interpret for Spanish-speaking parents (see "En Pocas Palabras III: Emergency Medicine and Latino Newcomers"); and public schools using bilingual students to translate for Spanish monolinguals (see Chapter 7). In all these examples, organizational routines result in the overwork of bilingual Latinos and fewer services received by monolingual Spanish speakers. Bilingual Latinos understand the inequity of the situation but, so far, are powerless to change it.

Many organizations have bilingual staff but do not assign them work in interpreting, even when it would make their organizations more efficient. Some onlookers might argue that the organizations have not yet had time to adjust because the influx of year-round Latino residents is so recent; however, all of these organizations have had Spanish monolingual clients and students from the migrant farmworker population for more than half a century. They have shown little openness to serving such clients in an equitable way. Anglos do not see the situation as racist but as an unfortunate consequence of many Latinos' deficiency: limited proficiency in English. Anglos thus place the responsibility for interpreting on Latino clients. Data in our study show that Spanish-speaking patients and clients are shortchanged throughout the rural Midwest in medical care, employment assistance, parent-teacher conferences, and classrooms because of the lack of interpreters.

The few organizations that we found in western Michigan that do provide interpreters include the huge chain stores (such as Wal-Mart), the community and migrant health clinics, and in a limited way, the Family Independence Agency (the state welfare department, which has a few bilingual staff, typically hired for the summer to serve migrant farmworkers). Organizations not typically providing interpreters in the communities in our study are schools, state employment offices, and hospitals, including emergency rooms. All of these organizations ensure that Spanish monolingual clients will receive many fewer services than do Anglos.

Anglo Perspectives on Local Latino History

Lack of attention by Anglos to the local Latino presence is a feature of daily life in the region in general. For example, in August and September 1999, the *Fall County Journal* published a millennium series of magazine inserts covering twentieth-century history in the county. A reader unfamiliar with the area would not learn of any significant Latino twentieth-century involvement, even though the series includes various articles tracing the agricultural history of the county. Only a couple of articles on agricultural production mention crops that "used" migrant farm labor. The articles emphasize farmers and crops, not the large number of migrant workers whose labor was essential to most agriculture in the region.

With their dramatic population increase in the last 20 years, Latinos have become the largest minority group in the area; however, no pictures of Latino families appear in the newspaper articles and advertisements. The few passages in Spanish are in announcements paid for by churches, Latino stores, and Mexican restaurants. The history of a significant population segment is missing, implying that this newspaper did not consider Latinos a part of the population of Fall County in the twentieth century.

Many Anglos hark back to the European immigrants whom they view as the county's founding population, living in poverty on newly logged land and working hard to become prosperous farmers. This selective recollection of local history omits the large number of Native Americans who formed a critical part of local economies, particularly in the maple sugar industry in the latter part of the 1800s. The typical Anglo expectation is that Latino newcomers will follow the trajectory of earlier European immigrants; thus Anglos see Latinos as having little real need of social services. That view, however, falls apart upon inspection. Latino newcomers do not earn wages at a level that would allow them to quit jobs as farm employees and buy farms, and they lack access to credit for buying land, which is much more expensive than in the 1800s. Latinos also lack access to credit for starting businesses; thus their stores tend to be poorly stocked and low in sales. Restaurants selling Mexican food can provide a living for a family willing to invest a tremendous amount of time and energy, but a town can only sustain a few such enterprises.

Farmworkers, Latino Settlers, and Eligibility for Services

Many rural Anglos think of local Latinos as migrant farmworkers and, in fact, the distinction between migrants and settled Latinos is not always clear. The definition of migrant farmworker varies among organizations such as migrant clinics and the state social services agencies, and in some cases migrant farmworkers can maintain their eligibility for services for several years after settling down. The high incidence of poverty and associated needs of migrant farmworkers have led to the creation of special programs at the state and federal levels. Some companies have taken advantage of these programs as subsidies, by recruiting a workforce that they can define as migrant farmworkers. For example, at least one food processing plant in our study employs "migrant workers" nearly year-round; they return south only for two to four months a year and depend solely on work at the plant for a living. They live on company property in company-provided housing.

Many people and state agencies nonetheless consider them migrant workers; the workers do not claim membership in the local Midwestern community, and they do not vote there (if they did, they would overwhelm the local population). Federal and state governments thus subsidize agricultural production, food processing, and work in other sectors employing "migrant farmworkers" (forestry, lawn mowing, greenhouse production, and so on).

In addition, some workers in food processing plants in Mapleville, Michigan, work in the fields seasonally.

> Ellen (a farmer): During peach time, we hire probably 20 Hispanics, and cherry time we have these people too. They have two jobs. Even during cherry time, they work with us from six in the morning and they quit at one. Then from two to ten, they work for Mapleville Freezing Company.
>
> . . . They want to work for Joe [a farmer], and Joe pays 'em real good and especially peaches, too, 'cuz they get paid by the box and they're there with a flashlight practically [to start as early in the morning as possible]. And they'll take their vacation time to work for us for three weeks.
>
> They fill a big box and they get paid anywhere's from, if you're fast enough, they're getting paid, like, $20 an hour or more.
>
> Interviewer: Well, you talk to people and from what they say, you know, you definitely have potential to make much more money working in the fields than in food processing plants.
>
> Ellen: Yeah, but you can't get white people to do that.
>
> Julie: That's right.

Many Anglos in talking with us have voiced the opinion that "no one works like a Mexican"—that "Mexicans" are the hardest-working labor force available. They are also viewed by Anglos as the most docile—a key characteristic in the Midwest, with its long, once bloody history of labor-management conflict. Along with this view comes a series of stereotypes about Latinos and their contrasts with Anglos.

As has been true of Mexican restaurants in the Midwest throughout most of the twentieth century, El Portal Restaurant in the town of Mapleville, Michigan, serves partly as a recruiting location for Latino workers. On the restaurant wall is a hand-lettered work-recruiting sign (see Figure 5.1).

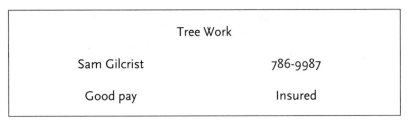

Tree Work	
Sam Gilcrist	786-9987
Good pay	Insured

Figure 5.1. A sign at a Mexican restaurant in Fox, Michigan

This sign and other, similar postings in restaurants and "Mexican" stores in the communities in this study imply an abundant supply of Latino workers ready for hire. In fact, we saw these signs when farmers in Michigan were complaining of a lack of workers. When farmers are unable to recruit enough workers through hand-posted signs in local restaurants and stores and through word of mouth, they say there is a labor shortage. Employers have extended this approach to recruiting workers for food processing plants and light industry.

The issues of medical care, bilingual education, and government-subsidized housing are particularly volatile among Anglos. Some resent Latino access to government benefits, while others justify them as aid to the deserving poor, that is, the working poor. For example, some Anglos in Shelby, Michigan, resented a government-subsidized apartment complex built for farmworkers, as shown in "En Pocas Palabras II" on Chapita Hills. The housing does not explicitly exclude Anglos, but it does exclude people who have not worked as agricultural day laborers for three years, and very few Anglos take such work.

Exacerbating the tension over Latinos' use of benefits, Anglos grossly overestimate the extent of assistance they receive. There is a local clinic that serves migrant workers, and Anglos believe that Latinos receive free health and dental care there. Actually, a sliding scale is used to calculate the bills of patients at the clinic. All patients must pay some amount, and services are available to all, not just Latino migrant workers. Nonetheless, many Anglos are convinced that the services are exclusively for low-income Latinos, who receive them at no charge. This example of Anglo misunderstanding of health clinic policies was repeated in every town in our ethnographic study.

In a focus group, several Anglos criticized the local discourse of resentment against government benefits for migrant farmworkers. Noting that the political system supports corporate welfare, they challenged the arguments that migrants do not deserve federal and state assistance.

Ellen (a farmer): I think they [local low-income Latinos] kind of take the bum rap, you know, locally, because . . .

Tom: They do, they really do . . .

Ellen: You give tax abatements to businesses. You give farm subsidies. You do all this kind of stuff, but everybody hollers about the free clinic or they get some food, you know.

Julie: I know too many people on welfare and they get everything for nothing and they could be working. They could be working and these people want to work . . .

Ellen: I don't think they should take the rap.

Julie: They want, they're working . . .

Sarah: And they work hard.

Julie: They work terribly . . . [They sometimes even work at] two jobs.

Ellen: They deserve what they get, I feel.

Bob: I can say that.

Ellen: If you ever pick pickles [cucumbers for pickling], they get everything they got coming.

People were quick to point out that Anglos in Fox and Mapleville generally were on public assistance much longer than Latinos, sometimes for years, and that many more Anglos than Latinos abused the system. In the Anglo focus group one woman commented:

A lot of the low-income white families here are third- and fourth-generation welfare people. They just don't work, just don't want to work . . .

Several Latino participants made a special effort to refute the complaints they have heard all of their lives that Latinos abuse the welfare system and do not work.

Many people [Latinos] are proud. They will find other people to help them out to keep from using welfare. Of course, there are always the people who do use welfare, and the few who abuse it.

Latino government workers and Anglos often differentiated between the working poor and those on welfare. Some Anglos saw local Latinos with jobs in food processing plants as hard workers who need assistance from the state because of their low wages. Anglo farmers, some Anglo business owners, and many Anglo professionals, some of whom employ Latinos for low wages, all expressed this viewpoint. Few Latinos with low-wage jobs receive health benefits in the communities in our ethnographic study. As they are paid at or barely above minimum wage, many live below the poverty level and cannot afford to pay for medical care or health insurance on their own. In some cases, employers offer medical benefits beginning six months after hiring, but with high worker turnover employers can minimize such costs (see Gouveia, Sanchez, and Saenz 2001).

Compounding this problem, hospital staff assume that Latinos without health insurance will not pay their bills (Millard, field notes from central Michigan, 1994). Spanish-speaking patients and migrant clinic staff see the hospital as unconcerned, and the result has been considerable suffering on the part of some patients and their families.

Commerce and Consumption

As noted in Chapter 4, ownership of the major sources of employment lies in the hands of Anglos in small Midwestern towns. Anglos own the larger restaurants, stores, and farms and all factories, while Latinos own "Mexican" restaurants and "Mexican" stores that sell Mexican and Mexican American food and merchandise. These differences probably relate partly to differential access to business loans.

In focus groups, Latinos reported that they are often treated badly in local stores. When they pay with food stamps or cash a public assistance check, Anglo store employees respond with dirty looks and sarcastic remarks. They approve when Latinos pay with cash or a paycheck. Other Latinos reported that when they went shopping in neighboring areas, store employees followed them to make sure they were not stealing.

In the Anglo focus group, one woman observed:

It's kinda hard at the grocery store to catch their eye. They always are looking in another direction, they don't expect friendliness. If you keep looking right at 'em until they finally look at you, and you say, "Hi," they'll smile.

Her focus group colleagues teased her about being a weird little old lady following people around in the stores, staring at them. None of the Anglo focus group members were aware that Latinos commonly experience racism in the community.

Latino newcomers thus face considerable discrimination as consumers and community members because of their poverty, lack of access to credit for starting businesses, and segregation in the workforce, as well as the high cost of farmland. The limited English proficiency of many newcomers contributes to these difficulties but does not explain them; English-speaking long-term Latino residents face many of the same barriers and patterns of discrimination.

Summary

The Anglo participants in this study in most cases were people of goodwill who would not describe themselves or their social circle as prejudiced, discriminatory, or racist. No Anglos in our study consciously made white supremacist statements. In some cases, they sought to act in egalitarian ways with Latinos and members of other ethnic groups and expressed disgust toward prejudice and discrimination against Latinos and other groups as well.

Although many Anglos and Latinos agree that low-income Latinos work very hard trying to improve their economic situation, there are still some Anglos who view Latinos as abusing the system and exploiting other people's resources. Many Anglos are ideologically opposed to racism and see themselves as fair-minded people, but few recognize the Latino economic contribution to their communities. Generally, both Anglos and Latinos commented on the fact that most Anglos were raised in a climate of prejudice.

Individual Latinos experience different forms of prejudice and bias to varying degrees, related to several structuring factors in their lives, including the language they speak, the color of their skin, length of residence in the community, education, work experience, social networks, and social class. Some of these differences are evident at work, as described in Chapter 6. Latinos say Anglos cling to stereotypes about Latinos because they lack personal relationships with Latinos that could disabuse them of their views. In many communities, Latinos are racialized, that is, assumed to have a given set of common characteristics subsumed under the label "Mexican." Many local factors determine the degree to which this racialization occurs, including the length of time Latinos have lived in the community, the relative proportion of Latinos to Anglos, the type of employment that typically brought the Latinos to town, and the attitudes of local officials and of the community residents.

Subtle and covert racism and institutional discrimination are widespread in the communities in this study. On the job (Chapter 6), at school (Chapter 7), and in church (Chapter 8), these forms of prejudice are part of the everyday lives of Latinos in the rural Midwest. The communities are to be respected for the efforts of some Anglos and Latinos to combat prejudice, but few people see the patterns of institutional discrimination that structure their relationships. Beginning to address this aspect of racism would be a big step forward for the rural Midwest, as well as for the nation as a whole.

CHAPTER SIX

On the Line: Jobs in Food Processing and the Local Economy

Maríaelena D. Jefferds and Ann V. Millard

It seems as though they [Anglos] accept us, but it's not that way. The truth is, they don't accept us. They accept us as machines for working. But they don't accept us as people. [Parece que nos aceptan pero no es así. La verdad es que no nos aceptan. Nos aceptan como máquinas para trabajar. Pero no nos aceptan como personas.]
Sofía, a Latina working in a food processing plant in Fall County, Michigan

You can't get white people to do that. They can't work as fast [as Latinos].
An Anglo woman farmer in Fall County, Michigan

Large numbers of Latinos are moving to Fall County for work, and their arrival has upset many Anglo residents. Although Latinos have become the mainstay of the local food processing industry workforce, most local Anglos think of them as outsiders rather than community members. Many Latino workers chafe under their working conditions, but most Anglos see them as content with their jobs. This chapter explores various experiences of Latinos at work and the views of their Anglo neighbors swept up in the social and economic change that is reshaping life in the communities of Fox and Mapleville in Fall County, Michigan.

Food processing plants have expanded in many regions of the rural Midwest, and they are the main attractions for Latino newcomers in many towns. In the grain belt, beef processing plants and feedlots have left Chicago and other cities with expensive land and costly union workforces for rural areas where grain is grown and communities have lower production costs. Similarly, pasta factories are located near grain fields in some regions. In fruit- and vegetable-growing regions, processing plants store, pack, freeze, and can harvest yields near orchards and fields. In addition to reduced production costs, improved road systems and changes in public policy may also have encouraged the movement of food processing plants to the rural Midwest. Some officials in Michigan say that public policy aimed at controlling pollution and safeguarding groundwater pushed food processing of Michigan crops into other states. In recent years, however, the state legislature passed "freedom to farm" laws that exempt farms, including their food processing operations, from local control. In addition, legal changes in the 1980s and 1990s (for example, the Immigration Reform and Control Act of 1986, discussed below and in other chapters) encouraged the influx of Latino workers by making it possible for many formerly undocumented immigrants to work legally and permanently in the United States. In recent decades, food processing has expanded rapidly in rural areas, making pollution and low pay hot-button issues for local people.

According to Anglo focus group members in this study, the consolidation of many smaller food processing plants has made the few existing plants safer and better environments for workers. The consolidation has occurred in nearby towns and counties as well, and several family-owned businesses have become corporate farms (i.e., businesses owned by regional, national, or multinational firms). (See Naples 1994 on the growing pace of economic restructuring in the rural Midwest beginning in the post–World War II years and continuing into the 1990s.) Local Anglos have described the Fall County Food Processors as "expanding every summer."

Despite recent improvements in Anglos' reception of Latinos in Fall County, some Latinos meet both overt and subtle bias, particularly on the job and at government agencies. Although food processing plants are providing the jobs that draw Latinos to the area, they are also the sites of working conditions and prejudice that bring bitter complaints from some Latinos.

In Fall County, most Latino newcomers are former migrant farmworkers who used to come to the area each year. Most have gotten jobs on the line in food processing plants, where they cull vegetables and fruits that are being frozen and canned. Many work in the plants under difficult conditions at minimum wage with no health or retirement benefits, which leaves them depending on government programs—food stamps, subsidized housing, subsidized health care, and, for their children, Medicaid and subsidized school lunches. Local Anglos generally refuse to do the same work that Latinos do for such low wages. Even Anglo high school students, who used to work side by side in the fields with Latino migrant workers, find the pay and working conditions in food processing unacceptable. Even as they comment that "someone has to do the work," many local Anglos resent the influx of Latinos and complain of their use of government services.

These two important dimensions of life for many Latinos—low-wage jobs and dependence on government assistance—have major social consequences. The current rapid growth of food processing plants in this region requires cheap labor, and this demand has drawn Latinos willing to work for low wages, especially because local people avoid jobs on the line in the plants. The result is a growing local population of working poor who differ culturally and ethnically from the mainstream. This chapter shows how and why Latinos have come to work at jobs in the rural Midwest and describes their experiences and the varying responses of Anglos to the transitions under way in their communities.

Latinos and Food Processing Plants

There is always work here. [Aquí siempre hay trabajo.]
Cristina, a Latina, on the advantages of the region

One comes here, not knowing the situation, but we all need to work.
[Viene uno no impuesto, pero hay que trabajar.]
Anita, a Latina who arrived in 1992

You work all day and it's very tiring; you make money, but it's hard.
Juan, a worker in the fields in the mornings and at food processing plants in the afternoons and evenings

Food processing plants in Fall County, the largest employers of Latinos, tend to have ethnically divided workforces: Anglo are the owners and high-level managers, while Latinos are workers on the line, doing the actual manual labor in the plant. Without Latinos, we were often told, the plants would not have enough employees. A few plants have approximately equal numbers of Anglo and Latino line workers, but an entirely Latino workforce on the plant floor is more common. The growth of the food processing industry is definitely a major reason that Latino settlement in the area is increasing. The largest plant in the area, which belongs to a farm, is also the focus of the most complaints by Latino workers. The workforce at that plant is approximately equal to those of the other five local plants combined.

Although Latinos come to the area for jobs, they do not always accept their treatment at work. Latino workers differed in their reactions to working conditions, their sense of a right to complain about them, and access to extended breaks and leaves for family emergencies. Many commented on a sense of being trapped in their jobs; they felt that they could not move to a new local job without a good recommendation from their current employer. Their discussions revealed that being treated respectfully matters a great deal to many Latino workers, but being treated in a just and fair manner by managers and coworkers matters the most.

Jobs in the plants vary considerably, and the most common work is on the line. Along plant conveyer belts, technology and human hands alternate in repetitive tasks of culling and washing. The plants have the latest high-technology equipment, including electric eyes detecting damaged produce and high-pressure air jets that puff imperfect produce off the line almost magically, but large numbers of workers are still required. Nearby warehouses keep crops such as apples in cool storage for months, to await processing or rising prices. Work on the line in the plants is physically difficult and dangerous. Both Latinos and Latinas work in these positions.

Another job is in the plant's laboratory, monitoring the quality of food products. The work is physically easier and allows more flexibility. A Latina who holds this job in one of the plants commented that she likes her work. She noted that she receives respect and consideration from the management. She has a high school education and is bilingual, putting her into a category different from that of most Latino plant workers.

Members of Latino focus groups defined a processing plant as "good" if it paid better than the other plants—working conditions and treatment by the management were not the most salient points of comparison. Some Latinos described their bad experiences at work as seriously demeaning, while others dismissed them. Among both men and women, views of jobs at the plants and expectations about treatment varied by employer, job assignment, control of English, and legal status in the United States. Because focus group participants who had worked in the plants were mostly women, much of the following information comes from their points of view.

Sofía's Experience at Work

In a Latino focus group, Sofía recounted at length her experience working at Fall County Food Processors. (She was introduced in Chapter 1.) She had moved to the county after 14 years of seasonal farmwork there. She was a single woman and thus was not pooling her income with a spouse, unlike other women in our study. She may have felt even more trapped at her plant job than did the other women.

Before she began to talk about her job at the plant, Sofía had seemed uncertain about participating in the focus group. She questioned us at length about what we would do with the information, including the purpose of the session, how the information would be recorded and used, and whether it would help other people. She seemed to be apprehensive about participating in the study but was willing to discuss her experiences with the idea that her participation could potentially benefit others. We had stressed that, although we hoped the study would lead to better conditions, we did not have the power to make those decisions.

Once she began to talk about her work, it was apparent why she had been so apprehensive. She expressed bitterness about how she had been treated and how the Latino workforce in general was treated. Sofía expressed no particular vendetta against a specific plant owner or manager, but instead she protested the system in general—working conditions, treatment by the management, and treatment by a specific Anglo coworker. It was clear that she had thought about her experience for a long time and had developed an analysis of employer-employee relations and Latino-Anglo relations at the plants.

Sofía spoke in Spanish, in a low, intense, clear voice, and moved from one topic to the next in a flowing narrative. She did not speak in a rabble-rousing style but earnestly, from the heart. The following excerpts capture the main points that she made as she spoke.

> I have been coming here from Texas for 14 years. And this last year has been the most horrible of my life! [Yo tengo 14 años que vengo de Tejas. Y este último año que vine aquí ha sido para mí el más horrible de mi vida.]
>
> . . . [When you work in a food processing plant,] you have to work from the time you wake up until you go to sleep at night. Yes, you have no time to rest. Fifteen minutes for lunch—you come, you rush to eat, and back

to work. Yes, and we go through this only out of necessity. [Uno tiene que trabajar desde que amanece hasta que anochece. Sí, uno no tiene tiempo para reposar. Unos 15 minutos en la comida—vienes, comes rápido, y otra vez al mismo trabajo. Sí, y éste es por necesidad, lo es.]

. . . If you are one minute late getting back to work, you get in trouble. You work for 10 hours and get a 10-minute break every 2 1/2 hours. In those 10 minutes, you have to go to the bathroom; you have to eat. And they don't count that time. They pay you for 9 1/2 hours' work. They don't pay you for 10 hours.

. . . We never get a raise, and the work is hard, the hardest. They have no right to treat Mexicans this way. Without us, the company could not even exist. They don't want to pay us one penny more, but they keep giving us more work. When the plant's really busy, you have to work seven days a week, ten hours a day. If you take Sunday off, they won't let you work for the next three days. So they punish you that way.

. . . The managers are in the office watching us through big glass windows. They're sitting there at computers, watching the workers. If you turn your head to say something to the worker next to you, a manager calls the boss to point out the one who's talking.

. . . They charge us for all the equipment we use, including plastic and cloth gloves, sleeves, aprons, and hairnets; $2.70 for the apron . . .

. . . All the workers there are Mexican. Americans [los bolillos (i.e., Anglos)] don't work in the factory, no.

. . . One woman got her finger frozen at the factory. They [the doctors] had to cut it off, and the factory didn't even give her a job after that. They would have nothing to do with her . . . One lady was injured when she fell . . .

. . . Assembling those cardboard boxes is really hard work, and some people can't breathe—the cardboard gives off fumes that make them sick. They feel as though their throats are closing up, and they'll suffocate.

. . . You can get an infection, but you don't have any money to go to the doctor. First, you have to provide for your children and pay the rent. The wages are so low you can't afford to buy medicine.

. . . I talked to the other workers; they said, "Don't complain or you'll get kicked out. You'll get kicked out, and you won't be able to get another job. Mr. Ferguson [the owner] will tell the other plant owners."

We did not hear anyone else make as clear and sweeping a criticism of working in the plants, but many other plant workers affirmed various aspects of Sofía's description, and some men also had severe complaints about their treatment at work, as discussed below.

Sofía's criticism of the plants was somewhat controversial, but on balance we found her description credible and her personal experience important to recount. In opposition to Sofía's position, a member of the second Latino focus group made a point of saying that she found local people extremely kind and not at all racist (see Chapter 5). She worked at the plant, but in the laboratory, where she had better working conditions, more responsibility, more flexibility to leave work to meet family demands, and probably better pay than typical workers on the line. She knew of a Latino family with a child suffering from cancer who had received considerable support from local Anglo employers and service providers; thus she argued that the local people were the most humane she had ever encountered.

On the other hand, other focus group participants generally supported Sofía's descriptions of working conditions and events in the plants, even though they did not express her bitter disappointment over them. Unlike the other women working in food processing, Sofía was single, and she faced greater economic difficulties than those in two-earner households. Other differences also may have contributed to her viewpoint, as discussed further below. We draw on her criticism not because it was typical but because it was a cogent statement of much of the grumbling we heard from other focus group participants.

Controversy among Latinas over Jobs at the Plants

As Sofía raised various points, other focus group members responded. Some agreed while others pointed out that their experiences were different, usually better. The two Latino focus groups raised many of the same issues—problems with prejudice, fear of injury, and the physical dangers and difficulties of their jobs. Everyone in the Latino focus groups was familiar with one of Sofía's major complaints.

> Sofía: . . . And another thing, when I was working there, the custodian comes in and says, "Oh, my God! Filthy Mexicans!" With the brush that she uses to clean the bathroom, she also cleans our lunch table. She's an American [Anglo]. When the people come, tired from work, they quickly

get their food out, they put their bread, their tortillas on that table—it's a horrible injustice [*injusticia horrible*].

Although Sofía was outraged, Liliana, in another focus group, disregarded the problems with the custodian.

The workers do make a mess at lunch. They should throw their trash in the trashcan—people should clean up after themselves . . . [Other focus group members argued with Liliana and emphasized that it was the custodian's duty to clean and not complain.] Anyway, that woman was fired. She was reported to the management and they fired her. Now Teresa's doing the job, and she's really careful.

All discussants expressed satisfaction in knowing that the custodian had been fired, that their complaints had been taken seriously. No one disagreed with Sofía about working long hours at the plant.

Rosario (a Latina, in an interview): At Fall County Food Processors, it's all fruit, and I spend 45 minutes packing apples, and then I get a break—it's 15 minutes for lunch, 10 minutes for a break, and you get paid for 10 hours.

Apparently Rosario was being paid for 10 hours of work at the same plant where Sofía was only paid for 9 1/2 (we have no explanation for this difference, but it implies that Sofía received worse treatment than Rosario).

It seems that Sofía may have been singled out at the plant, as she was not being paid for as many hours of work as others. (Among other low-wage workers, different pay for the same job was documented by Ehrenreich 2001.) Sofía also may have had other bad experiences in the plant that she chose not to discuss in the focus group. Out of her presence, other women speculated that perhaps because she was dark-skinned and did not speak English, Sofía experienced more problems than they did. Nonetheless, Sofía's criticisms of the plant raised legitimate issues, and other members of her focus group sympathized with her as she talked. It is hard to tell whether others were quiet because they did not wish to contradict Sofía publicly or because they were resigned to their working conditions. Finally, it is clear that a single person such as Sofía is in a much worse economic position than two-parent, two-earner households, even when they have children to support. Living on her own may have contributed to Sofía's extreme hardships.

The focus group discussions showed clearly that Latinas differ in their views of the plants, including their treatment by management and other workers. Cristina, who works in the lab at the plant, commented on the plant workforce and the length of breaks:

> Where I work, it's half and half [Anglos and Latinos]. When someone leaves the line, someone else fills in, and it can be an American. Everyone works fine together. There could be someone who replaces you [on the line] so that you could have longer breaks.
>
> Tomasa: I work the night shift, and the manager gives us longer breaks—20, 25 minutes.
>
> Anita: He's Mexican and there are no other managers around.
>
> Rosario (in an interview): We're not unhappy working at Fall County Food Processors. We have to pay for our own gloves and everything, but I'm happy [*contenta*] there. They give us permission to leave when we have an appointment.
>
> Cristina (in a focus group): When my daughter has a headache at school, I just punch out at Lake Canning Company. Then I go to school for her. They know I'm a good worker, and I wouldn't just take off without a good reason.

Many Latino focus group members were outraged at what they considered bad treatment by the management and owners of the plant. An example of injury on the job reveals a different orientation of workers from Mexico toward employers' responsibilities. Apparently, in Mexico, an injury on the job obliges the employer to continue to provide a job for the injured party. (In Michigan, this obligation applies in union shops but not among "at will" employees such as the workers at the food processing plants. Moreover, the Spanish-speaking, low-income workforce tends to have a poor understanding of worker's compensation, if they have any information about it at all.) Typically, in the factories in this study, those who were disabled at work would lose their jobs. Differences in work experiences and expectations clearly shaped workers' readiness to criticize their workplaces.

Experiences with Prejudice at Work

The Anglo owners and top managers at the plants speak little or no Spanish, and many Latinos who work there speak minimal English at best. Those without sufficient knowledge of English had to depend on others to speak for them, and at times they reported being taken advantage of, for example, by being assigned the more laborious tasks. They also reported instances of bilingual Latino coworkers lying about them to the Anglo management.

In focus groups, Latinos who spoke English reported fewer problems at work. Even for those who spoke English, though, it was not always comfortable to work at a plant.

> Tomasa: Everyone applies to Brown's [a local food processor]. They pay more, even though they are a little racist [*racista*]. They fire all the new workers [Latinos] in winter, and only the permanent workforce [Anglos] stays on.
>
> Cristina: There is some racism [*racismo*] there. It comes from the boss, but also a Mexican woman. (Everyone reacted in a disgusted way, as though the situation was familiar.) They [Anglo employees] ask, "Why do so many Mexicans come here to work?" They don't say this to anyone, but just say it out loud. I'm standing there, and I understand them, but they don't know it. They complain, "The Mexicans don't do good work. They need training. They don't work fast enough." But I think, "That's why they pay you, to train me!"
>
> Tomasa: We have to fix this [Tenemos que componer eso].
>
> Cristina: It's not so bad . . .

In Cristina's view, only this plant has a problem with prejudice; she does not consider the comments about workers as very derogatory (*despectivo*). Other focus group participants acknowledged that at work they had heard similar comments against Latinos. Cristina described it, not as overt prejudice, but small comments repeated by the permanent staff about the deficiencies of seasonal workers, the majority of whom are Latino. Cristina commented that most of the Latinos working there do not understand English, so it does not bother them.

> Interviewer: Have you heard about this kind of thing happening in other plants?

Anita: Not at Fall County Food Processors, because there are only Mexicans [*puros mexicanos*] there. It's great to work there.

Fall County Food Processors thus was alternately vilified and praised among Latinos. Some of the variation was related to the shift they worked and their treatment by the manager. As noted above, for example, a Latino manager on the night shift allowed more flexibility in breaks. The other contradictions in their statements are not easily explained, however, and may relate to comparisons with other jobs, first impressions as they started work at Fall County Food Processors, efforts not to complain to outsiders (e.g., to researchers), and other factors that cannot be analyzed in this study.

Prejudice on the part of Anglo coworkers occasionally leads to victimization and firing of Latinos. In a Latino focus group, we were discussing jobs, and when his turn came, Roberto spoke quietly, at first looking down at the table. He began in a very quiet voice, with the painful admission that he was unemployed. As he explained why, his voice grew stronger.

I worked as a welder in Westside City [a nearby urban area] until last week, when I lost my job. The other workers were all Americans [puro americano allá], and I had problems with the language.

The guy I was assigned to was difficult. He had worked there for years, and he was angry while he worked—angry for 59 minutes of every hour! He did not want to do his job, and I always had to work with him.

To tell the truth, he did not seem happy! [¡La verdad, no lo vi contento!] [The focus group laughed at this understatement.]

Eventually, the owners spoke with the guy to ask why our work was not getting done. The next thing I knew, they told me, "It's time for you to go." I was fired after working there for a year and two months.

It was somewhat my fault that I got fired; I've been here for five years and still don't speak English well. If I could have spoken the language, I could have defended myself.

Because he did not speak English, Roberto's coworker could make him a scapegoat. Roberto thus lost a good job after more than a year with that company.

Latinos' Reasons for Staying on the Job

Latino newcomers moved to Michigan for job opportunities and working conditions that were better than those where they had been working. In Texas, for example, jobs in fruit packing houses typically have unpredictable hours and require less than 40 hours' work per week. Referring to such work, Anita commented:

> When the trucks bring oranges in, you work two hours; then you go home. If I get home at eleven in the morning, soon, around three in the afternoon, they call me back to work at the plant. Then it's to work for another hour or half hour.

Focus group members explained that in Michigan they earn more because they work full days and occasionally overtime. Some commented that at overtime rates, they earned good wages. Families in which husband and wife both work year-round have higher incomes than typical migrant farmworkers in the area. Conditions are difficult for Latino plant workers in Fox and Mapleville, but having year-round jobs is crucial for them, and their earnings are better than they would be in Texas or doing migratory farmwork.

One reason that Latinos gave for keeping jobs under abusive conditions was that they feared the owners of the food processing plants. In a focus group, we asked why people would stay at Fall County Food Processors if the working conditions are so bad, especially if there are other plants in the area that do not treat workers badly. One woman stated, as had Sofía, that the workers are afraid ("tienen miedo") that if they leave, the owner will report them to the authorities for having papers that are out of order. That is, the owner will say the worker's documents of U.S. citizenship or legal residence are false. They are also afraid that the owner will complain about them to other area employers, thus denying them further local employment. Others at the table concurred that for these reasons, people keep working for Fall County Food Processors. They noted, moreover, that former workers had suffered both kinds of reprisals.

Anglos commented that Latinos prefer to work together rather than in an ethnically mixed workforce. Indeed, Latinos often mentioned this preference. Their reason, however, was that an all-Latino workforce allows them to escape prejudice, not that they simply prefer to be "with their own people," as Anglos tend to put it. Latinos concurred, moreover, that at a local plant where Latinos keep their jobs for a long time, the level of prejudice is low.

Anglo Views of the Plants and Latino Workers

Townspeople have mixed feelings about the food processing plants. They value the plants for providing local employment but complain bitterly about the stomach-turning smells of plant wastes that permeate nearby neighborhoods through much of the year. Furthermore, they complain about the living conditions of some Latinos, and they see the run-down condition of the housing and yards of some Latinos as phenomena belonging to "Mexican" culture rather than as resulting from poverty.

Although Latinos earn wages that put them in the category of the working poor, Anglos expect them to live as though they are middle-class. Latinos working on the line at the plants and packing houses receive low wages with no benefits, but Anglos criticize them for taking "government handouts." Without government assistance, they could not support their households. They pay for health care at a federally funded clinic that charges fees on a sliding scale, but Anglos complain that the clinic gives free medical care to "Mexicans." (This Anglo characterization is untrue.) Anglos note that other community members are just as needy as "Mexicans." Justice is thus a principle invoked by both Latinos and Anglos to explain their frustration over their working and living conditions and government benefits.

Views of the Shifting Workforce

Relatively few Anglos work on the line at food processing plants, and their reluctance to work in the plants and fields is a change compared to previous decades. Anglo teenagers no longer work in the fields either, whereas Latino adolescents do (children are allowed to work limited hours beginning at 12 years of age and can take regular jobs at the age of 16).

> Sarah (Anglo focus group): I did it [worked in the fields] for ten
>   years.
> Ed: All our kids did.
> Tom: Not anymore. You can't work as fast as what they [Latinos] do.

Sarah: Well, kidwise, you have to be so old before you can work for a farmer.

Ellen: Yes, that's true. My kids all picked and worked in the fields, but now it's 16 [years of age, the requirement for regular employment] . . .

Bob: Most of the [Anglo] kids work at Moon Lake [in fast food service for tourists], you know. You can't get 'em to work in the fields.

Sarah: Well, see, and they've got a law about how old kids have to be down at Moon Lake, but nobody enforces it because they want their kids to have a job. But a lot of what goes on down there should not be going on because of the age. They should not be handling money after certain hours [because of legal restrictions on work by young teenagers].

Interviewer: Oh, really?

Sarah: But everybody just kind of looks the other way.

Bonnie: Everybody in the family used to be out at harvest time, kids and all. You learned you didn't want to do that the rest of your life.

Sarah: Yeah, that's right.

Ed: Went to college.

Rick: That's right.

Sarah: But that's how you got your school clothes, you know, pick cherries.

Julie: Good economy.

Interviewer: There are other options?

Rick: Well, if you said, "Well, kids, would you like to pick asparagus this year or would you rather go and work at Flipper Water Slide?"

Bonnie: At the water slide . . .

(Conversation followed, including the point that the teenagers can earn more picking asparagus, but they are not as concerned about their own earnings as in earlier decades because Anglo parents typically have higher incomes than in the past.)

The Latino labor force for the plants suddenly became available because of an unusual historical juncture, according to some onlookers. Mrs. Smith, a local human services worker with over 20 years of experience, explained that the Immigration Reform and Control Act of 1986 (IRCA) was the mechanism that provided the labor force needed for the expansion of the local food processing industry. She said that many Latinos who had gained legal U.S. residency through IRCA stayed in Fall County because they felt indebted to farmers and other employers who had verified their employment. She argued that without IRCA, local food processing plants would not have had the labor force necessary for expansion, because few local Anglos are willing to work for so little money under such difficult conditions.

Anglo Resentment toward Food Processing Plants:
Pollution, Waste, and Low Wages

The growth of food processing plants is an ongoing point of complaint by many of the Anglos who do not farm. As James (an Anglo) explained:

> These plants are responsible for the increasing number of transient workers who have become full-time residents here.
>
> Lake Freezing Company is important because of its jobs. But if the plant weren't there, all those Mexicans wouldn't have come here either. They're not buying new cars or new mobile homes. They're buying used cars and old mobile homes. So they don't support our car dealerships, mobile home dealers, builders, or real estate agencies. Now, they do buy food at the grocery, but otherwise they're not contributing in the local economy. As a businessperson, it's hard for me to see the economic benefit of the Mexicans who are moving in.

When this argument was posed to a Latino, he responded,

> That's pretty short-sighted. When a Mexican buys a used mobile home or car, that previous owner can go out and buy a new one . . . It's not true that all Mexicans will be poor all their lives. We work in the food processing plants when we first get here, but after a few years, we try to move into industries that pay better.

In the Anglo focus group, residents discussed the future of local low-income Latinos. One woman theorized that it will take three generations for Latinos to improve their economic status and move from the lower to the middle class.

Without being able to speak English, it's hard to get a job. They have to depend on their children to help them at the store and anywhere else.

Later, the focus group discussed the work of newly arrived immigrants.

When they first arrive, many Latinos work in the fields and food processing. As they get better established, they reach a position where they can look for better jobs. From there they go to factory work—from farm to factory work, from factory work to better jobs. I can see probably, however many years down the line—might take 20 years—but I think they're gonna [better their lot].

This view is part of an Anglo ideology holding that Latino newcomers will go through the same struggles as their own ancestors and eventually reach prosperity. Anglos do not see that local conditions are creating the growth of a class of the working poor, most of whom will have little opportunity for advancement.

Anglos are quite ambivalent about local food processing plants. People living in Mapleville complain about the stench from one of the food processing plants located in the town. The waste ponds at the food processing plant, Anglo focus group participants say, stink "like rotting pumpkins" or like "flowers that have been in a vase too long" and "make you look at the bottom of your shoes to see if you stepped in anything."

The plant has sewer ponds that fill the air with a stench during the agricultural season. After 15 years, despite repeated complaints to the company, the odors continue.

Sarah (Anglo focus group): I was at that day care center near the plant. It was time for recess, the children started begging, "Oh please, don't make us go outside!" They can't stand to breathe it. If you can imagine, children who can't stand to go out to play!
Julie: I put in a window air conditioner to get rid of the smell, but it still doesn't take care of it.

Throughout the Midwest, Anglos are making similar complaints. For example, in the following letter to the editor, Kendra Kimbirauskas complains of contamination of food and pollution of groundwater by factory farms that the State of Michigan refuses to regulate. In fact, the Michigan state legislature passed a right-to-farm law during this study to protect farms from local control. Also known as Hog Hiltons in the case of pig farms, these farm factories are built on an unprecedented scale and overwhelm local communities in numerous ways.

Control Animal Factories

Factory farms make me sick . . . literally! Just imagine it, some 1,000 animal units crammed so tight in cages or stalls that they haven't even enough room to turn around. They are pumped with antibiotics and hormones in order to increase production and prevent sickness—all of which ends up in our bodies upon consumption of animal products.

As if we don't devour enough antibiotics and hormones with the food that we eat, we are also finding hormones and bacteria in our groundwater. These enormous facilities are currently producing more waste than a small city and haven't the means to properly dispose of it. As a result, thousands, if not millions of gallons of manure are stored in lagoons. These lagoons regularly have leakage and sometimes even burst or overflow.

Sound appealing? Apparently, the state of Michigan thinks so, since it has done nothing to regulate these monstrous facilities from poisoning her citizens! (Kendra Kimbirauskas, Stockbridge, letter to the editor, *Lansing State Journal,* June 19, 2001)

In Fall County, Anglos hate the smell of food processing plants, but on the other hand, they acknowledge that

it's kind of a give-and-take. We live in a rural agricultural area. We need something to process these things that we grow and, you know . . .

Over near Westside City, there's that paper mill. That stinks up the air pretty badly if the wind's blowing in the wrong direction.

I hate the smell [from the food processing plants], but I know that if I complain, I'll be talking about my neighbors' [losing their] jobs.

Fortunately, not all the plants in the area have this problem (whether that is because they are located away from population centers or because they handle their waste differently is unknown). At least in the case of the largest plant, Anglo neighbors have reservations about its presence in the community.

During focus groups with Latinos, we asked if they had heard people complain about the increasing numbers of low-income people attracted to the area or the presence of food processing plants. None had heard complaints about the growth of this industry.

> Carlota (a long-term Latina resident): Americans don't mind the food processing plants because they own them. They don't mind the Mexicans as long as we keep working in food processing. Americans complain when we leave the food processing plants and get other jobs. You hear, "Those Mexicans are taking all the jobs."
>
> The funny thing is, my aunt in Texas would say the same things about Mexicans who came across [the border from Mexico]. There were so many, wages were going down, and the situation was getting worse.

Many Anglos in Fall County see the shift of Latinos from farmwork to food processing as a big step forward.

> Nate (an Anglo): I've been working at migrant health clinics for 25 years. On the farm, workers have to depend—economically and socially—on a single farmer. In my opinion, the plant jobs have really improved the situation of migrant families. They've been able to break that dependency with jobs in the plants. It's a good thing.

On the other hand, Nate does not realize that many workers are trapped in the same way in their jobs on the line in food processing as they had been as migrant farmworkers.

Anglo Concerns about the Local Economy

Fox and Mapleville both have industrial parks that have attracted a number of companies to the area through tax incentives. The industrial parks have provided new jobs in light manufacturing companies that produce electronic and plastic components for cars and other products. We were told that since about 1996, the area has shifted toward this type of industry. The new jobs at these manufacturing companies were described as low-paying, and Anglos voiced their concerns that higher-paying companies had not been attracted to the area yet. Anglo focus group members had the following comments:

Interviewer: So the idea is, you want to draw more of these industries to the area then?

Rick: I think it would be nice. I wish, in the same place [where] we have jobs that are paying $8, $9 an hour, I wish we could have enticed a division of Aeronautics Enterprise to come up here with their union jobs; not that I'm pro-union or anti-union, but there's a huge difference.

Interviewer: How much do they make? How much would a union job be compared to that $8 to $9 job here?

Tom: Eighteen?

Rick: I was gonna say almost double.

Julie: At least, yeah, at least double.

Sarah: Plus a whole lot more benefits.

Near the end of the focus group session, we returned to this subject.

Rick: I'm personally worried about the effect on the school. In Fox Elementary School, 55 percent of the students have assisted lunch [subsidized by the government for children from low-income households] . . .

Ed: But that's not just Spanish. I mean, that's—

Bonnie: Yeah that's everyone.

Rick: I know, yeah, I know and my main concern, if I could change anything, we'd add $5 an hour to everyone working in Fall County Food Processors or working at Lake Plastics Company or—

Julie: How about day care?

Rick: Oh, whatever.

Sarah: I think you had a good point when you talked about union jobs.

Ellen: Oh, yeah.

Tom: We don't have any union jobs.

Rick: You know, we'll jump through hoops to get Lake Plastics up here, but you start out at seven bucks an hour and top out at $11. The managers at Fall County Food Processors average 55, 60 hours a week, and that puts them in the middle class, but that's a lot of overtime. I wish we could do something to shake up the economics . . .

What the [school] administration is concerned about is the high number of assisted lunch students. That could translate to lower MEAP scores.

The Michigan Educational Assessment Program (MEAP) evaluates schools through testing students, and the students' scores ultimately affect school budgets and autonomy and determine which students receive state scholarships for college. Low performances by students are thus a concern for entire communities.

Local leaders suggested that Fox and Mapleville may expand the size of their industrial parks in the future. One staff member of Michigan Works! (the state employment agency) spoke of two local trends, one toward manufacturing and another away from farming. She stated that there is a lack of migrant farmworkers, which has resulted in a decrease in farming and a diversification of agricultural industry in the area. She and others expect these trends will continue. (Although a number of Anglos referred to a shortage of migrant farmworkers, a number of state government staff were skeptical, as local farmers have not intensified their recruiting and have still succeeded in hiring adequate numbers of farmworkers.)

Currently there are economic difficulties for some farmers, while others continue to do well. According to Anglo residents, some farms are closing due to increased global competition, rising costs of running a farm, and lack of farmworkers. Last year, several apple farms closed, mainly because of competition from China.

Ellen (Anglo focus group): You couldn't pick up the juice apples for three cents a pound. It was more expensive to pick 'em up and sell 'em so [they stayed on the ground].

Despite this problem with the market for juice apples, Ellen and other farmers were doing well. They tended to view local farming as a continuing way of life and an economic mainspring in the county. Ellen commented on her own and other farms:

They're doing fabulous. In fact, Fall County Food Processors got a contract from Gerber's that they just can't keep up with [for] the peaches.

We could probably put in another 30 acres of baby gold peaches, too, if we had the land. They're contracting from Gerber. So it's fabulous, and even with cherries. If we can get the Japanese market and some of these foreign markets . . .

But it's just so much work, where the farmers are just getting burned out, and no one's taking the farm after them is the problem.

Thus, the pressure of global competition and other changes are driving some farms out of business, while others are in good financial shape. Local people predict, however, that the farm families will not continue in agriculture in the next generation. Some farmers have said they would rather have their land pass into the hands of Latino farmers than to those of housing developers. One view of the future is that the county will be made up largely of Anglo retirees and commuters, with low-income Latinos doing the hard physical labor on local farms and in the plants. Some community members hope to attract higher-paying jobs to the area to avoid a depressing future for Fall County.

Economic Dimensions of the Latino Influx: Discussion and Policy Implications

The Latino influx into Fall County is a response to job availability, as local food processing plants have recruited Latinos as a workforce willing to work for minimum wage and no benefits, conditions refused by most Anglos. Latinos have come to Fall County since 1918 as migrant farmworkers; the change in the last two decades has not been in the number of Latinos coming to the county but in the number settling there permanently. Although this change is only the culmination of a process that began early in the twentieth century, permanent residence of Latinos has startled and dismayed many Anglos.

In this respect, Fall County resembles the area of rural California studied by Allensworth and Rochín (1998a,b; 1999). There is little evidence, however, that widespread extreme residential segregation of towns as either "Mexican" or "Anglo" will develop in the Midwest. On the other hand, many of the tensions that exist between Anglos and Latinos in rural California (Allensworth and Rochín 1999; Menchaca 1995) also appear in the communities in this study.

The meatpacking plants in the Midwestern grain belt have recruited a mostly male workforce, and they pay above minimum wage and provide medical benefits after the first six months of work (Gouveia and Stull 1995, 1997). In comparison, the plants in this study have a larger proportion of female workers and pay Latino workers minimum wage with no medical benefits.

As with meatpacking plants in Nebraska, the expansion of the food processing plants in the present study has depended on and encouraged Latino settlement. Latinos value the plants as sources of work for themselves and their neighbors, but the pay places them at the bottom of the economic scale, among the working poor. Many are thus forced to rely on government aid, including food stamps and subsidized housing. Some Latinos complain bitterly of discrimination and arduous working conditions, but others report that they are generally comfortable at work.

Anglos insist that they are not concerned with the changing ethnicity of the population but with the changing class parameters, particularly increasing poverty and its social and economic implications. Although they appreciate the food processing plants because of the jobs they have created, many Anglos are angry because of the stench emitted by the plants in their neighborhoods. Middle-class Anglo children are leaving the community in search of employment that pays well, while wealthy urbanites are retiring along the beaches to the west of Fox and Mapleville—a pattern encouraging the growth of low-paying service jobs. Shifts in the farming and food processing sectors continue to draw new Latino residents, who join the low-wage labor force.

The economic changes at the local, national, and international levels that have encouraged permanent Latino settlement in the area are complex, as noted by Rochín (1995), Massey (1998), Massey and Espinosa (1997), and Hayes-Bautista et al. (1988). Anglos in Fall County often recognize that many Latino newcomers are going through hardships, but they expect that Latinos will make their way upward economically, as did the ancestors of local Anglo farmers and townspeople. They do not recognize that structural constraints consign most Latinos to the working poor, now and in the future (Chapa 1988, 1990, 1995). Latinos lack access to loans to buy farmland or start other businesses; shopkeepers cannot afford to stock their stores well enough to generate reasonable incomes and must compete to some degree with megastores within an easy drive.

Anglo leaders, businesspeople, and farmers could engage with Latinos in devising a constructive response to the situation; however, many of them are too involved in various factions that divide the Anglo community. A crucial part of this picture involves the few Anglos who profit from the status quo. They include the owners of the plants who employ the Latino newcomers as the cheapest laborers they can find and Anglos who rent housing to workers. Other townspeople oppose the run-down housing often used for this purpose, but they associate it with the tenants, not the owners. Various providers of services to low-income Latinos also benefit; there are workers in social services, education, and health care employed to deal specifically with Latinos. These organizations have Anglo ownership or management and usually employ bilingual Latinas to deliver services to monolingual Spanish-speaking Latino consumers. Local low-income Anglos complain of services made available to Latinos, because most Anglos do not realize that the services are not divided by ethnic group but by income level, occupation, and other economic categories. These misunderstandings discourage Anglos from working with Latinos to solve community problems.

Policy Implications

Any of a number of changes would allow Latino newcomers to meet their basic needs more completely, and most of these changes would also benefit the Anglo working poor as well. Paying Latino food processing workers a living wage with benefits, as received by most other rural workers in non-agricultural light industry, would allow Latino newcomers to exit the class of the working poor. Providing medical benefits on the job to Latino workers, as received by most employees in the state, would allow them independence from government-subsidized health care at migrant and community health clinics. Providing Latinos access to business loans would allow some to acquire farms and businesses large enough to support their households, and the resulting economic stability would allow them to follow the pathway of various immigrant groups toward a more prosperous future. Finally, providing a reasonable education to Spanish monolingual children would allow them to learn English efficiently, to graduate from high school, and to qualify for better jobs than their parents have. These changes would also reduce the proportion of working poor in rural towns and reduce government expenditures on services to them. These policy alternatives are not locally under discussion, however.

Anglo and Latino residents had the same projection for the future if Latino population growth continues: white flight. If business and industrial development continues in the present direction, bringing more low-income Latino settlement, it is expected that Anglos in the middle- and upper-income brackets will leave. This pattern of change would take Fall County in the direction of the ethnically segregated communities of central California (Allensworth and Rochín 1998a,b). As the low-income segment of the population expands, the tax base is forced to stretch further to meet the increased costs for schools, health care, and human services.

The failure of Anglos to engage with Latinos to settle the various questions posed by the recent influx rests, in part, on the fact that a few powerful Anglo employers and landlords are profiting from the current situation. Anglos also tend to see the influx as driven by Latinos taking advantage of government benefits, not as the result of the demands of local employers for low-wage workers willing to take jobs that do not pay benefits. Many local Anglos are prejudiced against Latinos as well.

Latinos do not participate with Anglos in discussions about the future of the community because the two ethnic groups lack basic social ties outside their few connections at the workplace. Latino children for the most part are receiving a level of education that will keep them in the same economic and social position as their parents. In newcomer families, most children speak English, giving them access to more jobs and perhaps slightly more pay. Latinos have little voice in political and other institutional decisions, a situation not expected to change for some time.

Anglo community leaders suggest an alternate future for the community. They want steps to be taken to encourage growth in middle-class employment. They propose that the county attract high-end industry and improve the appearance of towns to attract middle-class residents from nearby cities. At this point, it is unclear whether Anglo leaders will pursue this path, but they apparently will continue to determine the future of the county and its institutions. As long as this situation holds, Latinos will continue to have little say in the agenda for the county, minimal power over economic development, and practically no voice in a political future that will govern them and shape their livelihoods.

CHAPTER SEVEN

Mexicans, Americans, and Neither:
Students at Wheelerton High

Ken R. Crane

In Fred Peralta's high school study hall for students in English as a Second Language (ESL), I chatted with some of the Latino students about where they were from. One came from Chicago, one from Tamaulipas, one from Zacatecas, and several were from the Mexican state of Aguascalientes. They jokingly told me they were nicknamed Las Aguitas (The Little Waters), and in English they were sometimes called Hot Waters (the literal translation of the state's name). They were among the 550 students in Wheelerton's school system in the year 2000 who spoke Spanish as their first language and whose families moved to this area in the 1990s from Mexico and the Texas-Mexico border region. The Latino population began to soar in the school system in the early 1990s. In 1992–1993 Spanish-speaking students were 7.6 percent of students in Wheelerton's school system. Wheelerton Elementary School had almost 9 percent. Two years later, the proportion for the elementary school had increased to 14 percent. The middle school went from about 5 percent in 1993 to almost 16 percent three years later. From 1994–1995 to 1995–1996, the Latino student population in the middle school more than doubled in number (partly due to fifth grade moving to the middle school from the elementary school). The influx of Latino students has added to a school system that has been growing steadily; from 1983 to the present, it has had annual increases of about 30 students. To meet this demand, the school system had plans to expand classrooms by the 2001 school year at a cost of $7 to $12 million. The high school principal reported that over the recent years, the student increase was about 1 1/2 percent per year (or about 9 students), with about two-thirds of that increase being Latino students.

I spent several hours over a period of three weeks observing the high school study hall and talking in depth with the ESL coordinator, Megan Saavedra, and the bilingual tutor, Fred Chavez. Megan was stretched to the limit, since she had to teach ESL at all the schools in the district. The various perspectives of students and teachers described below shed further light on how Latino students are experiencing the classrooms and social life of schools in Wheelerton.

ESL Study Hall

My first day at school, I thought, was going to be the best. I was going to a new school; I was going to meet new people. I was wrong! I was scared because I was the only one who did not speak English and everyone looked at me strangely. At recess all the girls came up to me; they stood in a circle with me and talked. They wanted me to talk too, but I could not. I felt so bad that I cried. I wanted to go back to where I was from, back to my friends, back to someone I could talk to.

Tonia, a Latina newcomer

The ESL classroom provided a gathering place and learning area for many Latino students. Below are some observations:

Megan was doing ESL instruction (for students in level 3 and one in level 4, to whom she was giving some extra work). Fred didn't have any study hall students at this hour. Juan, a student from a migrant family, was especially talkative. Several guys were getting ready for baseball practice (the first of the season). José stayed for next period as well but did some kind of learning game on the computer. Then he sat down to my left at the table with a guy named Padilla. I talked to José and a friend about their homework. José quickly changed the subject and asked if I knew any pretty girls in Michigan. I said, "Only mi esposa [my wife]."

During the next hour, scheduled for students in levels 1 and 2, a much bigger group came in—a larger ESL class and a study hall group, all in Fred's room. It was a much rowdier group, partly because there were so many; they were definitely more rambunctious than earlier or later classes. José and another guy were walking around and tended to speak more assertively to the teachers. Megan broke the students into groups, mixing some of the more advanced with the less advanced. Several had joined the class at midyear and were behind the rest.

A young man who had not said much got up from the study hall table and sauntered to the door. Megan asked him for his work; he replied it was on the table and prepared to go out; she told him to give it to her. He sauntered back and handed her his work; she thumbed through it making comments. Later she told me he was almost failing. He was wearing sagging jeans, hip-hop style, head almost shaved. To my left a girl was helping Fred by taking attendance and making photocopies at the office. We chatted. She didn't need any help. I asked if she was an Aguita (from Aguascalientes), and she and her friends just laughed.

[On another day,] some of the students were taking tests. One student had finished his work and was listening to a tape. Another student who was taking a test asked him to turn it down. I walked over and asked him if I could listen. I put on the headphones and heard a Mexican rock band. I asked him the name; he said, "La Tri."
Crane, field notes

Megan believes that students who were good students in Mexico are also good here. They tend to overcome the language barrier and catch up quickly. Fred feels that some use the ESL classroom as a crutch; they don't want to graduate out of it. He warns them that they can't be calling him up years later for help in filling out application forms.

Teacher Perspectives

In interviews with teachers, I asked what kind of challenge the growing Latino student population poses in the classroom. A counselor thought it was tough for the average teacher who does not want to stop the class for several students who are having difficulty with English. Teachers have had to learn how to deal with this challenge. The ESL coordinator felt that some cope with the learning needs of these students by sending them to ESL study hall too frequently, outside of the normally scheduled ESL study hall period. She explained that when students have time in other classes to work alone on homework, they often ask to go to ESL study hall with the actual intention of socializing with their Latino friends. The bad side of this is that ESL study hall becomes sometimes too crowded (as I witnessed). She thinks teachers should check more carefully on what their ESL level is, if they are in ESL classes at all, and try to work with them in the classroom as much as possible.

Others remarked that there are some teachers who don't know how to deal with students who have any kind of learning challenge, whether it is language or special needs. This perspective views such teachers as having difficulty with any kind of special needs student, including "Limited English Proficient" (LEP) students. According to this perspective, their aversion to such students therefore should not be seen as racially motivated.

The school counselor asserted that those who plan to go into manual work of some kind do not care about school. They are not even interested in vocational programs, according to her. One teacher noticed that dropouts tend to be older males who work in addition to going to school. Several 18-year-olds had worked the third (graveyard) shift, then had come to school after work, and they dropped out after a while. Another student worked the second shift, and he still managed to graduate.

Boyd, who mostly teaches English literature and honors English, has not had large numbers of Latino students in his upper-level classes. In his lower-level classes he has had more, occasionally as many as eight or ten. He said they are always courteous and respectful, although if a group of them are in class they are more vocal and less reserved and tend to chatter with their friends in Spanish. He believes that those who are lazy academically are that way because they see no use for formal education—one student had a job lined up that did not require a high school diploma.

Bilingual Education and English as a Second Language

Several teachers emphasized to me that a true bilingual educational program is needed. Generally, in such a program, courses are taught in two languages by a certified teacher. One elementary teacher sees students as falling behind and insists that such a program could prevent this problem. She went on to argue, from a pedagogical standpoint, the various reasons true bilingual education is needed. If students whose first language is Spanish learn the principles of Spanish grammar, they can learn English grammar more efficiently than by focusing on English alone. This sequence is more efficient for learning a new language than trying to take on the grammatical rules, vocabulary, and sound system of a new language all at once. The teacher asserted that it is unfortunate that many teachers and administrators use the "deficit model" of language, focusing on students' lack of English skills but ignoring their strengths in their first language. Bilingual education acknowledges a student's strengths in the mother tongue.

It is argued that this keeps the student from falling behind in the subject matter and better prepares the student to learn English. A high school teacher had pushed for a limited bilingual education model in which one subject, such as government, would be taught in both languages. Her idea was never adopted.

The school district has had an ESL program since the late 1980s, but the rapid increase in "language minority" students created a need to expand the program. According to the superintendent, they eventually got more funding in the mid-1990s. The West Wayne elementary, middle, and high schools have an ESL coordinator, and each school has an ESL study hall with a bilingual tutor. One responsibility of the ESL program is to test students to determine whether they should be in an English-only program. Those who test at low proficiency levels are placed in one of four categories (level 1 being lowest, level 4 being the highest). Later tests determine if they are ready to move to higher levels or out of the program altogether.

The academic performance of the Latino students has caused some concern among teachers and administrators because their grades and test scores lag behind those of other groups. Administrators acknowledge that tests may give an incomplete picture of how the students are doing. Students with extremely low English ability (level 1) do not even take the standardized tests; those who do take them encounter a cultural bias. Fred, a bilingual tutor and Mexican American who grew up in Wheelerton, claims that he experienced cultural biases in the test, and he commented that Latino newcomers would experience many more. The way standardized tests are given could also be a factor. A bilingual tutor assists ESL students with tests given for regular classes but not with standardized tests.

High School Dropouts

One staff member who works closely with the Latino students believes their dropout rate is much higher than that of Anglo students. She noted that Latino student enrollment is always high, indicating to her that they "know the value of a high school education." The reasons for dropping out are different for men and women. Some men work a full-time second-shift job in addition to attending school.

> If things get tough, it is usually the education that goes. Often times they pledge to come back, and sometimes they do. There are so many jobs in

our area, and they don't require a diploma to make $10–15 per hour, so it seems tough to keep them in school.

She also noted that more Latinas quit school nowadays due to pregnancy than 20 years ago. In addition, the newly arrived students have a higher dropout rate than those who grew up locally. "So the dropout rate is high for both groups, but I still feel they know the importance of school, but circumstances interfere."

Tensions have arisen around students speaking Spanish in the classroom. For example, Julio and a friend had been given detention slips by a teacher for speaking Spanish in class. The teacher had provided some written ground rules for his class regarding foreign language use, which stated that only English was allowed unless special arrangements had been made explicitly. Megan, suspecting that this was in violation of students' rights, intervened by discussing the matter with the principal and was given permission by the superintendent to research the matter further. Megan discovered that it is against U.S. Department of Education guidelines related to Title VI to punish a language-minority student for speaking a language other than English during free time or time to complete homework. She and Fred were advised by the superintendent to draw up some guidelines to circulate to the teaching staff. A one-page sheet of guidelines was circulated on translation, discipline, disrespectful behavior, and students' right to express themselves in any language, "as long as it is not vulgar or profane, in the cafeteria, hallways, restrooms, and during free time in class." The language issue remains a sore point between a number of students and their teachers.

Another staff member noted that Latino students are not well represented in vocational and career-related courses. "The exception is cosmetology, where the Latino may be the majority. The girls also do a good job of taking office and computer classes. But we do not get many boys in auto, building trades, or printing." She believed it may have to do with both language and parents' opinion that school is for academics, not preparation for the trades. Citing the case of one girl, she said that her parents wanted her to learn all she could, because she would work for many years after high school. At the same time, few Latinos are college-bound. Some tend to be interested in some subjects, such as art, and begin to see possibilities of studying for the sake of learning; however, many do not choose to take the classes that prepare them for college. More young men than young women are going on to college, although some young women are "very motivated and have college goals."

Ethnic Relationships

Several teachers and administrators told me of positive trends in relationships between Anglo and Latino students. Boyd, the English teacher, says he sees much more acceptance of Mexican students by the student body. He notices more mixing. In contrast to 1993, when he had a student who would openly blurt out racist remarks in the presence of Latino students, he hears none of those remarks anymore. The middle school principal observed that he has noticed more three-way conversations where one person is translating.

Another improvement is the increase in ethnic diversity which, I was told, was "badly missing" in earlier days. One teacher sees that the presence of other cultures can be harnessed as a learning tool. The celebration of Cinco de Mayo in a school assembly, for example, exposed Anglo students to the history of the Mexican struggle against colonialism. Megan, the ESL teacher, mentioned that some Anglo students wanted to learn Spanish by assisting at ESL study hall. The Spanish teacher believes that there is actually more tolerance among students now than when there were fewer Latino students; as their numbers have grown, so has tolerance toward Latino students in school.

Some teachers remember that during the middle part of the decade, when the influx of Mexican students was a new phenomenon, there were more problems. One middle school teacher remembers that Mexican students would stick together in large groups and there were more fights than there are today.

The athletic program staff generally noted that sports activities tend to incorporate Latino students with others. One coach stated that when Mexican students become involved in sports, they end up making friends with Anglos. Most of the quarrels he has seen involving sports are between people of the same ethnicity. Another coach said that language barriers present fewer challenges in sports: "Football is the same in Texas as it is here." He went on to add, however, that "you might think you're communicating but they [Mexican students] don't know where you're coming from." Mexican students had both positive and negative experiences to report from their involvement in sports (see below).

Student Experiences and Perspectives
Antonia

During one of the ESL study halls, I met Antonia, a senior at Wheelerton High who is headed for college with a scholarship. During fifth hour, she assists the bilingual tutor by helping other students who are less proficient in English with their homework. She is bilingual and talks easily with both Mexican and Anglo friends. She is tall and attractive, with full, wavy hair falling below her shoulders. She seems mature for a woman her age, with a self-confidence forged through a tough past.

Her father came to Wheelerton from Aguascalientes via California in the 1980s, seeking an industrial job. She and her younger sister came in 1990 (she was about seven years old at the time). She said she didn't want to come here. Her mother worked picking apples. Other family members have come to the area since she did—three uncles on her father's side, one on her mother's side. Most of the family still resides in Aguascalientes.

When she arrived, Antonia started in the third grade in Wheelerton. She remembers it as a very difficult time. She cried a lot during the first week because she didn't know the language. Some of the children were kind to her; some were not. There was one other Latina in her class. She would be given assignments different from those for Anglo students (e.g., coloring instead of writing). She was homesick a lot. At home, she taught her younger sister the English she had learned to spare her the same misery.

It took three more years before she began to feel like she had adjusted to her new environment. As she moved into high school, making friends with both Anglos and Latinos, things were better but never without problems. She sometimes found herself having to choose between loyalty to one group or the other. "It was also hard because my Mexican friends were racist, and they did not want me to talk to the *bolillas*. I could not choose between my race and the other race because I liked them both." In high school sports, she would be criticized by opposing teams for speaking Spanish to teammates. She hasn't forgotten how someone wrote "Spic go home" on the cafeteria table where Latino students normally sat.

To complicate her difficult transition at school, there was instability at home. Just after her mother had their last child, her father left.

Her mom had a third-grade education and wanted to help Antonia with her homework but really could not. Nevertheless, she says her relationship with her mother is very good—her mother is her best friend; she gives her lots of good advice (*consejos*). She is also close to an aunt who comes from Mexico to visit them regularly.

Her dad wanted to take them back to Mexico because he felt she was becoming too Americanized. For example, he would get very upset when she could not remember certain words or translate something properly. She had no desire to return—she had come to like it here, had lots of friends, liked her new way of life, was doing well in school and had even grown to like school. She believes this contention over returning to Mexico is one of the reasons the family split up.

Besides church, she is also involved in volunteer activities: Charger Care (involving community work and visiting nursing homes); PRIDE (a drug-free club that helped raise $70,000 for a child's kidney transplant); the soccer team; and Drama Club—she had a part in the play *Our Town*. She also participated when the Spanish Club performed traditional Mexican folk dances for a special Cinco de Mayo show in the auditorium.

Cinco de Mayo

On May 5, the Spanish Club presented a special assembly to celebrate Cinco de Mayo. The Spanish teacher and Fred organized the program. One of the Mexican students, a girl who originally came from Tamaulipas, had studied dance at an institute in Mexico. She taught the other Mexican students a number of traditional dances from different regions of Mexico.

Crane, field notes

The program was well received by the student body. The dancing was expertly choreographed and performed. Fred's Tejano band performed several songs, during which the dancers went into the audience and paired up with Anglo students. You could see a lot of mixed couples; people seemed to be enjoying it. Fred then made several acknowledgments and song dedications to the principal, who was retiring that year.

Anglo Student Perspective

Later that day, we asked a focus group of Anglo students how they felt about the program and about relationships with Latino students. The majority thought it was a good program; they enjoyed the music and dancing and the good feelings it seemed to produce. One student said she had not wanted to go because she did not know what was being celebrated. She commented with irritation, "I'm not Hispanic and I don't know their beliefs. I honestly did not know what to expect, so you know, why attend something if you don't know what you're celebrating?" In the past, a speaker had been invited to talk about the historical significance of Cinco de Mayo; this year the written program explained its place in Mexican history. Evidently, this student had not read the program.

Overall, most Anglo students exhibited an attempt to understand the situation and behavior of Latino students. They were quick to differentiate themselves from racist or negative comments made by adults in the community (including their own parents in some cases).

> Brittany (focus group interview): In general I think the community isn't very accepting, but I think we're more accepting—like the student body . . .
> Rick: We've grown up more with it.
> Brittany (who had moved here from California): I mean, in California, you know, this is pretty much normal—having a lot of Hispanics or, you know, Cubans or whatever you have. I mean, California, it's just normal and then, you know, you move here and there's a lot less Hispanics than where I used to go, and I hear a lot of people talking bad about 'em.
> Interviewer: In the community?
> Brittany: In the community, yeah. The school is pretty well accepting but, I mean, a lot of people in the community don't like 'em, you know, and I just don't understand the need for it. I mean, they're just normal people. They're just like us.

During their discussion of negative or positive feelings about Latinos in the community, they recognized the influence parents had on their attitudes and those of others.

James: I think a lot of it stems down from how our parents . . . I mean, like I hear sometimes, they don't pay taxes. All they do is have 40 families in one house, and they don't have to pay taxes, and they're taking our money, and they're taking our jobs. But around school, we don't have to deal with it. We're not competing for jobs. We're not, we're just here to go to school, but, um, there's none of that because it's just not a big deal.

Brenda: I have to agree with [James]. I do believe that it stems down from our parents, and that's one of the first things my parents taught me—was not to be a racist. So I was very accepting and my very first babysitter, who I have fond memories of, was Hispanic. And they were awesome people 'cause, you know, right from the beginning I was accepting it.

When I was little, though, it was rare to see a Hispanic in this community, and as I'm getting older it's just progressed slowly and now everywhere you look you see it, and so it's kind of a shock to the community. We're really conservative and it's the whole change thing, I think, you know. This community is conservative and it's used to being set in a certain way and now it's starting to change and people are not liking that.

Students were very aware of the unstated differentiation that many in the community make between "good Hispanics" (more assimilated, bilingual, church-attending) and "bad Hispanics" (young, beer-drinking, and "illegal"). The Anglo students didn't care about the legality issue and felt that, facing the same circumstances, they would do the same as Mexicans who cross borders illegally.

Brittany: It's the illegal Hispanic people that come here. I mean, I've been to Mexico and my dad has told us, you know, if we lived in Tijuana, you know, if we had that kind of lifestyle, he said he'd do anything to get us across the border, you know, I mean, if I had a family—

Mark: I don't really blame him.

James: I would do that, too.

Mindy: If they can make it here, good for them, I think, 'cause I would do the same thing.

Students believed that racism was not a problem in their school and that it did not characterize the relationships between themselves and Latinos. From their parents and others they hear comments such as "They don't pay taxes," "They take our jobs," "They have forty people in one house." The students, however, present themselves as more accepting than people in the community and more tolerant of difference.

In narrating their experiences with Latino students in classes and clubs, the Anglo students were generally positive. Most had friendships or positive interactions with Latino students and coworkers. Some students raised concerns, though. Some Anglos felt there was too much voluntary separation of Anglos and Latinos, and they blamed it on the Latino students. One girl complained that she had made unsuccessful overtures of friendship to several Latinas in her class: "You try to be friendly to them, but they're not friendly back." (She admitted, however, that these girls were not fluent in English, which could explain their unresponsiveness.)

In sports, several students had observed that even when on the team some Latinos kept to themselves: "Yeah, they just, they just kind of wanted to wrestle with themselves, you know—they didn't really try to mix in real well. I mean, it was kinda different." Another student (on the football team) admitted there were negative feelings about the mostly Mexican soccer team.

Rick: Yeah, they play soccer. That's their way of getting away from it—I mean, a lot of negative stuff comes from the football team. Like, we don't want to hear about that communist sport and that kind of thing . . . they do tear up our football field. They make holes and stuff in it and I—that's probably where a lot of negativity comes from, soccer, 'cause we don't like ruts in our [field].

Several perceived a lack of interest on the part of Mexican students in seeking friendships with non-Mexicans. Most, however, did not see the separation of Anglos and Mexicans as a significant issue.

James: One thing that usually happens is, like, in the lunchroom and stuff. Usually most of the Mexicans and Hispanics, they sit at one table, and a lot of the white people sit at another table, but it's not— I mean, you can still mix. It's just kind of the way they do it.

Rick: It's just like that's who their friends are and they're all Hispanic and they like to speak their own language, you know, around their friends. And I mean, if we say hi to them, it's not like, "Oh my gosh, you said hi to me."

Mindy: Yeah, but if the groups do mix, it's not really a big deal. It's just kinda, they know each other better, maybe.

The Anglo students did not perceive the separation of groups as being motivated by, or a consequence of, racist attitudes. Rather, they attributed it to the natural tendency of youth to hang out with those of similar interests, background, and language: "There are plenty of Hispanics, so they can find friends to talk to, so they do not have a problem fitting in." From the other focus groups and interviews, however, we know that Latino students have encountered racist remarks and attitudes from teammates and Anglo students.

On the social scene, it was widely believed that more and more Anglo girls were dating Mexican boys. The question of dating came up several times in the context of parental concerns. The parents of several Anglo students discouraged them from dating Latinos. One woman said her father would prefer she dated an African American rather than a Hispanic man because he believes Mexicans treat women badly. In a separate interview, a recent Anglo high school student reported that her sister dated a Latino, and they found they had many cultural differences, including pressures on Latinas to dress to please men and disapproval of their going to college.

Latino Student Perspectives

Focus groups with two sets of Latino students revealed that their overall experience at school was mixed. Interactions with Anglo students and teachers were generally positive, but their experiences varied according to the length of time they had lived in the community. "Old-timers," as some were called, had some significantly different approaches to the questions of ethnic identity and group relationships from those who arrived in the area more recently.

Old-timers

Students who were better established or who belonged to the second generation (i.e., who were born in the United States) had a view of group relationships that differed from the views of both Anglos and newly arrived Mexicans. Most of these second-generation Latino youths (nicknamed "old-timers"), grew up in Wheelerton, with its small but strong and tight-knit Mexican community. Some grew up in nearby towns or villages as the sole Latinos of those communities. In school, many of the old-timer students struggled to learn English, because they had grown up with parents who spoke no or little English. Sometimes they ended up in readiness class (remedial English) because they spoke English mixed with Spanish. Sometimes they were given assignments different from those of the rest of the class; sometimes they were told to wait for the teacher to explain the subject after class.

As they grew up, they encountered discrimination. A Latino student who managed to make the basketball team was told, "This is a white man's sport." A Latina spoke in a focus group about the lunch table where she and some other Mexican students sat. One day when they arrived, they found written there, "Go back to Mexico." Some of the Latino students who had been born in the United States commented on the ignorance of Anglo students. They managed to find acceptance from some of the white students, though, and many counted one or a few white students among their close friends.

Cultural differences made dating and friendships more complicated. Estela remembers missing out on all those sleepovers with her Anglo friends:

> Estela (a Latina in a focus group): You know, one thing that always bugged me, like when my friends would be, like, "We're having a sleepover. Do you want to come?" I'm like, "Mom, can I go to the sleepover?" And my parents are like, "No." "Well, why not?" and Mom's like, "'Cause you can't." And I'm like, "Well, why not? You know her family is going to be there." She's like, "You have your own house. You sleep in your own house!" That's one of the biggest things. I'd miss out on those sleepovers. I was always mad about it.

Like other second-generation Latinos, Estela found herself having to reconcile expectations of Anglo friends with the stricter rules of her parents.

She related how the customary Anglo dating practice, going out with a boy in his car, was seen as reprehensible by her parents.

Okay, going on dates and the guy picking you up in his car, you do not get in the guy's car. That's just, they're [your parents are] like, "If you get in a guy's car, you've lost respect for yourself." That's like, you're in the guy's car and they think you're off having sex or something. I'm like, "No we're not," and my mom's like, "Well, why can't you just meet him there?" If you do [ride in the guy's car], they're like, "Take your little brother with you." I'm like, "Why?" [All the focus group members were talking and laughing.] That's the worst thing.

Estela remembers her mother saying frequently, "But our *costumbres* [customs], don't forget our *costumbres!*"

What many old-timers find disturbing is being looked down upon by the more recently arrived Mexicans. An example of this is Rosa, who was born in Texas and grew up in the only Latino family in an Amish town ten miles from Wheelerton. She feels the newer Mexicans see her as "just a white girl."

Rosa (in a focus group): I'm just a white girl, you know—I'm not with Mexicanos, I'm just a white girl and that's still hard right now. Right now it's just like, oh well, Mexicanos, they don't treat me as a Mexican because I'm not Mexican, but then white people are like—well, I'm not a white, you know. I'm not American. So I'm right in the middle. So I'm not there and I'm not here, you know, so it's very hard for me—you know, you don't speak any Spanish, so you're white. You're an *americana* and that's what they call me, like *gringa* or that kind of stuff. Oh, that gets me so mad—I'm Mexican American and I'm not Mexican and I'm not American. I'm just right there in the middle, you know, and it gets me so mad because like they're, they think that I'm white and I'm not, and they think I'm Mexican and I'm not, and oh that gets me mad. That gets me really, really, really mad.

The old-timers believe they are seen by Mexicans as no longer truly Mexican but Americanized; they are called, e.g., *gringa/gringo* (white boy/white girl wannabe or *preprancholo* (combination of *prep* [preppy], *ranchero* [unsophisticated], and *cholo* [low rider]). Having Anglo friends makes them suspect; they are called *bolillos* (white bread), a term often used to refer to Anglos. They find this experience of rejection by more recently arrived Latinos troubling. "You're, like, racist against your own race—if we're all Mexicans, how can we be racist against Mexicans?"

Conversely, their judgment of the recently arrived is not complimentary either. They joke about the yokels from the ranchos in their boots and jeans, women in shorts and high heels, trucks with names on the back window (and lots of fuzzy ornaments inside and 20 antennas), and guys wearing too many gold chains and not enough deodorant. They are not *bien educados* (polite). The old-timer women students complained of the stares and comments made by the men. "You can't wear a skirt because all the guys will be there staring at you." They spoke of being embarrassed by them and observed that their behavior perpetuated the stereotype that all Latino men are like that.

On the other hand, they also have empathy as they watch the newcomers go through experiences similar to theirs in the classroom. They notice when teachers send the Mexican students unnecessarily to ESL study hall. They watch painfully as their Anglo friends make disparaging comments, as discussed by one Latino student.

> Virginia (in a Latino focus group): Antonio came in and they're like saying, "Oh great, another one that doesn't speak English." Then he's like, "I speak English," and they're like, "Oh, oh, you do." And it's like, I don't know, I feel like, I feel bad inside, you know, but it's like I want to say something but at the time I'm like, "No, I can't say nothing 'cause then they'll talk about me." I usually end up saying what I feel, but I get in trouble.
>
> Estela: Or sometimes the teachers say something that, like, gets to you. They're like, "Other Mexicans are like . . ." And it's like, "No, I'll just keep it to myself," you know.
>
> Interviewer: When you say it gets to you, is it—
>
> Estela: It makes you feel bad.
>
> Interviewer: Is it said towards you as a, as a person, as a Mexican?
>
> Estela: They're not racist towards me 'cause I mean, 'cause they already think I'm white, you know, but like sometimes I'm just like, I feel bad 'cause I mean, they're like, they're still my people, you know, and I feel bad 'cause my, all my, my parents are from Mexico and

everything. And I'm just like, I'm like, you know what, just put your-self in—I always just tell people to put themselves in their shoes and just, how would they like to be, if they were treated that way? People wouldn't appreciate it, so I don't know.

They also resented the way they were treated as de facto teacher's aides for newcomers.

Rogelio (in a focus group): Also, in sixth grade, I guess some teachers aren't patient enough 'cause in sixth grade, they, two new Mexicans, came in and they gave 'em to me right away, told 'em to sit by me and I would translate for 'em because they just didn't want to bother with that and it was my job to teach 'em actually, and I guess some teachers aren't patient enough. The teachers thanked me and all, but I kind of was thinking, like, I wish we could work individually and we could have gone a little bit slower with them, but still, you know, she should have taught them, instead of making me teach them.

The arrival in the mid-1990s of large numbers of new Mexican students from Mexico and the border states has created a paradoxical situation for the old-timers. The old-timers, being bilingual and having white friends, were considered the cool Mexicans by Anglo students. Showing solidarity with the newcomers made them targets of the same "Spics go home" remarks that characterized the backlash from some Anglos. On the other hand, hav-ing white friends made them suspect in the eyes of Mexicanos, who had initially kept to themselves.

By the late 1990s they found themselves part of a large minority of La-tino students. To the extent that ethnic solidarity began to override mutual in-group suspicions, so that old-timers and newcomers alike considered themselves part of a larger Latino presence, old-timers experienced a sense of group power: "It's better now; they [Anglos] always talked against us, but now there are more of us and they're afraid." Along with power came a heightened sense of ethnic identity and pride, articulated when Latinos competed at sporting or academic events.

Rogelio (in a focus group): Once I went to a track meet . . . When a Mexi-can wins first place and stuff, I don't know why, I'm not even winning it, but when I see a Mexican getting the first honors, second honors, beating all these people, I guess I feel proud.

The net result of this greater sense of power and pride is that social success is less dependent on assimilation into Anglo student culture. Latino students can now impose their own boundaries: "We don't let them [Anglos] in—you talk to Hispanics because you talk about more of the same stuff."

Newcomers

Many students at Wheelerton High have arrived within the last five years, and one of the women in our focus group had been here for only two weeks. Most who are from Mexico come from the states in north central Mexico, especially Aguascalientes. Their parents had family connections in Wheelerton, and those in our group say they are here "de necesidad" (out of necessity) because of "mucha pobreza en Mexico" (a lot of poverty in Mexico). Their parents work in the industrial park, and a few of them have done some agricultural work in the summers with their parents.

Several of them spoke of tense encounters with police and frequently being checked for their identification. They also told of fights and racially motivated confrontations. In one incident, a group of local Anglos stopped a van (the music was loud and they could hear that it was Mexican). The Anglos demanded to see the identification cards of those in the van. When one of the passengers, the brother of one of the students in the focus group, did not have ID, the Anglos called the police. The student's brother was arrested.

In another case, a student and his friend were pushed off their motorbike by a white youth and his friends, who followed the student to a Dairy Queen. They were going to confront him, but a police officer was there, so they did not. Several students said it is common to have "Beans!" yelled at them as they walk down the street. They seemed to think this was peculiar and somewhat funny. Others, however, felt they were well treated.

The students referred to *racistas* (racists) as a category of people in a matter-of-fact way. When I asked, they said that there are racists who live in Wheelerton; they were emphatic about this; they don't just live in other communities. They said that there are people in Wheelerton ready to beat up a Mexican if they are in a situation where they have the advantage, and you have to figure out a way to negotiate your way out or escape; the police and other Anglos will not help.

When speaking of experiences at school, they said there are no racists at school. Nonetheless, they did report experiences that seem to involve racial prejudice on the part of white teachers and students. One student had joined the track team and he was so good that he was threatening to become the school's best runner. A white track team member pulled his pants down to his knees in public one day, and everyone laughed. The Latino student dropped off the team and, even though the coach pleaded with him, would not reconsider. He said he was more concerned with getting a job to help support his family than participating in high school sports.

Several said that speaking Spanish could get a person into trouble with some teachers, and they told of a recent case where two students had been given detention for speaking Spanish in the classroom. On the other hand, one argued the importance of speaking English at school. "Si no nos ponemos a hablar inglés, ¿cómo vamos a hablar inglés?" ("If we don't put ourselves to the task of speaking English, how are we going to speak English?")

They identified teachers who were particularly helpful—the Spanish teacher and the math teacher, because she worked hard with Mexican students. The ESL coordinator was identified as having assisted a number of students with family problems. Some felt it would be good to have more teachers who spoke some Spanish, because students drop out when they cannot speak and understand English. They said those students "lose hope" (*desesperan*).

Several referred to certain Mexican students who have been here a long time. One student said that there are local Latinos who don't want to speak Spanish. "If you ask for help, they tell you, 'No hablo español.'" This group hangs out together and they "think they are better than others." The members of the group are students who have grown up here.

When we asked these students about the future, there was a mixed response. One or two considered the possibility of college. Despite some of the negative experiences, three students intended to stay in Wheelerton because their families are here, and there are also jobs here. Several intended to go back to Texas or Mexico.

I asked administrators whether the growth in the number of Latino students, which must have required additional programs and staff, was perceived as a crisis or just another challenge. The middle school principal responded that funding problems are a routine challenge in public schools. He recalled being told (by state authorities) that ESL funds were being cut,

although they were also getting more ESL students. "It is definitely a problem, but these kinds of problems are routine." [1] The elementary school principal summed it up by saying that the word "crisis" is too strong. It is definitely a "situation of upheaval," a "unique event," but not a crisis.

Earlier in the 1990s, there had been fights in school between Latino and
Anglo students. In the period of this study there were no fights, and the
administration, faculty, and students reported improvements in ethnic relations. After I left the school, however, fighting again broke out between
Latino and Anglo students, and relations seemed again to be on the decline.
This suggests how premature it is to make claims about trends moving in
either positive or negative directions. Hopes expressed by teachers that a
new chapter had been opened in relationships between Latino and Anglo
students, (e.g., fewer racist comments, observations that "they know each
other better"), were suddenly dashed by renewed outbreaks of fighting and
tension. Perceptions and interactions between Latino and Anglo students
continue to fluctuate, as they do in the other communities of this study.

The Virgin of Guadalupe: Admittance in Question
Maríaelena D. Jefferds and Ann V. Millard

In Mapleville, Michigan, a Catholic mass has been conducted in Spanish on Sundays since 1995. In 1997 a struggle began between the Spanish-speaking and the Anglo congregations at the church. The focus of the controversy was a carving of the Virgin of Guadalupe, a Mexican image of the Virgin Mary widely revered as a religious—and sometimes political—symbol among Mexican Americans.

The Latino congregation members wanted the image inside the parish church. They described her as "our Virgin," and the carving at issue was by a parishioner. A group of Anglo parishioners, however, rejected it. They argued publicly that only one Virgin was allowed in a Catholic church, but they privately also asserted that the carving lacks a style that would fit with the rest of the imagery in the church. Anglos repeatedly removed the statue.

One Latino said, "The Anglos get their way because they are wealthier." Anglos provided the primary funds for the parish, because most Latino members were low-income workers who could not make substantial donations. The struggle over the Virgin of Guadalupe was a focus of growing tension that magnified Anglo-Latino differences.

A number of other Catholic churches in the region, however, contain an image of the Virgin of Guadalupe, including an upper-middle-class church in a resort town with no significant Latino membership. The dispute in Mapleville continued unresolved for years, and Latinos were hurt and worried. Some went so far as to attend two masses on Sunday, one in their local church and another an hour's drive away at a church housing an image of the Virgin. They felt it necessary to attend the two masses, and they complained that doing so was a burden.

A number of Anglos in this study commented that Latinos preferred to socialize separately from them, and they pointed to Latino attendance at church services in Spanish. Some Anglos supported this pattern, saying, "It is important that they have the opportunity to be together." Other Anglos argued that separating Latinos and Anglos reinforced distinctions between "us" and "them." The situation with the Virgin of Guadalupe shows that Latinos often were not welcome in Anglo congregations, however, especially when they tried to practice their own traditions in ways they saw as appropriate.

Culturally specific expressions of Mexicans and Mexican Americans are often seen by Anglos as inappropriate infusions into local practice, even though Anglos have long incorporated German, Belgian, Italian, and other European traditions.

I've never been assigned to an area as religious as this. I've never served such a small town with so many churches.
Father Joseph, a middle-aged Catholic priest

Fox and Mapleville, Michigan, each have over 15 churches, even though they only have populations of 4,000 and 1,700, respectively (figures from 1998 for the two townships, published in the local paper, August 1999). Latinos and Anglos agree that attending church is the main social activity of Latinos, aside from home life. Churches with growing Latino populations in Fox and Mapleville include the Catholic Church, the Seventh Day Adventist Church, and the Jehovah's Witnesses. Church services are often directed to Anglo congregations, but there are a few churches that offer separate services for Latinos in Spanish. Those in Spanish are culturally contoured for Mexican and Mexican American members. There are no bilingual services, and we heard of none throughout our community studies.

The effect of separating services by language is to divide church membership into an Anglo, English-speaking congregation and a Latino, Spanish-speaking congregation, and the separation allows mutual incomprehension to continue. With the controversy over the Virgin of Guadalupe, the Catholic church in Mapleville became a site of struggle between Anglos and Latinos over iconography appropriate for their place of worship. The churches in Fox and Mapleville generally give Latinos second-class status by welcoming them as long as they do not make their presence felt by requesting changes in the practices and appearance of the church. Although not discussed in these terms, the struggle over the Virgin of Guadalupe also addressed the character of the church and the broader community regarding ethnicity, class, transnationalism, and the acceptability of Latinos to the local Anglo community.

Epilogue

After we had finished collecting information about the Mapleville controversy, some Latino parishioners took the issue to the bishop. The result is
that a temporary statue of the Virgin of Guadalupe was placed in the church,
and as this volume was being concluded, an image was being carved of
wood to be added permanently to the church.

CHAPTER EIGHT

"To Be with My People": Latino Churches in the Rural Midwest

Ken R. Crane and Ann V. Millard

Well, my parents, they're from different parts. My dad was born in Aguascalientes, and my mom was born in Matamoros, but she lived all her life in Arlington, Texas. My dad came up here when he was 20 with Grandma and Grandpa to look for work, and my mom came up too. She came up to Fort Wayne with her dad 'cause her dad was a minister, and so they started the church in Fort Wayne and then . . . my mom got a job in Botech that was here . . . and they started a church [Templo Cristo Rey] with the Morales family, with my grandpa, and then my dad started working at Botech and that's how they got hooked up. They've all been here, ever since. That's what happened.

A Latina high school student in Wheelerton, Indiana

Two miles out of Wheelerton stands a modest new white church, Templo Cristo Rey (Christ the King Church). The church was started by several large Mexican American families who settled in the area in the 1960s and 1970s. Being recruited for jobs in the rural Midwest, bringing families with them to settle there, and establishing new churches in their new hometowns is a common sequence in the communities studied in this project. Church membership is not a universal feature among Latino newcomers, but it is widespread for the spiritual, material, and political reasons discussed here.

Templo Cristo Rey is now home to 300 Pentecostal believers of Mexican and Mexican American descent. It is affiliated with the Assemblies of God denomination, which claims a membership of about 2.3 million in the United States. Some Latinos also attend a local, mostly Anglo, Assembly of God church. A good number attend St. Martin's Catholic Church, but Templo Cristo Rey (which we will call the Templo) has a larger Latino congregation and more influence as a Latino organization in the larger community.

My uncle José picked Wheelerton because he and Uncle Luis were looking to settle in a town that had more churches than bars. In 1960 Uncle Luis took a job with an Amish popcorn grower near Wheelerton. Two

years later, Uncle José settled in Wheelerton and started working for Botech. Then Uncle Luis came and started working at Botech too.
Niece of José Morales

In 1968 about 20 believers began meeting in the home of José Morales in Wheelerton. The two Morales brothers joined with the extended Domínguez family to form the church. A Morales daughter married the son of a Pentecostal pastor in Fort Wayne, whom they invited to help lead the church. Later they invited a third Morales brother, who was a minister in Mexico, to pastor the church. The name Rosa de Sarón (Rose of Sharon) was suggested for the new church, but the members voted in favor of Templo Cristo Rey, the name of the hometown church of the Morales and Domínguez families in Nuevo León, Mexico.

During the 1970s, the congregation was a tight-knit group whose members were drawn from a small number of extended families. In fact, nearly all the Latinos in Wheelerton at that time went to the Templo. Each week, a family would sell tickets to the church members, who would go to that family's house the next week to eat tacos and tamales. The family used the money to buy the ingredients and gave the surplus to the building fund. Then church members started selling Mexican food to the public on Saturdays. They soon raised enough money to purchase an old brick United Methodist Church building. About 20 years later, they bought land and built the white, steepled church just outside of town.

As the "Mexican" population grew dramatically in the early 1990s, so did the Templo. The church growth continued throughout the decade, despite some growing pains when a few members left to form new congregations. In 1995, the members broke ground for the present building, and Wheelerton's mayor Lainge was there to lift the first spade of dirt, alongside Pastor Guzmán.

The Templo is famous for its long, lively services with music, group prayer, and dynamic preaching. The pastor and worship leader encourage demonstrations of feeling, including clapping and praying aloud. Center stage is a gospel band with lots of brass instruments, a full acoustic drum set, keyboards, electric guitars and bass, and words of the hymns projected onto a screen. The lyrics and melodies come partly from young evangelical musicians in Mexico, who have developed a dynamic, contemporary style of religious music. The Wednesday youth meetings and Sunday evening services are usually somewhat louder and more enthusiastic than the Sunday morning service. Guest speakers and guest musicians frequently visit the congregation, and Christian Mariachi bands, such as Río Jordan, are brought in for special occasions.

> In one sermon, Pastor Guzmán preached the story of Gideon's victory at the Battle of Jericho, and when telling how his men blew the trumpet, the pastor held up a trumpet and pretended to blow while one of the band members played "Oh, when the saints, go marchin' in . . ."
> *Crane, field notes*

The Templo has grown to have a large congregation that organizes important public events, such as the celebration of Cinco de Mayo.[1] The pastor has made efforts to get to know the mayor and other important Anglos in town, with whom he has worked to enhance Latino-Anglo relations. In conversations and sermons, he characterizes Latinos as the latest of a number of groups who have come to Wheelerton seeking peace, refuge, and prosperity. He thus seeks to explain to Anglos and to Latinos themselves that the recent Latino influx belongs to a historical pattern of the populating of the Wheelerton area, which drew various refugee and immigrant populations from Europe in the 1800s and early 1900s, and Appalachians in later decades of the twentieth century. In evoking the history of settlement in the area, Pastor Guzmán seeks to legitimate Latino newcomers in the eyes of Anglos and to provide newcomers with a sense of their rights to membership in the town and village populations of the region.

St. Martin's Catholic Church, Wheelerton, Indiana

By the late 1980s, numerous Catholic Latinos had moved to Wheelerton in response to the demand for labor in the growing manufacturing sector. Many were from the central Mexican states of Aguascalientes, Guanajuato, Michoacán, and Zacatecas. Catholic parishes around Indiana with growing Latino membership advertised openings for bilingual lay workers; and Deacon Ramón Pacheco applied from Texas and got the job at St. Martin's. He arrived in 1994 when there were about 25 Latinos attending mass. In June of 2001, a Mexican priest began serving in the parish, and two masses in Spanish were started. The leaders believe a third mass might be necessary in the future. Now, on a typical weekend, about 700 attend Sunday services.

Deacon Ramón [of St. Martin's] is the kind of person who makes you feel like you are an old friend. He is a large man, with Roman nose, a barrel chest, and somewhat leathery chestnut skin, frequently wearing a flannel shirt and jeans. I accompanied him on visits to parishioners' homes, where he easily related to them. He once commented on Latinos in Wheelerton, "They are good people." His energy and compassion, as well as his ethnicity, in my thinking, have been keys to making Wheelerton and his church a place of welcome for Latino Catholics.
Crane, field notes

Ramón is aware of the cultural differences between Latinos and Anglos at church. He appreciates the devotion of the Mexican people. He says jokingly, "I've noticed a difference between the Anglo and Mexican members. The Mexican members all go to confession, but few take communion; the Anglos all take communion but only a few go to confession!" Through the efforts of people like the deacon, many of the new Latino families in Wheelerton now congregate at St. Martin's. This is a departure from earlier times when most Latino newcomers were Pentecostal.

St. Barbara's Catholic Church, Ciderville, Michigan

> Stayed here at the age of seven
> Never went back to my Texas heaven
> Didn't know why we had to stay
> Why we had to work and play
> —in Michigan
> *Guillermo Martínez*[2]

Summer or winter, Spanish mass at St. Barbara's in Ciderville, Michigan, is always crowded. Music in the *corrido* style shown above is central to the feeling of the service. Three or four guitarists, an accordionist, and a vocal group with a Mexican folk sound serenade the congregation. Carlos, the music coordinator, walks back and forth, vigorously leading the enthusiastic congregational singing. When communion begins, the musical group sings, "Somos el cuerpo de Cristo" (We are the body of Christ) and "Cristo está en nosotros" (Christ is in us). The musicians create a light, joyous atmosphere as people line up to take the bread and wine.

The use of traditional instruments and language combine to make St. Barbara's a culturally familiar place for Latinos of Mexican origin. The music and liturgy, however, are by no means simply transplants from Mexico. The music is a style of "Mexican gospel" with a hint of the Tejano music style, developed in the United States. Most of the songs come from *Flor y Canto*, a hymnal by Mary Frances Reza, a Catholic laywoman from New Mexico. The book's music draws from a range of Latin American music, with expression in a Mexican American style. In the hymnal preface, Archbishop Levanda of Oregon anticipated this transnational fusion when he stated, "*Flor y Canto* helps bring the gifts of the past and present to us, to each other . . . for our common future."

The parking lot overflows with pickup trucks and vans, spilling out along the street. Inside, there is standing room only; it is full of young, single men and families, including small children. Teenage males stand in the back, hanging out with friends; gold chains and crucifixes are de rigueur. Most people are dressed neatly in street clothes—men in new jeans, cowboy boots, and shirts without neckties. Older women wear dresses; younger women and girls often dress in fashionable pants.

St. Barbara's is a multicultural and multilingual parish, with separate English-speaking and Spanish-speaking congregations. The Anglo membership numbers about 150, and the Latino about 400. Some Potawatomi Indians also belong to the church. The transition to a predominantly Latino parish has been difficult at times. According to Joyce, a longtime lay leader of African American and Native American heritage, Father Rafael "has been good at bridging the communities. When they come together for meetings and make a decision, he says, 'The people of the church have said this.'" She believes the parish has already been through its hardest transition.

> Fortunately, now we have been through turbulent and strong winds, we are now over the mountain in the foothills on the other side—they [Anglos and Latinos] are growing together . . . The pain is a lot less. I feel there is a lot less bias than before—the majority are looking for ways to come together.

St. Barbara's has a long history of ministry to the newly arrived and migrant Latino population. The bishop made a decision in the 1970s that the church would reach out to Latinos, even those living outside the parish boundaries, by offering mass in Spanish, in the church. The former practice of priests holding mass in agricultural labor camps still continues, but the bishop's decision was to draw local Latinos into full membership in the parish. In 1989 he assigned a priest, Father Bill, to be diocese coordinator for Latino ministry and a parish pastor. He had extensive experience in the camps and spoke Spanish; upon his retirement a priest from South America, Father Rafael, took his place. In the summer, when migrant farmworkers are in the area, he holds mass twice on Sunday for approximately 400 Latinos who drive to his church from communities throughout southwest Michigan.

Three cultures shape the services at St. Barbara's: the Mexican American culture, particularly that of south Texas; the Mexican influence of recent immigrants; and the culture of Anglo members, recently the majority, who still dominate the council and financial decision-making. Particularly during the mass in Spanish, the Latino influence dominates the atmosphere, ritual, and interactions. Within that Latino cultural matrix, the influence of the large number of recently arrived Mexicans is preeminent.

Latinos as Founders of New Churches in the Midwest

One of the first things that Mexican American families did when they settled in Wheelerton was to organize themselves into church congregations. In many cases, they recruited pastors to move to their new locations and head their new churches. Those who were Roman Catholic sought out churches where they could attend mass in Spanish, and many continue, including numerous bilingual Latinos. Through these practices, Latinos have created their own institutions in their new Midwestern locations, and they have done so not through confronting existing authorities but by expressing their will in a respectful, consistent, and gentle manner. Essentially, Latinos have brought their churches with them—their denominations, their religious interpretations, and their organizational approaches.

Their approach contrasts with that of middle-class Anglos, who tend to join existing church congregations even if it means changing denominations. Latino religious practices in the rural Midwest are, in sociological terms, a major expression of human agency in the sense that as they create new churches, Latinos change the conditions of their lives; they show that they can create organizations that significantly benefit their constituencies and represent them in their new hometowns. In so doing, they contradict the Anglo stereotype that Latinos are a passive, powerless population incapable of organizing themselves. It is no mistake that churches have often become major Latino instruments of cultural, social, and political expression. Churches, after all, are generally regarded by Anglos as unthreatening, as assisting those who need help, and as controlling people who might otherwise threaten the social order. In short, churches are the only expression of human agency—of Latinos' autonomous ability to influence events—that many Anglos will accept with equanimity.

The importance of churches as refuge under conditions of oppression links the situation of the Latino newcomers in the Midwest to that of many African Americans. The history of African American churches suggests that Latino churches too have the potential to develop social movements, political protests, and nationally prominent political leaders. Thus, the struggle over churches' responses to Latino newcomers reveals not only cultural differences between Latinos and Anglos but also their different positions in a system of social inequality.

What surprises many Anglos in the Midwest is the great diversity of Latino religious expression; the stereotype that all Hispanics are Catholic is negated by Spanish-speaking services held in Midwestern Protestant churches of every type imaginable—Baptist, Adventist, Methodist, Mennonite, Pentecostal, Jehovah's Witness, and numerous independent evangelical churches.[3] Some Latino newcomers to the Midwest have for generations been Protestant, bearing witness to the strong presence of Protestantism in the U.S. Southwest and in Latin America. Pastors from Latin America are recruited to lead congregations in the United States, and many Latino immigrants arrived as Protestants.

Here and there, in isolated cases, a Roman Catholic diocese had designated a certain parish to meet the needs of Latino members, but only when a bilingual deacon or priest began to officiate at mass in Spanish did Catholic Latinos join in the life of parishes in this study. Protestant Latinos, as the example of Wheelerton illustrates, acted in a more independent and energetic fashion than Catholics. Within three years after the first Pentecostal families arrived, the Templo had a pastor and an organizational structure and had received official recognition from the Concilio General de las Asambleas de Dios (the Hispanic branch of the Assemblies of God in the United States), even though they did not yet have a building to house their activities.

The Templo congregation follows the pattern of most Latino Protestant congregations that have been founded and led by Latinos, many by pastors from Latin America. One variation occurred in Berryville, Michigan, where Adventists from another town in the region started a church, for which the Adventist administrative office for the region later hired a pastor from the Dominican Republic. In Wheelerton, the Templo congregation met in homes until they had raised enough money to acquire their own building. A frequent variation of this pattern is for a Latino congregation to rent space from an Anglo church, sometimes even from a different denomination, until they can acquire their own space.

The decentralized and independent manner in which Protestants (particularly *evangélicos* and Pentecostals) have operated has worked to their advantage in creating Latino churches. They can organize themselves quickly into tight-knit, semiautonomous units and recruit their own leaders. The same characteristics, however, make them more vulnerable to division. Latino congregations are quite diverse in terms of liberal versus conservative doctrine, newcomers' values versus those of long-term residents, national origin, and socioeconomic characteristics. These differences may result in subgroups splitting off and forming new congregations.

Protestant and Catholic congregations also contrast in other ways. Protestant congregations tend to be owned and operated as entirely Latino organizations, which lends greater linguistic and cultural unity. Catholic parishes, on the other hand, operate as multicultural entities when they expand to include a mass and religious education in Spanish, as at St. Martin's and St. Barbara's. While developing a commitment to creating cultural space for Latinos, the leadership also must strive to maintain a parish in which all groups feel comfortable. It is a challenging task; separate masses are one step, but it is even more difficult to provide religious education for 300 children whose first language is Spanish, as required in one of the churches in our study. Tension rises as budget priorities and human resource allocations begin to address the needs of the majority group, Latinos, while the minority Anglo group still provides the funding for the parish. Most newcomer Latinos are unable to bear the financial burden of substantial church donations, as they are often low-income wage earners who can barely support their own families. The challenges, however, are not completely insurmountable. St. Martin's and St. Barbara's have demonstrated that where there is a commitment to creating a multicultural community, a constructive outcome for Latinos and Anglos is possible.

The Congregation as Locus of Community
Ministering to Newcomers and Other Vulnerable Parishioners

Many of the newer Latino residents in Midwestern communities have found a home in parishes and churches. This can be illustrated by the experience of Antonia, a high school senior who arrived from Mexico in the mid-1990s.[4] Antonia's father came to Wheelerton from Aguascalientes via California in the 1980s, seeking an industrial job. She and her younger sister arrived in 1990 when she was about seven years old.

> I had my friends [whom I had to leave behind]. At first it was strange; I couldn't talk to anyone, watch TV, or listen to the radio [because I did not understand English]. I used to cry every day after school because I couldn't understand what people were saying.
> *Antonia, a high school student*

To be with other Mexicans, Antonia went to the only "Mexican" church in town, Templo Cristo Rey. She described her family as "strongly Catholic," but says they felt welcome at the Templo, where they also got help with food and clothing. Her mother gave birth to a last child, born four months premature and hospitalized for a long time. "She is our little miracle," Antonia commented, as the baby survived and grew to be a healthy child. Just as the child was born, Antonia's father left for Mexico and returned only briefly. Her mother took a job picking apples. Antonia said, "It was tough, because my mother did not beg from anyone. Sometimes we had only beans and potatoes in the house." They did receive assistance from Medicaid and WIC.[5] For a period, they coped with being homesick by calling relatives in Mexico twice a week. They were grateful to the Templo for assistance but stopped going because Templo members began to criticize the Catholic Church.

They started going to St. Martin's Catholic Church about six years ago, when mass in Spanish began. Antonia speaks of a time in her life when she became "very devout." When she was twelve years old, she went to a spiritual retreat and was moved by a woman speaker's message. In her spiritual life, this was a defining moment. "I came to know how much God is involved with us," she commented.

Latino churches have generally made an effort to welcome newcomers, and some, like St. Martin's, have Latino membership comprised mainly of newly arrived families. Many of the adults in such congregations work the second and third shifts at factories, have an elementary school education, and are isolated from sources of community support. Their foothold in the community is tenuous because of their vulnerability to economic downturns, when layoffs frequently mean they must move elsewhere to find work.

Latinos in many of these communities have experienced hostility and marginalization. The leadership and staff of some churches have a reputation for being trustworthy, making their congregations safe places for Latino newcomers. As illustrated by Antonia's family, St. Martin's is trying to meet the needs of people who have had to struggle hard against hostility and instability while adjusting to their new hometowns. As described below, Latino congregations serve the purpose of being safe places to congregate with friends, relatives, and those of similar cultural profile.

Social and Emotional Support

Sister Consuelo, a Mexican American nun of the Our Lady of Victory Missionary Sisters (Victory Noll), has served the church for 56 years, mostly in California and Texas. She then came to Indiana, where she became a vital part of St. Martin's ministry to Latinos in Wheelerton. Seventy-six years old, she plans to work "until the day I drop." "I serve the people," she says simply, which means anything from teaching confirmation class to taking pregnant women to the emergency room in the early morning hours. She works much of the time with the poorest Latinos, who live in crowded downtown apartments and trailer parks. She is no stranger to hardship and poverty herself, having grown up in a migrant farmworker family in California.

> When I was eight, my mother sent me to get water from the common faucet (in the labor camp), and I saw another child getting water. I remember it was cold. The girl had no shoes; her feet were blue; she seemed neglected. I went back to the cabin and told my dad, "I want to be helping people like that." I told him I was going to be a nun, but he didn't believe me.

In Wheelerton, Sister Consuelo ministers to Latino families living in unstable conditions. While she is involved in the distribution of material assistance, a larger part of her work involves the social and emotional support she provides wherever she goes. "I laugh and cry with the people."

Sister Consuelo never complains about the intense, unending demands that she faces; rather, she stresses what she receives from those she serves. "I guess I touch their hearts, and they give me so much more." She speaks of the joys she and Latino families have experienced from the birth of a child and from spiritual growth and of the sadness that accompanies death. "Occasionally I am asked if I regret not having children, and I tell them 'I have a thousand children.'" A powerful experience occurred when she took a woman in labor to a neonatal intensive care unit on Holy Thursday. The woman had high blood pressure, and the doctors performed a delivery by caesarean section on Good Friday.

> I spent Good Friday till 6:00 P.M. with them. The baby girl only weighed three pounds; I've never seen such a little human being. I call it the Paschal mystery—the baby struggling between life and death, death and life. I was privileged enough to be there and see that. That was my special day.

Sister Consuelo also spoke of accompanying another pregnant woman to the hospital in the middle of the night; the baby was born prematurely en route and died after several days. The child's father had asked the nun to stay with them through the ordeal. Similarly, she counseled and consoled at length the mother of a three-year-old who had died.

Spiritual Transformations

During the Saturday morning church service (*culto de adoración*) at the Iglesia Adventista (Seventh Day Adventist Church), two things stand out: *testimonios* (congregational testimonies) and children. Characteristic of many Protestant and Pentecostal sects is the time given to personal testimonies of how people have experienced God in their lives. This is a high point in the service in which young and old, men and women, laborers and professionals, enthusiastically take part. At Berryville Adventista it is the women who are especially vocal at this point in the service. People's testimonies span a range of life experiences: a child asks the church to pray for her family as they leave for Texas; a grandmother gives thanks that her grandchildren are being quiet in church; a girl in middle school gives thanks that her basketball team won that week's game; a five-year-old boy thanks God for his brother's birthday. Some deal with the realm of the miraculous—a mother tearfully rejoices at her son's recovery from a brain tumor or because her child with a learning disability passed a test. Some deal with human tragedy—Arturo's mother testified that God had helped them during a very tough family situation; a cousin was in solitary confinement and her husband and a friend had gone down to help. The testimonies not only praise Heaven, but also inform the entire congregation, who thus learn everybody's troubles and joys.

At the Templo, Pastor Guzmán calls for those with special needs to come up to the front, where they kneel. During these times, there is praying and crying throughout the church. The pastor goes to people, puts his hand on their foreheads, and occasionally prays and praises God loudly. Several men and women assist, going from person to person to offer prayer and lay hands on them. I (K. Crane) asked the pastor about the laying on of hands, and he explained that Latinos don't deal with emotional and psychological problems by going to professional therapists. They confide in, and get counsel from, older people and friends, and they go to pastors. They come to the front of the church for emotional and physical healing.

Protestant Latinos frequently said that a religious experience transformed them so that they became more productive and healthier.

Arturo of the Iglesia Adventista told of his conversion experience, after which everything changed. He had been a heavy drinker who would return each night from picking crops in the hot sun and drink a liter of beer. He'd be drunk three or four days out of the week. He became ill and went to the doctor, who told him his liver was so swollen it could burst. Arturo quit drinking and attributes success in doing so to his religious faith.
Crane, field notes

David, a lay leader at the Templo, told of a more dramatic transformation.

I was involved in drugs and a gang when I lived in Houston as a teenager. I dropped out of high school in my sophomore year. One day, I overdosed. I knew what it was, because I started shaking uncontrollably. I started thinking about my family, that I would die, and then God came to mind. I prayed that if I survived, I would quit drugs and serve God every day. I recovered and that same day I went to Mexico. I knew that if I stayed in Houston, I would keep doing drugs. I needed to get away from that place. Later, I came to Wheelerton to live with my sister. From that point, my life changed totally. Drugs do not come to my mind any more. I know it's because of Jesus.

David recognized the seriousness of his situation as a drug addict, and he attributes his conversion experience to saving his life and ending his craving for drugs.

Latino Congregations and Cultural Identity

It's not because I'm racist that I go to the Templo, it's just that I'm more comfortable with my people.
A Latino high school student

Celia grew up in Liberty, a small Amish town about five miles from Wheelerton. Her parents, both trained as lay pastors, helped start Templo Cristo Rey. Celia's family was one of two Latino families in Liberty. The other family was Catholic and opted to attend the Mennonite Church, an English-speaking congregation which previously had no Latino members. Celia recalls that the parents in that family did not allow the children to speak Spanish at home, and the family assimilated quickly. For Celia, however, it was Spanish at home and church.

These two families represent two different modes of involvement in Latino faith communities by Latino youth in the Midwest. The path taken by Celia's friend illustrates a strategy of assimilation adopted by many blue collar and lower-middle-class Mexican immigrants and Mexican Americans, who do not speak Spanish to their children in the belief that it will detract from their children's success in school and the workplace. The path taken by Celia's family, however, was a means of resisting the pressures of linguistic assimilation and acculturation to Anglo ways. The Templo served as a resource that reinforced the socialization taking place at home. Upon reflection, Celia believed her involvement in the Templo strengthened her ability in Spanish. She had to read the Bible in Spanish and to speak Spanish at church. She said she also learned to respect her parents. Pentecostalism lacks some religious and cultural expressions often expressed by Latinos through Catholicism and seen as central to Latino identity. Pentecostalism, though, did not diminish Celia's identity as a Latina, as evidenced by her later position as president of the Latino Student Association at her university.

At St. Barbara's Catholic Church in southwest Michigan, Fernando and other Latinos found a Catholic congregation that also reinforced Mexican American culture. Fernando, a mechanic in his mid-40s, was born in Querétaro in 1962 and has worked in the United States since he was 14. In 1984, he and his wife (whom he had met earlier at St. Barbara's) stopped migrant farmwork and settled in rural southwest Michigan. Fernando speaks English fluently as the result of great effort to learn the language well, and he and his wife are raising their children to be bilingual. Fernando has also become a legal resident of the United States. He and his family attend mass regularly at St. Barbara's. I asked Fernando what his involvement with the parish meant to him and his family.

> Fernando: I go there for two reasons. It's in Spanish, and there I can be with my people.
>
> K. Crane: What do you mean by "my people"; do you mean friends?
>
> Fernando: No, to be with other Mexican people.
>
> KC: Why do you require your children to go to church?
>
> Fernando: Mostly because it's in Spanish.
>
> KC: Do you think it helps preserve the language?
>
> Fernando: Yes.
>
> KC: Would you go if the mass were only in English?
>
> Fernando: Probably not—they [my children] speak only Spanish at home.
>
> KC: Will being Mexican keep your children from getting ahead?
>
> Fernando: No, I want them to be proud of their culture. Like at home, they listen to mostly norteño, ranchero, and mariachi music.

Fernando represents a substantial group of first-generation Latinos of Mexican descent who settled locally in small towns in the late 1980s through the 1990s. They now live in primarily Anglo communities, where they have struggled to find decent jobs and homes and stability for their children.

While Fernando and his family could attend a mass in English five minutes from their home, they prefer to drive a half hour to St. Barbara's. Fernando implies that the affirmation of cultural traditions is important to him and his family. Mexican traditions are a routine part of baptisms and other rites at his church. Fernando sees the church as a setting where his culture, including language, values, and traditions, is respected, taught, and reinforced. He is interested in these aspects of religion for himself and for his children. (He, like other parents, takes spiritual reasons for granted as an aspect of church membership.) The church as an important cultural resource supporting speaking Spanish and Mexican American culture emerged as an important theme in interviews with parents, although they did not always speak of intentionally using it to socialize their children as had Fernando. Sometimes parents would simply state a preference for the language, or talk about the congregation as a place to see friends and family.

Views of Adolescents: El Día de la Virgen de Guadalupe

The mariachis from Chicago had begun serenading the Virgin at 5:30 A.M. with their repertoire of religious songs. A deacon who was a Potawatomi Indian performed a prayer ceremony to the four winds, beginning with the east, burning a bundle of sage and stoking it with an eagle feather. The altar held a painting of the Virgin and was surrounded by flowers. Some parishioners videotaped the entire service; others had their photographs taken by the altar; after mass, many knelt there to pray. In the social hall, the mariachi band started to serenade the people who had followed the mouth-watering smell of *menudo* (tripe soup) and eggs fried with *chorizo* (pork sausage). Many commented that they had never seen so many people before at St. Barbara's.

This day, December 12, the Day of the Virgin of Guadalupe, is celebrated widely in Mexico and among Catholic Mexicans and Mexican Americans in the United States. The Virgin of Guadalupe is a widespread, powerful religious symbol for them for a number of historical, political, and social reasons. For many years, Mexican and Mexican American parishioners of St. Barbara's have celebrated a daybreak mass in her honor. Extensive planning and fund-raising, including selling homemade Mexican food after mass, led up to the December 12 celebration.

Many church-going Latinos will drive 50 miles to attend the services for the Virgin of Guadalupe and the Sunday mass in Spanish, while they could have walked to mass from their home. Danny, a high school junior whose parents work in the fruit packing houses, explained his family's reasons for doing so.

Danny: I think it means something important to me. That's the only
time a lot of Hispanics get together, do something, then sometimes
they have games, see friends.

K. Crane: So it's important because you can get together with others?

Danny: Yeah, other Hispanics.

Danny's statement that mass in Spanish at St. Barbara's is "the only time
a lot of Hispanics get together" refers to the weekly gathering of a group
of 400 to 800 people (depending on the season). There are also weddings,
quinceañeras (celebrations of a girl's fifteenth birthday and her presentation
to the community as a young woman), dances, soccer games, and *norteño*
concerts that attract big crowds. Danny's perception is correct in a social
sense, though. Nowhere else in the region is there such a large, organized,
regular gathering of Latinos.

While it is clear that Latino parents see churches as affirming traditional
values, it is equally clear that their children, especially those born in the
United States, experience the faith community differently. Rubén, whose
parents came to Wheelerton in the 1970s before he was born, illustrates an
experience different from that of his parents:

My experience is different from my parents'—I am 100 percent American, although I'm proud of my Mexican roots. I'm not Mexican but hold
to some Mexican customs. I'm a mix, a Chicano; we are attempting to
create something else. You see this in my clothes, baggy jeans, preppy
shirt, K-Swiss shoes. We grew up with MTV.

Rubén uses the word "Chicano," although it is not a common part of the
Midwestern vocabulary, in an attempt to identify the unique experience and
culture of the second generation. Many Latino Pentecostal parents would
find Rubén's views disconcerting. Nonetheless, if they listened carefully,
they would see he does not in any way diminish the significance of his religion. In fact, his faith community remains an integral part of his bicultural
identity. His presence there and that of the second generation in general,
however, does present challenges. Rubén felt that he was one of the members of the second generation who had been neglected by previous youth
pastors, who focused on newly arrived youth from south Texas and Mexico.
One of the challenges facing Latino congregations is how to incorporate

newly arrived "Mexican" youth and those self-identified Chicanos of the second generation. Pastor Guzmán of the Templo realized that the second generation was on a different cultural trajectory and tried to let them express some of their identity through music, especially by singing and playing in a gospel band of teenagers.

The Templo congregation today is formed mostly of long-term residents, their children, and their grandchildren. The first generation has largely passed leadership on to their children. A third generation of middle school and younger children has now emerged, and they will help chart the direction of the congregation. Pastor Guzmán knows that the Templo must be involved in recruiting youth to ensure the continuity of the church.

The statement by a member of the congregation about being more comfortable with "his people" strongly suggests that a sense of ethnic solidarity, based on shared experiences, common culture and language, and feelings of *familia* (family togetherness) draw Latinos into Spanish-speaking congregations. Latino youth in small Midwestern towns are part of a spatially dispersed minority, and churches can affirm their identities as Mexican and Mexican American.

Mobilizing Resources

In the early 1970s, southwest Michigan was the flash point in a crucial chapter in the history of farmworker struggles in the state. At the time, some farmers were denying agencies serving farmworkers access to farm labor camps. One large grower, Mr. Hassle, near Ciderville, vandalized cars of social service and legal staff who were visiting workers in his large labor camps (for details about these incidents, see Valdés 1991). On a number of occasions, he threatened them at gunpoint. In one encounter, he physically assaulted and injured Mr. Folgueras, an outreach worker from United Migrants for Opportunity (UMOI). Mr. Hassle charged him with illegal entry to his farm; later he dropped the charges, and then several parties, including UMOI, brought a case against Mr. Hassle. In 1971, the Michigan attorney general ruled that the trespass law could not be used to bar visitors from the premises where farmworkers lived (i.e., farmworkers had the same rights as other tenants to have visitors at their homes).

In the mid-1990s, St. Barbara's became involved in a controversy that was an outgrowth of its ministry to farmworkers. A local agency approached the church to purchase some adjacent diocese property for farmworker housing. The church held town meetings on the matter. Many community members opposed the project and attacked it. One parishioner remembered that during one really packed meeting, Anglo residents made some "racist" remarks such as "It's going to bring down the neighborhood—there will be junk around and low-rider cars." She said, "You could see the lines drawn." Most Latinos (with some Anglo supporters) were on one side of the room, and huddled on the other side was a huge block of Anglos (with some Latino families). Some Latinos, mostly those whose families had lived in the region for several generations, opposed the project on the grounds that proximity to the church would place too many burdens on the priest. While they supported housing for farmworkers, they were uncertain that the agency implementing the project was truly competent and fair.

While many in the congregation supported the plan, a consensus emerged in the church community that it would not be a good idea. Two factors converged and led to a veto of the project: (1) objection from the Anglo community at large; and (2) opposition of some church members who felt it was not good for the church. Father Bill could have proceeded with the plan, since community approval was not required, but he and the council did not want to be seen as doing something in opposition to the community. The ordeal left relationships between Anglo and Latino members strained. Over the long term, though, the parish has welcomed Latino newcomers. Father Bill ministered to them and worked with the Anglo membership to promote full membership for Latinos and good relations among ethnic groups. A succession of bilingual priests (including Vincentian priests and several others from Colombia) fully welcomed Latinos to the church, and their membership exploded.

Material Assistance, Linking People to Resources, and Family Counseling

The Latino congregations in this study have seen their mission as more than addressing spiritual needs in culturally relevant ways. They have also dealt with the practical needs of the Latino community, especially migrant farmworkers, newly arrived families, and youth. St. Barbara's operates a distribution center named after a "Mexican" family whose father's generosity was so great it "exasperated his family and friends." During the fruit season, the center stocks used clothing and household items. Templo Cristo Rey houses a lunch program that provides meals twice a week and activities for children and their parents.

Overall, however, the direct distribution of material assistance is less important than the service provided by staff in connecting people to services from nonprofit and government agencies. Sister Consuelo, Deacon Ramón, and other staff, being bicultural and well established in the wider community, provide important bridges to resources for the newly arrived. They frequently help people negotiate resources and services, including visits to the emergency room, social service agencies, and officials in the legal system. Sister Consuelo is frequently called upon to accompany women to the hospital for emergencies and births; she also helps guide people through the application process for establishing residency or citizenship.

She sometimes also mediates among family members, for example, in intergenerational conflicts.

> The girl comes home late at night, and the parents think she's up to nothing good. So the girl comes to me and says, "They don't want me to come back to the house anymore." I say, "Why?" "Because they told me to be there at 11:00 and I came home at 12:00." Of course, I ask where she was, and she says, "I was having a good time." So I go to the house and explain to her mother, "You know, nothing happened," and this and that, "so why can't we make peace?" Then her mother accepts her back [into the home].
> *Sister Consuelo*

Churches have also responded to requests to provide English as a Second Language (ESL) classes. For example, St. Martin's teamed up with a nonprofit organization that addresses the literacy needs of groups throughout the county. Both the agency director and Sister Consuelo recognized that most Spanish-only parishioners do want to learn English, but language classes are often scheduled at inconvenient times. They realized they would need to schedule classes around the work schedules of factory workers, many of whom worked the more inconvenient second and third shifts. Evening classes would not work for most people, but a Saturday slot before second shift would be the most accommodating time. In April of this year, they began registering people at St. Martin's. Sister Consuelo contacted 45 people, and 27 showed up at registration. An agency staff member attributed the successful turnout not only to more convenient scheduling but also to Sister Consuelo's efforts, people's trust in her, and the safe environment of the church. Currently, between 40 and 50 people of all ages attend Saturday morning classes.

Leadership and Modalities of Activism

While the affirmation of cultural values is an important function of Latino churches, some Latinos argue that it is not enough. The church must help people deal with the here and now of life in this country—not just help them remember what they have left behind but empower them for life in the present. Indeed, many Latino churches in the Midwest provide vehicles of engagement with the present and future. The extent to which churches are involved in creating their own solutions revolves around the quality of leadership and the ethnic and generational composition of congregations.

Lay member activism is also a feature of many churches, both Protestant and Catholic. Federico, a church musician whose family settled in Michigan in the 1950s, was part of the radical farmworker rights movement in the 1970s. He now works with other members of St. Barbara's to make the school system more responsive to needs of Latino students.

Ken, it's like that old Stevie Wonder song, "Just Enough for the City." They give us just enough to get by on. They zero in on bilingual issues, but other needs of the population, for example, physical and mental handicaps, are ignored. Kids are left to themselves. They have no Latino teachers to encourage them. The school districts want to get as many [Latinos] as they can for the fourth Friday count [the enumeration of pupils that determines the annual state allocation of funds for a school district], but you don't see the same effort being made in the spring to recruit Latino students.

Federico, several professors from a nearby university, and a large number of teens, parents, and grandparents from St. Barbara's have formed an organization to look into these issues. In focus groups of students at several churches, the research team found that many were angry at school counselors for steering them into non–college preparatory classes. The interviews also revealed some surprises for parents, namely, that many of the things facing their children had not changed since the days of their own youth: language issues, communication, and discrimination. The driving force behind this initiative is that schools need to do something beyond counseling and bilingual education for Latino youth. Their immediate goal is to pair up Latino high school students with local college professors in mentoring relationships.

The involvement in activism also reveals a difference between newcomers and older residents. The newcomers, whose foothold in their new community is more tenuous, have opted for forms of engagement with society that are less militant than those of better-established groups. St. Martin's leadership has so far chosen to work in a largely pastoral and nonpolitical fashion. The new literacy program is therefore a big step, and the strong response indicates that it provides a form of engagement that people are ready to embrace.

The pattern seems to be that as Latino congregations become more established, more challenging issues, such as working conditions, housing, and education, are addressed. Whether the modalities of engagement are pastoral (Sister Consuelo), or social activism (Federico and Pastor Guzmán), they are all significant ways that Latino congregations develop local responses to community issues.

In terms of the role of leadership and community engagement, these faith communities represent different modalities. The involvement of Templo Cristo Rey with the mayor's efforts to reconcile the community contradicts the common critique of Pentecostalism as a "mechanism for social disengagement" (León 1998:164).[6] Pastor Guzmán was fortunate to represent Latinos who were firmly in the middle class and whose public cultural expressions had been protected by the veil of religious legitimacy. This is not to minimize the risk of bringing the congregation under criticism, and indeed his actions brought racist sentiments out into the public square.

The St. Martin's leadership has so far chosen to work in a quieter, largely pastoral fashion. As deacons and religious sisters and priests, their orientation was toward training, evangelism, religious retreats (*cursillos*) for teenagers, religious education, catechism, and counseling. In various discussions, the priest who ministered to the Latino congregation (and who was from Mexico) and the lay and religious staff of the church defined their approaches to their work as separate from liberation theology, which they disavowed. Furthermore, the parish priest, an Anglo, took an assimilationist view toward the new "Mexican" parishioners. Unless inspired by a charismatic leader, people whose foothold in a new community is tenuous will generally not put themselves at risk through high-profile actions. The high number of participants in the new literacy program indicates that it provides a form of engagement that people are ready to embrace.

Religious expression, whether it be through Pentecostal tongues or *fiestas patronales* (celebrations of the feast days of patron saints), is often criticized in Marxist terms for having no instrumental value in dealing with the present social order. Some would argue, however, that religious expression is its own form of engagement with society. The psychologist Ainsley (1998) believes that religious symbols and expressions are important to Latinos engaged in "cultural mourning"—the psychosocial process by which migrating people come to terms with the distance from family, home, and the loss of familiar culture and community. If we accept Ainsley's argument, then we should see music, processions, and important cultural icons such as Our Lady of Guadalupe as more than nostalgia, as ways that people deal with the present. This approach opens the possibility for religious expression, in its own right, as a mode of engagement with the present order.

Conclusion: The Place of Churches in the Lives of Latino Newcomers to the Rural Midwest

For many Latinos in Midwestern towns and villages, churches are key places for face-to-face interaction with other Spanish-speaking members of their culture. It is not unusual for families to drive more than an hour to attend services in Spanish at St. Barbara's, St. Martin's, Templo Cristo Rey, Iglesia Adventista, and other churches. Churches like these hold the largest regular public meetings of Latinos in the region. They provide the primary social space for maintenance of ethnic solidarity and integration of youth into Mexican American and Mexican ways of life. Thus, it is likely that Latino congregations will continue uniting people in a geographically dispersed community and, in that process, will continue to develop diverse cultural and religious values, with the possible emergence of new and surprising forms of leadership.

Latino congregations of southwest Michigan and north-central Indiana publicly celebrate their faith in different ways that illustrate their unique forms of spirituality. Whether it is the gospel band at the Templo or the sing-ing of corridos at St. Barbara's, they have developed liturgy, music, and wor-ship services inspired by a rich cultural heritage, mainly from Mexico and south Texas, that resonates with their experiences of migration, struggle, and building community.

The congregations discussed in this chapter each reflect a facet of the Latino communities in which they are situated. The demographic differ-ences among congregations reflect ethnic and religious pluralism among Latinos in rural Midwestern communities. The Templo currently represents an established Latino community that is beginning to produce a third gen-eration of members. Most members of the congregation are blue-collar and lower-middle-class people with double-earner households and have been vigorously upwardly mobile. St. Martin's, on the other hand, reflects the community of the first-generation Latino newcomers to the region—mostly monolingual Spanish speakers whose children are learning English rapidly in school. St. Barbara's is a combination of both demographic groups, with a well-established, lower-middle-class Latino core membership which sup-ports the newly arrived. Both Catholic parishes, while having Latino majori-ties numerically, still have influential non-Latino parishioners. The Templo, by contrast, has been Latino from the beginning, founded by Mexican and Tejano Pentecostals.

The communal and individual narratives presented here are consistent with other Latino congregations in the United States, which have often played the crucial role of mediating between marginalized groups and insti-tutions of the dominant society. What this chapter describes, however, are the nuanced modalities by which this is accomplished. Both Protestant and Catholic congregations, in their own unique ways, have presented moral challenges to fellow Christians and their communities at large. Their dif-ferent cultural configurations continue to push their ministries in different directions, but of greater importance is the way the leaders of faith com-munities have responded to new social and spiritual needs. These different leadership styles have had implications for culture change, including mo-dalities of community engagement.

In the future, Latino churches may collectively address challenging is-sues, such as the housing shortage, discrimination, and labor conditions. Fortunately, the major Latino churches are willing to cooperate in meeting the needs of the Latino population, but the increasing diversity of congregations, as well as some residual sectarian suspicions, will have to be overcome. Much more could be said about the Latino churches in these communities and about the congregation members, whose stories are so rich in spiritual detail. Current circumstances present great opportunities for Latinos in the Midwest to play an important role in the spiritual, cultural, and political life of their communities. The experiences of Wheelerton, Ciderville, and other communities in this study in accepting new strangers within their gates are being replicated in hundreds of similar towns. Fortunately, the stories recounted here show that Latino churches can play a vital role in both advocating social justice and building bridges to the wider community.

The "Mexican Situation" and the Mayor's Race

Ken R. Crane and Ann V. Millard

This account deals with Ligonier, Indiana, and a race for mayor that turned on the "Mexican question." In many ways, these events typify political struggles in Midwestern towns through the 1990s and into the twenty-first century as the low-wage Latino population has grown. In Ligonier, it grew from less than 10 percent of the townspeople in 1990 to over 40 percent in 2000. Many Anglos saw this change as a dramatic, threatening transformation in their community of about 4,000 residents.

The flashpoint of tension in reaction to the Latino influx was highly visible in the town in the mid-1990s. The public reaction of Anglos and the consequences for public officials were openly expressed in the local newspaper, which provided the information for this analysis. It was evident in our study, however, that the entire region was undergoing a similar change in the ethnic composition of its population, for similar reasons and with similar reactions. The town of Ligonier was simply representative of many small towns and cities in northern Indiana, although other places may not have articulated their experiences with the same degree of candor.

Mayoral Politics: 1993–1995

In January 1993, the same year that in-migration of Latinos became quite noticeable in Ligonier, a new mayor took office. Glenn Longardner began his tenure confronting a mounting series of complaints to the mayor's office regarding certain practices of the now highly visible Latino population. One of the early complaints was from an agitated Anglo neighbor of a "Mexican" family who had slaughtered a goat and left the entrails "laying around." The neighbor was concerned that the dogs were going to drag these things all over town. Some townspeople were not surprised in the least, recalling their farm days when it was customary to leave the remains of slaughtered animals for the dogs.

Others, however, did not understand; it was hard for "city folks" to take. The city authorities had to send someone out to get the people to clean up the goat remains. This was the end of that matter but only the beginning of a series of complaints about loud music, loitering, drunkenness, and fixing cars in the backyard. It was the beginning of what became known as the "Mexican situation," as it was called in the local newspaper. The Mexican situation, first of all, did not concern all Latinos or all people of Mexican descent. Latino families had lived in Ligonier for more than 30 years without coming into the political limelight. In fact, these longtime residents had established themselves as hard working and industrious factory workers, businesspeople, and professionals. The complaints were directed at the public presence and behavior of certain newcomers. The Mexican situation concerned what was perceived to be a particular segment of the population, often profiled in variations of the following: young, male, rude, monolingual Spanish speakers, illegal, and prone to drinking too much, loitering, and listening to loud music; also, there were "too many" of them. The complaints were prompted by the public presence and behavior of certain newcomers, but the description of the problem was generalized to encompass the entire ethnic group "Mexicans."

The mayor felt strongly compelled to do something to bring the two communities together. At his request, the council agreed to form the Intercultural Committee (ICC) to "bridge the cultural gap." This committee consisted of the mayor, two members of the town council, and members of the Latino community. The mandate of the ICC was to build understanding between the Mexican population and the Anglo community, finding ways to build rapport and trust.[1] Their official motto was Bridge the Gap.

The first step in cultural bridging was to provide some ways to incorporate the Latino community more fully into the town. One approach was to educate the newcomers about local ordinances (e.g., regulations limiting the number of people per residence, car maintenance at residences, and goats), and to provide information about using services such as banking, mortgages, language classes, and the steps for gaining citizenship. Information was to be disseminated through a monthly newsletter and the town newspaper, whose editor agreed to publish notices in Spanish. The committee also organized a group of volunteers to conduct a census of the Mexican population.

As another step toward bridging the gap, the mayor honored the request of the Mexican community to use Town Square to celebrate Mexican Independence Day in September. The newspaper advertised the event in both English and Spanish. A church brought in a Christian mariachi band from Ixmiquilpan in central Mexico. The three-day celebration was a big affair; in addition to the music, it included poetry contests, prizes for best traditional dress, and a soccer tournament at the park. Here is how the local press described it:

> For a moment, it felt like downtown [Ligonier] by some freak act of nature slid south of the border and into the heart of Mexico. Hundreds of native Mexicans, including one mariachi band, saluted the Mexican flag and proudly sang Mexico's national anthem Wednesday night. Then the Cry of Independence rang out—"Viva México!" . . . "I think it's great," Mayor Longardner said. (*Ligonier Advance Leader,* September 23, 1993)

The Mexican community perceived this event as a gesture of welcome and goodwill from the city. The event ended with Pastor Gutiérrez, the pastor of the largest Latino congregation, presenting a plaque to Longardner for "allowing Ligonier Mexicans a chance to celebrate publicly." "Perhaps we will make this an annual event," the mayor said (*Ligonier Advance Leader* September 23, 1993). Some Anglo members of the Intercultural Committee also thought it should perhaps be made an annual event. A Latino paid a visit to the mayor's office to thank the mayor personally for allowing the celebration to take place, saying, "This is first time we have felt welcome here."

While goodwill was flowing between town authorities and the Latino community, other members of the Anglo community began to criticize the situation. The mayor was criticized for promoting a Mexican independence day celebration but not a celebration of the Fourth of July. (Ligonier has never had an official U.S. Independence Day celebration, nor are there plans for one, despite this outcry and even though the mayor offered to support such an event.)

More complaints about the presence of Mexicans in public space began to find their way to the mayor's desk and onto the editorial page. One woman (unidentified) wrote, "I can't take my grandkids to the park and I don't like to go to the stores in Ligonier because of the illegals' always saying things about the white people in Spanish" (*Ligonier Advance Leader,* September 22, 1994).

Apparently many took literally the newspaper description of Ligonier sliding "south of the border and into the heart of Mexico," for the criticism became much more open and virulent after the celebration took place again the second year, with twice the number of people (about 1,000) attending. The day after the festivities began, the paper had a front page article with the bold headline "Viva Mexico or Long Live Ligonier?" A photograph showed a sign by the approach to town that said "Welcome to Mexico" (someone had stenciled the word "Mexico" over "Ligonier"). It was at this time that the movers and shakers of the town became quite vocal in their negative sentiments about the Mexicans, the ICC, and the mayor. Some said that the public interpreted the committee's actions as promoting Mexican culture at the expense of American culture. One community member said it was the Mexican independence day celebrations that really turned the tide of public opinion against the mayor and the ICC (which reportedly sponsored the event, although no city funds were spent).

Latinos could not ignore what they perceived to be some of the underlying sentiments being expressed. In response to comments made during the council meeting, Latino residents defended the Mexican population, pointing out that many had lived in Ligonier for over 30 years. "How in the hell can you claim we don't belong here, you arrived in 1964 and I was already here in 1960 . . . as long as we are legal residents of the U.S. we have the right to live anywhere in the country we want to," said one of the first Latinos to settle in Ligonier. He also added that the Latinos are extremely hard working and conscientious, and are trying hard to adapt to a new country (*Ligonier Advance Leader* November 3, 1994). A local Latino pastor also urged Anglos to be patient: "I ask the Anglo community to try to understand the Mexicans . . . Be patient with the Mexicans. We [are trying] to teach the Mexicans how to assimilate, absolutely" (*Ligonier Advance Leader,* April 16, 1995).

Sensing that they were in a potentially volatile situation, the mayor and ICC decided a change of strategy was needed, so some of the Mexican members of the committee suggested that instead of an independence day celebration they would have an ethnic celebration in 1995. According to Mayor Longardner, "They realized the problem it [the independence celebration] was causing in the community and kind of took the bull by the horns" (*Ligonier Advance Leader,* May 11, 1995).

A local Latino pastor stated, "It's better that it's all ethnic groups instead of just Mexicans. Some people think it's not good for Ligonier to have a festival for Mexican Independence if they don't have one for American Independence" (*Ligonier Advance Leader* May 11, 1995).

Publicity was optimistic, with the theme "Unity and Diversity." The newspaper announced the event on the front page with the opening lines, "They say the way to a man's heart is through his stomach. With seven food booths at Ligonier's first ethnic festival, the way to ethnic unity may also lie through the stomach." The ICC and mayor were equally optimistic about their hopes for the community. "The goal is that it helps bridge the [cultural] gap," Longardner said. "That's been the whole idea of the Intercultural Committee since it began in June 1993." However, still reeling from the heavy round of criticism the previous year, he added this proviso: "I haven't heard any complaints, although I probably will next week when it's over." Pastor Gutiérrez was also hopeful: "I expect to see better understanding from both sides. I know there is prejudice, not only from the Anglo side, but sometimes the Hispanic side also has prejudice. It will be a kind of celebration of better understanding" (*Ligonier Advance Leader* May 11, 1995).

Meanwhile, despite the dismal weather, a mariachi band made its first appearance in the northern Midwest, and booths sold food from Mexico, Ethiopia, Germany, Italy, and the United States (ice cream). Organizers felt it was a success. The mayor said he would like to continue the event, possibly even holding it next year on July 4, with fireworks. The ICC said they would study the idea. Another dark cloud appeared on the horizon just before the festival weekend. The Immigration and Naturalization Service (INS) notified several local factories that some of their workers were illegal. One of the largest plants had to dismiss 45 workers. The link of the ethnic festival to the dismissal of workers may have been coincidental, but it suggested again to Latinos that they are not welcome in Ligonier.

Mayoral Elections: 1995

The year of the ethnic festival, a mayoral primary and election were held. One of the hot issues was termed "the Mexican situation." The incumbent mayor and his Democratic opponent had similar opinions. During the Democratic primary, Charles Musselman, who would eventually run against Longardner, articulated his position:

I would treat them ["Mexicans"] as I could any other citizen . . . I think they should be educated to our way of doing things. Maybe that could work both ways—we could be educated a little in their ways . . . Since they are here, they should live the way we do; I think most of them probably do. (*Ligonier Advance Leader,* April 27, 1995)

He admitted the mayor doesn't have any control on immigration into Ligonier. "I don't see how you could stop [Mexicans from moving here]. I don't know how it started in the beginning" (*Ligonier Advance Leader,* April 27, 1995). Later, during the fall campaign against the incumbent mayor, Musselman made these statements:

They're here and we have to live with them, but we do have city ordinances. We have to use these ordinances and have them live like we have to live, then we can get along with them. (*Ligonier Advance Leader,* October 15, 1995)

Longardner's position was similar:

People want to know why there are so many Mexicans coming in. I say it's because there are jobs here. It's amazing how many jobs there are in this town for its size. (*Ligonier Advance Leader,* January 9, 1995)

We must recognize that they're here and here to stay. They're here because of jobs and they're welcome here. We have to help bridge that cultural gap. That will take education both ways. The Hispanic people have the responsibility to learn that they're living in Ligonier and not in Mexico. Our laws, our ordinances, our customs are different. They have to adjust; they can't expect the Anglo people to adjust to their customs. (*Ligonier Advance Leader,* October 15, 1995)

Longardner expressed hopes the Hispanics could be "assimilated" more into the Ligonier mainstream, but recognized that it will take more than festivals for that to happen (*Ligonier Advance Leader,* October 15, 1995). Throughout his tenure as mayor, he had stressed his belief that the process of "assimilation" was happening and that most Hispanics in Ligonier wanted to "fit in."

Longardner's and Musselman's publicly stated positions were strikingly similar. Musselman stressed the importance of educating the newer Hispanics into "our way of doing things"—learning English, knowing the laws, and understanding the consequences of disobeying the laws. Longardner's position was essentially the same, perhaps with a somewhat more inclusive tone if taken in the context of his proactive approach through the Intercultural Committee. Musselman sounded as though he would continue working to bridge the gap but with a tone of conditionality: "Then we can get along with them." He said he would continue the efforts of the Intercultural Committee. Some claimed that supporters of Musselman off the record took a much harder line than his public statements.

In the November election, Mayor Longardner and his Republican supporters on the council were voted out of office. Perhaps the bridge they were building was one that few were willing to cross. In any case, the Bridge the Gap approach had backfired. In 1996 no ethnic festival took place, neither in May nor on July 4. The ICC was disbanded soon after the new mayor assumed office.

Many who thought they knew the community were surprised. The editor of the local paper told Longardner that he was "utterly surprised," given the similarity of opinions about the "Mexican situation." Longardner believes it was his closeness to the Mexican community that was the deciding factor. He says there is a nonacceptance of any outsiders by natives of Ligonier who trace their families back to the original founders. They did not accept the later waves of Jewish in-migrants[2] or the succeeding wave of white Appalachians. "Even we are not considered real natives, because we've only been here since 1977." His efforts to mobilize enough votes from the Latino community to override this opposition failed. Longardner's editorial summed up his disappointment with a warning to those who had cast their vote to counter his conciliatory stance toward Ligonier's Mexicans:

To be criticized and defeated in an election because I recognized a need to bridge the cultural gap between the Caucasian and Hispanic people hardly seems fair. I know nobody said life had to be fair. If the 1,150 registered voters who did not vote or voted against me believe that the Mexican people will be packing to move or will have already moved by Jan. 2, 1996, they will be disappointed. The Mexican people are here to stay. They moved to [Ligonier] before I did and they will be here after

I am gone. Do not feel sorry for Glenn Longardner but feel sorry for Ligonier because of its discriminatory attitude. (*Ligonier Advance Leader*, November 16, 1995)

The local editor followed the same line of reasoning in an editorial in the same issue, arguing that Longardner's policy is the only viable option, working toward educating newcomers and developing mutual understanding. Alternatives such as laws against newcomers, indifference toward them, or harassment of them will only cause retrenchment and bad will. Privately, the editor told me there were other factors. Local business leaders felt the mayor had not done enough for the local economy, and they felt his opponent could serve their interests better.

The new mayor took office in January 1996; shortly afterward he had a heart attack and was absent for the next three months. Musselman served one term and lost his reelection bid to a former policeman who proclaimed himself a redneck. (Longardner believes he meant to say "blue collar.")

Thus was the door of Ligonier generously opened to Latino newcomers, only to be slammed in their faces. This opening and closing of doors was symbolic, and it was very emotional for everyone involved, including our research team, who were beginning to be optimistic that a small Midwestern town could welcome Latino newcomers. The welcoming of Latinos did not work in this instance and resulted in an upset in the succeeding election. Latinos nonetheless continue to move to the area, regardless of the symbolic aspect of their reception. They continue to seek jobs that pay well and provide benefits, and the region continues to provide them.

CHAPTER NINE

E Pluribus Unum? Discussion, Conclusions, and Policy Implications

Ann V. Millard, Jorge Chapa, and Ken R. Crane

Downtown, Ligonier, Indiana, AKA "Little Mexico"
A community survey asked, "What three things in Ligonier do you NOT show to an out-of-town guest?" "Downtown," was a frequent response. There is a perception that the downtown area has deteriorated. Residents complain of brick facades in disrepair and houses turned into multiple family rentals. Shops like the Dollar Store have moved out to a strip mall to the south. In the early 1990s, Latinos moved downtown to run businesses and rent housing, and the deterioration there tends to be blamed on them, even though they do not own the buildings.
Crane, field notes

In or Out: One Community or Many?

Generally, Anglos in the rural Midwest disapprove of the Latino newcomers to their communities. A widespread stereotype is that Latinos arrive destitute and have come simply to live on welfare benefits. Contributing to this image is the fact that they nearly all are poor when they arrive, and the jobs they acquire generally pay so poorly that they qualify for government assistance. The close concordance of Latino ethnicity with poverty under these specific circumstances magnifies the stigma attached to the newcomers. On the other hand, employers and others in contact with Latinos emphasize that "Mexicans" are ideal workers and that they are proud of supporting themselves. Key underlying factors not generally discussed in rural communities are two actions by Midwestern employers. Employers recruit the newcomers and usually pay them low wages with few or no benefits; thus employers often ensure the newcomers' dependence on government services. Latino newcomers, in their poverty, thus embody a process created largely by Midwestern Anglo employers. Local Anglos, however, view the newcomers as symbols of economic, cultural, and racial change reaching into their communities.[1]

As we observe throughout this book, Latinos in the communities we studied maintain a social network separate from rural Anglos. Our analysis shows that Anglo suspicion and hostility play a larger role in maintaining this separation than does any aloofness on the part of Latinos. The ultimate question to be faced by each town, and our nation, is whether Latinos will become part of the U.S. mainstream or whether they will maintain a separate status.

This chapter describes some of the positive actions taken by rural people to improve ethnic relations and solve local problems related to the Latino influx. These actions provide concrete suggestions for other rural people and government agencies to use in making Latinos full members of their communities. In this chapter, we also briefly review our findings and discuss policy implications. We find that several factors act to maintain Latinos as a separate community, especially current immigration policy. We see the major dimensions of the problems associated with the Latino influx as the history of Latino migration to the Midwest, population dynamics, employment, education, and church policies. Many local low-level policy changes can contribute to a better situation for Latinos and their new communities; however, as discussed at the end of this chapter, a major change in U.S. immigration policy is required to transform the current exploitative, unethical, and illegal system.

Community Problem Solving

During the course of this study, we were fascinated to find a number of solutions to conflicts about the growing Latino presence being worked out in various villages and towns. We hope this study will be useful as a resource for policy options for dealing with the Latino influx into the Midwest. We were surprised to find that even when a policy initiative had proved constructive, it was not necessarily sustained in the community that originated it. In many cases, these initiatives are not being communicated to other villages and towns.

Much of the following material comes from Ligonier, Indiana, and consists of model activities conducted by students at relatively low cost but with considerable positive effects. We selected these examples because Ligonier is a typical community in regard to levels of prosperity and the severity of problems noted by Anglo and Latino residents. It is important to note that Ligonier's lack of prosperity has not kept the town from taking many steps to improve conditions for Latinos.

Middle School Students and the Gus Mack Tournament

Jennifer, a teacher in the middle school in Ligonier, described what school was like in 1995, when tensions between Mexican newcomers and Anglo residents were high. She commented that the "Mexican students didn't mix outside of their group. Boys especially stuck together in large groups; there were more fights than there are today."

In 1995 some middle school students in an honors program planned an event to help bring groups in the community together through a basketball tournament. The students called their group Community Problem Solvers. The remarkable fact is that the students planned and implemented the whole event from beginning to end, under the sponsorship of Sally, a middle school teacher. The students were eight boys and girls, including two Latinos and some other non-Anglo students, who brainstormed to come up with a focus and a program. They decided to address the tensions among ethnic groups through a community-wide 2-on-2 basketball tournament (a "Gus Mack tournament") with teams mixed by ethnicity, for example, an Anglo paired with a Latino. "After all," they said, "sports are universal."

While competitive events do not necessarily translate into racial harmony, the organization of the event revealed the students' considerable insight into group relations. Students and adults were invited, and the pairing of Anglos and Latinos was done randomly within age groups. Players who already knew each other could not be on the same team. The players were to lunch together at tables where servers would offer both Mexican and Anglo food.

The students named their project UNIDOS (Uniting Neighbors, Interracially Diverse, with Organized Sport; also meaning "united" in Spanish). They printed T-shirts for all participants and advertised the event with posters and flyers in both English and Spanish. They announced the event in the newspaper, at churches, and at shops to reach a variety of groups.

The students also sought support from the community. The mayor loved it; it fit perfectly with the goals of the Intercultural Committee. The students talked to teachers, some of whom actually said it wouldn't work. (The students even had a photograph of one teacher telling them it wouldn't fly!) They talked to principals and the press. They got coverage in the local paper. They applied for and received a grant to cover some of the costs, which amounted to over a thousand dollars, including lunch, T-shirts, referees, and prizes.

On March 18, the day of the tournament, 78 people entered the contest, and most of the 36 nonwhite players were Latino. Sally, the middle school teacher, said, "The feeling that day was very positive. Many Latinos came out to watch the event; the participants were really positive about the event."

A write-up by the local editor quoted many participants who confirmed that feeling: "From all indications the project was a success." One Latino man said, "This was a very good idea, I'd like to do this more often . . . I work around American people and I like American people, but I don't get to play with them often." Commented another, "Like it says, 'One nation under God.' That's what it should be." An Anglo member of the community said, "I'd like to see it each year, bigger and better." Another said about his partner, "I found out he has a kid about the same age as mine." A longtime Latino resident said he would like to see it expanded to softball as well (*Ligonier Advance Leader,* March 2, 1995).

One pair of seventh graders found themselves facing a serious language barrier. Geraldine spoke no Spanish, and Juanita, who had been in Indiana less than a year, spoke no English and hadn't played much basketball. Geraldine sought out Juanita a few days before the game and practiced with her; with the help of translators and sign language they pulled it off. Juanita's inexperience showed in the tournament as she fouled by pulling an opponent's arm down as she went for a layup. Geraldine laughed while telling this story, saying that the penalty for the foul didn't bother her, and she congratulated Juanita on the good game afterward. Juanita was contemplating trying out for the middle school team the next year (*Ligonier Advance Leader,* March 2, 1995).

In the following days, the students were asked, "When are you doing this again?" Sally spoke modestly of the students' achievement, "I'm sure we didn't do anything earth-shaking. It'll take some small steps. I think we took one of those steps" (*Ligonier Advance Leader,* March 2, 1995). One of the student organizers said, "Not everybody got to win, but they met people and talked." A lot of people said they had fun. The students got a double bonus; beyond the reward of having done something positive about a community problem, they also went on to win the first place award at the national competition of Community Problem Solvers.

Although the event was successful, it was not repeated in succeeding years. It is evident that events of this kind are valuable, and they should be supported by local governments, schools, and other organizations to foster a person-to-person understanding to build mutual respect, trust, and communication.

Students and PRIDE

Another accomplishment by students in the Ligionier schools involved their work in a PRIDE organization, a school club that campaigns against drug use. The club includes Anglo and Latino students. They raised $100,000 for a kidney transplant for Carlos, a 12-year-old boy from Mexico who was living in the area. They also submitted a petition asking the U.S. government to allow his family to stay in the United States to ensure that necessary medical treatment would continue. The PRIDE chapter received a local prize and went on to Louisville, Kentucky, to compete for broader recognition. Although the chapter did not win, the members dramatized a humane approach to some of the problems confronting Latino newcomers and countered the general pattern of opposition to Latinos in the region.

The Total Quality of Life Initiative

The Total Quality of Life Initiative (TQLI) came from collaboration among the town of Ligonier, the Indiana Chamber of Commerce, and Ball State University (DUP 1994). The TQLI study focused on local people and their choices to improve their lives. Two thousand questionnaires were sent out with telephone bills. The responses were presented in a 43-page Community Quality of Life Profile and discussed at several town meetings. Housing was identified as a major obstacle. Economic growth had been "too successful" (*Ligonier Advance Leader*, February 23, 1995).

The 43-page report did not contain the words "Hispanic," "Mexican," or "Latino," even though much of the downtown was being transformed into a Latino enclave. The Latino presence was addressed during a public meeting by the director of the initiative, however, who identified the

communication problem with an unnamed ethnic group. You all know what I'm talking about and it's time to stop complaining about it. The immigrant population has also grown very quickly, but it's a reality, so start involving them and their leaders. They are now part of the town's heritage. (*Ligonier Advance Leader*, February 23, 1995)

Similarly, in Logansport, Indiana, the town government collaborated with Iowa Beef Processing Company (IBP), which opened a plant there in 1996 (*Actionlines* 2001). They instituted diversity classes, a central communication center, and a program cultivating leadership in minorities. They also promoted home ownership for Latinos, provided free transportation services to "anyone in need," informed Latinos about measures to take in an emergency, and offered ESL and Spanish classes. The ESL classes were free and IBP reimbursed tuition to employees who took the Spanish classes. In Postville, Iowa, efforts were made to "reach across ethnic boundaries" of Jewish, Russian, and Latino residents through a movie festival, community gardens, an international market, and various efforts by religious leaders (Marbella 2001). All of these towns, and many more, have first faced turmoil and then moved on to take constructive steps in problems solving. The policy changes that we would recommend, as a consequence, include disseminating these innovations in rural areas before turmoil occurs and informing local communities about the ramifications of promoting economic development through the opening of large manufacturing plants.

A Summary of Local Initiatives Fostering
Good Anglo-Latino Relations in the Rural Midwest
In the course of our study, we found a number of constructive actions taken by different organizations in dealing with rural Midwestern controversies over the Latino influx. Our proposal is to support these initiatives and to see that they spread. These actions are summarized in Table 9.1. They deal with the areas of language, institutional discrimination, business, schools, churches, medical and social services, and local government. All of these areas need to be addressed to adapt a community to a low-wage Latino influx. In the communities that we have studied, it is apparent that many Latino newcomer families intend to stay, and it behooves Anglos in those communities to see that they prosper. Anglo families are more dependent on the livelihood of Latinos than they realize in most cases, and the future of their communities cannot be separated from the status and well-being of Latinos or other substantial population segments.

Table 9.1. Ways to Improve Anglo-Latino Engagement in the Rural Midwest

1. Language policy regarding the use of Spanish and interpreting
   A. Schools should implement bilingual education to facilitate the transition of Latino students to classes in English.
   B. Medical and social services should organize to make interpreters available, and the interpreters should be trained. Staff and monolingual patients should press for interpreters.
   C. Schools and medical and social services should make written materials available in both English and Spanish, with the translations placed side by side to assist staff and clients in communicating. Teachers, physicians, nurses, and social workers should ensure that translations are available.
   D. Monolingual English speakers should not assume that Latinos do not speak or understand English.

2. Institutional discrimination
   A. Organizations should review their practices to see how they might be engaging in institutional discrimination and revise their policies and practices accordingly.

3. Businesses
   A. Have Anglos and Latinos on the same work shifts.
   B. Reward members of the workforce and managers who are bilingual.
   C. Be sure that Anglo and Latino workers have the same information. If a significant number of workers do not read English, have written information translated.
   D. Follow worker safety and labor laws without regard to the ethnicity of the worker.

4. Schools
   A. See 1A, 1C, and 1D above.
   B. Arrange for bilingual staff to be available for non-English-speaking students newly arrived at the school. Arrange ways to assist students in learning English as efficiently as possible.
   C. Arrange for communication with parents who do not speak English. For example, have translations of homework assignments written out in the form of templates, so that teachers need only fill in the blanks (with the chapter number or the math problem numbers, for example).
   D. Communicate with Anglo parents about Spanish-speaking students, their use of resources, and how they benefit the school.
   E. Recruit Latino students to be involved in school activities.
   F. When Anglo and Latino students get involved in an activity together, support it. One model of an organization that attracts both Anglo and Latino students is the Spanish Club, with free picnic lunches and trips to amusement parks or other popular spots.
   G. Include material from Mexican and Mexican American literature, history, geography, and politics in classes.

Table 9.1. (*continued*)

H. Celebrate Cinco de Mayo or another holiday or event with Mexican roots by having Latino students invite Anglos to dance and teach them how to do "Mexican" dancing.

I. Make sure that teachers get continuing education credit for learning Spanish and taking trips to Mexico.

5. Churches

A. As community organizations with a major mission to assist others and to ensure religious freedom and social justice, churches without Latino members need to undertake efforts to educate their congregations about the issues. They need to make Latino newcomers welcome in the community and to encourage respect for them.

B. Anglo and Latino clergy need to communicate and model cooperation for their congregations.

C. Churches should sponsor unity prayer breakfasts where Anglos, Latinos, and other ethnic groups can meet one another and discuss working together for the benefit of the town.

6. Medical and social services

A. See 1B, 1C, and 1D above.

B. Make sure bilingual staff are available in large enough numbers that their client loads are no greater than those of other staff.

C. Make sure that programs that are available to Anglos are also available to those who speak only Spanish.

7. Local government

A. Seek ways to connect members of Anglo and Latino communities socially. For example, a multicultural breakfast could be held once a month with members of each ethnic group sitting together at each table.

B. Encourage activities that bring Anglos and Latinos together. Example: the Gus Mack Tournament.

C. Seek Latinos for membership on councils and boards.

D. Examine local policies to see how they can be modified to serve the interests of Latinos as well as Anglos.

E. Endorse ways in which workers from Mexico can have the same rights as U.S. citizens.

F. Ensure that various parts of local government, including fire and police departments, implement policy evaluation and change.

8. Federal government

A. Create a legal structure authorizing immigrant laborers to work in the United States.

B. Support other policies that encourage communication between Anglos and Latinos.

C. Support policies on language and training to encourage the above actions.

A Brief Overview of Our Findings and Their Implications for Policy
Latino Population Dynamics, Employment, and Rural Growth

Historical studies show that Latinos have a long history of migration to the Midwest in response to Midwestern factories and farms, which have been recruiting people in south Texas and Mexico since the last quarter of the nineteenth century. One of the ultimate ironies of the contemporary situation is that while many rural Anglos deplore their presence, Latino newcomers are key contributors to local population growth and rural economic development. Without their growing numbers, many villages and towns would be losing population. Without their labor, many light industrial plants would have to pay higher wages or relocate abroad, and agriculture and food processing would have to pay higher wages or stop producing labor-intensive crops. As previously noted, these contributions of Latinos to local populations and economies are understood by few Anglos, but most see Latino newcomers as threatening the rural Midwestern way of life, not as sustaining it. In analyzing the challenges of the Latino influx into rural Midwestern communities, we have traced the anatomy of prejudice against Latino newcomers, and we caution again that discrimination against the newcomers erodes the broader community, as well as Latino households.

As noted in Chapters 4, 5, and 6, the workforce in food processing plants tends to be stratified by ethnicity. Some plants have all-Anglo workforces, and in our observations they are the factories with high technology and better wages and benefits than other plants. Some plants have one or two shifts that are virtually all Anglo and another that is all-Latino. In one plant producing auto parts, for example, Latinos have the late-night shift. The only plants we learned of that have all-Latino workforces are those that pay near minimum wage and have the most difficult and dangerous working conditions; these plants do food processing, including meatpacking. A later section of this chapter makes the argument that the immigration policies that have led to this situation need to be changed.

Education

The relationship of Latinos to the school system is complex and thought-provoking. As shown in Chapter 7, the educational system is a microcosm of society-wide prejudices against Latinos. At the same time, our high school study reveals some optimism and idealism on the part of students.

We propose changes in school policies to take advantage of the Latino influx as a teaching opportunity, prompting teachers and students to focus on Mexico and the rest of Latin America in history, geography, social studies, government, and foreign language studies. The presence of students from Mexico in the classroom could help to bring alive the studies of another country, Mexico, the largest neighboring country of the United States, an important trading partner and a leading nation in Latin America in many endeavors. We know of no high schools teaching Latin American history, geography, and literature; and although some teach Spanish, it is usually viewed as less valuable than French and German. Promoting the study of Spanish would encourage Anglo students to communicate with incoming monolingual Latino students and provide Anglos with a skill valuable on the job market and in other endeavors.

A number of teachers support the use of bilingual education to assist immigrant Latino students in making an efficient transition to all-English classrooms; however, ordinary rural people and the U.S. public at large have no understanding of this advantage of bilingual education. Perhaps because the issue has become so politicized by organizations like U.S. English, teachers are unwilling to risk criticism by publicly advocating bilingual education.

To blame Latinos for a low educational level is common and oversimplifies a complex situation. The stereotype is widespread among Anglos that Latinos do not value education. Weak research has supported this view by taking statistical findings of low educational levels of Latinos out of context. Studies typically quantify schooling for the population 25 years of age and above; on this measure, numerous Latino populations have less than a high school education on average. The conclusion is that they have many high school dropouts. The problem with these analyses is that many of the immigrants from Mexico have met educational norms for the general Mexican population, not the 12 years of education required in our system. Currently, Mexican law requires school attendance from 6 to 14 years of age (*Encyclopaedia Britannica* 2003). To categorize those with less than a high school education as high school dropouts is therefore erroneous. Statistical analyses of educational levels should examine foreign-born Latinos separately from those born in the United States.

Many U.S.-born Latinos do face educational barriers, on the other hand. While many low-income Latino parents want their children to finish high school and go beyond, the children themselves are often alienated by their experiences of discrimination in school, as described in Chapter 7. Our study thus confirms that there are pressures on Latino youth that prompt them to drop out of high school, but we assert that the educational level of those over the age of 25 years is a misleading index of dropout rates. To address dropout rates, we advocate the educational policy changes presented above. Orienting classes toward Mexico and Latin America can enhance respect for Latino newcomer students. Teaching Spanish will also provide means to bridge the communication gap between Anglo students and Latino newcomers. In addition, it is important for school staff to communicate with parents who are monolingual in Spanish. We talked with parents who have not gone far in school who did not realize that their children need to attend school daily and complete all homework to be successful. Midwestern schools need to inform parents in Spanish of these requirements.

Churches and Extended Families

As they have settled in the Midwest, Latinos have brought many institutions with them that provide assistance to the needy. In effect, they have brought their own social services system with them, contrary to the stereotype that Latinos have come to the Midwest simply to live on welfare benefits. A major organization brought by Latinos to many communities is a church, often beginning as a congregation holding services in rented or borrowed space, later gathering resources to purchase a building, as noted in Chapter 8. Latino pastors, recruited from the U.S. Southwest, Latin America, and the Caribbean, collect and distribute resources to those in need, including food, clothing, information about housing, and various referrals to service agencies. Pastors often negotiate with local authorities on behalf of Latino community members, especially those who literally have no voice in local affairs because they cannot speak English.

In addition to their churches, Latinos often bring parts of their extended families with them, and they provide all kinds of child care and assistance to one another, ranging from food and shelter for new arrivals to assistance finding jobs, understanding the school system, knowing where and how to shop, and obtaining services ranging from car repairs to prenatal care.

The family and the church carry out service work that otherwise would be demanded of agencies that provide welfare and refugee services. The Anglo stereotype of the newcomers as highly dependent stands in ironic contrast with the reality of a highly self-sufficient Latino population.

One reason that Latinos bring institutions with them is that they are usually not welcome in Anglo organizations. Our research team is not particularly surprised at this, although it is disappointing to see Latinos rebuffed by Anglo churches. Each town has Anglo residents who try to welcome Latinos, but their efforts are undermined by other Anglo community members through actions ranging from taunting to beatings. Several policy changes are called for by this situation in order to improve Latino access to health and human services, to increase tax monies flowing to rural communities, to include and address the needs of low-income Latinos in rural economic development policy formation, and to enhance relations between Anglo and Latino congregants in various churches.

Demographic Trends and Their Policy Implications
Older Anglos, Younger Latinos: Population Growth and Differences in Age Structure

Three major demographic trends are shaping the role Latinos will play in the future of the Midwest, as noted in Chapter 3. First, we see that Latinos are becoming a larger part of the population and the low-skilled local workforce. Second, Latinos are not achieving educational parity with Anglos for reasons discussed above and in Chapters 2, 3, and 7. Third, Latino population growth is mainly in younger age groups. Many Latino newcomers arrive during their family-building years, and many Latino teenagers plan to stay in their new rural Midwestern communities as adults. The growing proportion of young Latinos may well be an encumbrance to future economic growth if Latino levels of education and work skills do not improve. These three trends in combination suggest that the growing Latino population may remain lower-class outsiders who hold low-paying jobs and are unable to contribute fully to the collective well-being of rural Midwestern populations.

Changes in population composition are accentuated by differences between Latinos and Anglos in age structure (i.e., age distribution), and these contrasts have important ramifications for the future. Rural populations will have increasing percentages of Latinos in the youngest age groups and more Anglos in the oldest age groups. These ethnic differences in age structure will have significant policy implications in at least three policy-relevant areas. First, returning to the issue of education, we note that much of the school-age population in numerous rural communities will be Latinos if current trends continue. Second, a larger proportion of the working-age population will also be made up of Latinos. This trend will be particularly evident among younger, entry-level workers. The negative impact on the local economy will be significant if Latinos do not improve their educational and skill levels. The third policy-relevant area involving this shift in ethnic composition according to age structure is that almost all of the burgeoning population of seniors and retirees will be Anglo. Numbers and percentages of elderly residents will increase greatly in the future. The policy relevance of this trend can be found in the fact that senior citizens put large demands on public services. These demands will occur at the same time that Latinos are becoming a larger part of the workforce. Increased demands by the elderly for public services may further exacerbate economic problems flowing from the low incomes of Latinos and other minorities.

"The Whole Enchilada" Proposals and Problems with the De Facto Guest Worker Program

As analysts, we are obviously sympathetic to Latino newcomers in the rural Midwest. We join the call for immigration reform on the basis of our experiences and analyses. A number of the Latinos who informed this study are undocumented immigrants, that is, they lack official U.S. permission, in the form of a visa or other document, to work in the United States. For many years, undocumented Latino immigrants have provided the United States with a "de facto guest worker program" (Massey et al. 2002). (Guest worker programs take many forms around the world, but they all involve government permission granted temporarily to workers from abroad ["guests"] to be employed in a given country.) Many of the benefits to employers and workers, as well as costs to workers and their new Midwestern communities, were reviewed in Chapters 2 and 3. Regarding the debate about whether their tax payments outweigh their use of benefits, undocumented workers do pay into the federal budget without being able to collect Social Security, whether in retirement or in cases of disability. On the other hand, they typically use locally funded services at rates that outstrip their tax payments.

The de facto guest worker system has existed for many years but with many problems. As noted in Chapter 3, it benefits employers and places many costs on workers. Enforcement against undocumented immigrants in the Midwest tends to be erratic.[2] Fear of deportation is ever-present and shapes many aspects of the lives of the immigrants. Their undocumented status limits employment opportunities and the redress they could and would seek for work-related problems. It also limits access to health care, driver's licenses, and other public services, as shown in other studies (Massey and Espinosa 1997).

There is a debate over whether undocumented status forces immigrants to lead "shadowed lives" (Chavez 1992). According to one commentator, "Countless news stories highlight illegal immigrants as proud homeowners, successful businesspeople and ambitious high school graduates openly seeking admission to California's public universities" (Skerry 2001). Even though some undocumented immigrants have become publicly known, however, it does not mean that they have nothing to fear. The degree to which undocumented immigrants are free to go public varies regionally (Leiken 2002:71) and over time. We observe, though, that immigrants are deported from all over the United States (INS 2002, table 60) and that undocumented status was a major source of stress in some families in our study.

Moreover, a perverse aspect of any de facto system is that the terms and conditions of the system can be changed at any time. The history of Mexican immigration to the United States offers many examples presented in earlier chapters, including the mass repatriations of the 1930s and Operation Vanguard (see Massey et al. 2002).

One cost to society at large that is not generally discussed, however, is the widespread understanding that laws do not apply when it comes to U.S. citizens who profit from undocumented workers. Those who employ, rent to, and deliver various government and private services to undocumented immigrants generally understand that at least some of them have problematic legal status. The current system is thus inherently corrupting, not only of workers but also of those whose livelihoods depend on them.

One of the top policy priorities of George W. Bush, as he began his U.S. presidency in the year 2001, was the resolution of some of the problems inherent in this de facto system. This was also a top priority for Mexican president Vicente Fox, who was the first foreign head of state to meet with

Bush. During the first week of September, Fox had a highly visible, successful trip to Washington, including White House meetings and an address to Congress. Bush and Fox were developing an initiative to "legalize" the undocumented immigrants. The Mexican president had already put forward a comprehensive proposal, whose representative, Jorge Castañeda, said, "It's the whole enchilada or nothing; we can't slice it one piece by one piece" (Zoellner 2001; *Economist* 2003). It included a "full range of civil rights benefits for Mexicans in the United States, including Social Security numbers, drivers' licenses, health care, resident college tuition, and the right to join trade unions" (ibid.). The proposal also included "regularization" of the status of undocumented workers through a formal, de jure guest-worker program.

Before the September 11, 2001, attacks on New York City and the Pentagon, some states had begun to implement one aspect of regularization, allowing undocumented immigrants to get driver's licenses. The Mexican government had also been providing Mexican citizens with *matrículas consulares,* consular identification cards to be used in the United States in opening bank accounts, obtaining driver's licenses, and getting access to other instruments for daily life. Increased security concerns ended the regularization trend in the United States, though, and some states reversed their policies (T. Sharp 2002; D. Sharp 2002). The September 11 attacks occurred just days after Fox's visit and stopped all talk of regularizing or legalizing undocumented immigrants.

The U.S. Border Patrol has increased its vigilance at the U.S.-Mexico border since the mid-1990s. The heightened U.S. emphasis on security has also changed the terms of the de facto guest worker system. The U.S. Department of Justice launched Operation Tarmac shortly after September 11 and arrested hundreds of undocumented airport employees (CNN.com 2002). A public defender representing some of the arrestees said they were "basically the working poor. We're talking about Starbucks and Burger King employees who happen to be taking jobs at the airport" (Kobell 2002). This example documents the dispersion of undocumented workers throughout the low-paying strata of service, agricultural, and industrial jobs nationwide. The security responses to September 11 have made the de facto guest worker program more onerous for laborers and employers alike.

We agree with Robert Leiken that "Mexican immigrants are not a direct threat to homeland security." We also agree that the "active market for illegal documents" required by the de facto system creates a threat to security (UPI 2002). In short, the move away from regularizing Mexican immigrant workers is against the security interests of the United States, even though it is politically expedient in a simple-minded way.

Another source of strain on the de facto system was a U.S. Supreme Court decision, Hoffman Plastics, decided on March 27, 2002 (*Hoffman Plastic Compounds, Inc. v. NLRB* (00-1595) 237 F.3d 639, reversed). In this decision, the Supreme Court reversed lower court awards of back pay to an undocumented immigrant who had been laid off because of his support of a unionization drive at the plant. While the Supreme Court's "decision does not mean that undocumented workers do not have rights under other U.S. labor laws" (U.S. Department of Labor 2002), the Hoffman Plastics decision undermines an important part of the legal scaffolding supporting de facto laborers.

Given these facts, the obvious way to end the demand for forged documents and many of the problems with undocumented immigrants in the United States today is to document the immigrants—to legalize or regularize their status so that they can live, work, and drive in the United States legally. (This chapter is not the place to develop the details on how this should be done, but we endeavor to show that it is necessary for many reasons.) The ongoing flow of undocumented workers from Mexico and the rest of Latin America to the United States is a disgrace. It leads to their exploitation, lack of enforcement of labor and safety laws, low wages, the growth of the working poor, and many other negative effects. By changing policy so that the only people working in the United States have legal authorization to do so, we would greatly reduce many of the problems on that list. Not only is working as an undocumented laborer dangerous for the employee, but it also can be dangerous for the rest of us. The large number of undocumented workers from Mexico has created large markets in the United States for falsified identification documents. If the U.S. government authorized Mexican immigrant laborers to do their jobs, many customers would leave the underground market for documents, potentially allowing easier government control of official identification documents and thus tighter control of U.S. borders.

Summary: Policy Changes Needed at Many Levels

As this discussion has shown, changes in policy are appropriate at many levels, ranging from local school systems and town governments to the federal level. Local changes are possible to make immediately, and many could receive support from local foundations or could be carried out cost-free. Many of the changes that we suggest do not require any massive change of heart on the part of the general public, and they would encourage people to develop greater understanding across ethnic lines.

Fundamental to changing the situation of Latino newcomers, however, is the larger issue of immigration status for those workers who lack documents. Although they do not account for all Latino newcomers, the general Anglo public assumes that they do, leading to the treatment of Latinos in the rural Midwest as though they lack permission to be there. Some observers would hold employers responsible, and we have in our analyses. We would add, however, that in our capitalist system, employers find a low-wage, docile workforce almost irresistible, and we should not expect employers to desist out of idealism. The immigration reforms of the 1980s set forth provisions to penalize employers for hiring undocumented workers; however, those provisions generally have not been applied, for political reasons. (The employers tend to be quite powerful locally and in some cases nationally.) For these reasons, a policy change is required either to create a formal guest worker program or to allow official immigration of Latino workers.

Many towns have failed to forecast the rather large cost to local government of adding a new food processing plant to their area. They have provided various corporations with tax abatements that have resulted in considerable expense for local governments to extend public service infrastructure, increase the capacity of schools, and deal with an a large influx of low-income people. On the state and federal levels, companies like Buckeye Egg Farm have been costly because of the efforts required to regulate them, especially legal suits involving fines and orders for them to change their way of doing business and to stop illegal treatment of workers, pollution, and other exploitative practices.

Immigration reform should require that those in the U.S. labor force are conferred with the right to be in the country where they work and that they have the same fundamental rights as other workers in the United States. As shown in our analysis, it is exploitative to have laborers come to Midwestern towns for the purpose of contributing to the economy without taking all of their human dimensions into account—their need for safe housing, medical care, and emergency social services, and their children's additional need for schooling. These costs, which were initially hidden from rural communities, provide good reasons for rural people to pursue policy changes. The inhumanity of the megafarm, as it is often put into practice, and other production systems where Latino newcomers find work, should be given close scrutiny. Many of these concerns are safety hazards for entire rural communities and watersheds, in addition to their Latino workforces.

Our policy recommendations, therefore, are to do "the whole enchilada"—ranging from changes in immigration policy to actions by local governments, schools, landlords, employers, service providers, and others to accommodate rural Midwestern communities to Latino newcomers and vice-versa. Appropriate policy changes can diminish the turmoil experienced by rural communities with the construction of manufacturing plants and a consequent Latino influx. Policy changes can set the stage for improved wages and working conditions for Latino newcomers as well. The consequence can be strong economic growth for rural communities, changes in local culture in ways that are not threatening to long-term residents, and acceptance of Latinos with respect. Without such policy changes, the consequences will be a furthering of the racism currently shaping much of Anglo-Latino relations and the creation of a low-income stratum of Latinos in rural areas who are disenfranchised and denied a chance for the American dream.

Methods Used in the Community Studies

Ann V. Millard, Maríaelena D. Jefferds, and Ken R. Crane

The community studies focused on employment and relations on the job, education and relationships at high school, and religion and relations to congregations. In addition, we also examined housing and politics (see Table A.1). To address these questions, Millard, as manager of the qualitative research component of the study, designed approaches based on the California study of Allensworth and Rochín (1999) to fit the Midwestern context and maintain comparability with their research.

Methods Used in the Community Studies

The methods we used to study community clusters included surveys, participant observation, interviews, focus groups, and reviews of written sources. Each community study focused on a cluster of two to eight communities defined according to the focus of the investigator and the local geography and economy. For example, in studying the relationships of Latino newcomers to public schools, Crane examined a high school and therefore focused on the communities in that school district.

Selection of Communities

We identified communities appropriate for this study by beginning with a quantitative analysis that showed which areas had relatively rapid growth of the Latino population and which had few or no Latinos. We then carried out brief regional surveys to pinpoint communities with rapid Latino population growth in the 1990s to study in detail. A researcher then visited a specific community to collect data over a period of two to six months.

Each fieldworker began by trying to study one community, but we had not anticipated the extent to which rural people move among different towns and villages in their daily routines, to get from home to work, school,

Table A.1. Foci and Methods in Community Studies

Focus	Communities	Methods of Data Collection and Researchers for Each Study
Communities with rapid Latino growth		
Housing of migrant farmworkers and newly settled Latinos	Oceana County, Michigan	Review of newspaper accounts and letters to the editor (Burillo, Millard)
Employment of Latinos, working conditions, wages; relations with Anglo employers and fellow employees	Fox and Mapleville, Michigan	Participant observation, semistructured interviews (Jefferds); focus groups (Jefferds, Millard)
Education of Latinos; relations with Anglo teachers and students	Wheelerton, Indiana, area, with information from Fox and Mapleville, Michigan	Participant observation, interviews (Crane, Jefferds); focus groups (Crane, Flores, Millard; Jefferds, Millard)
Religion, Latino congregations and their relationship with Anglo churches and congregations	Berryville and Ciderville, Michigan, with information from Fox and Mapleville, Michigan, and Wheelerton, Indiana, area	Participant observation, interviews (Crane, Jefferds)
Politics, Latino newcomers as a political issue	Ligonier, Indiana	Review of newspaper accounts and letters to the editor (Crane)
Corporate, mass-production agriculture	Columbus, Ohio, region	Interviews by phone with state workers, review of local newspapers and field trip (Chapa, Jefferds, Millard)

(Continued on page 224)

Focus	Communities	Methods of Data Collection and Researchers for Each Study
Constructive responses	Ligonier and Wheelerton, Indiana, with information from rural Michigan	Interviews, review of newspaper accounts, letters to the editor, documents, and research literature (Crane, Chapa, Jefferds, Burillo, Millard)

Communities with few Latinos

General conditions	Rising Sun, Indiana	Interviews and site visits (Chapa)
Amish commerce and social life	Various communities in Indiana and Ohio	Site visits and research literature (Chapa, Millard)
Egg farm communities	Columbus, Ohio, region	Interviews with state workers and residents, site visits and review of newspaper accounts (Chapa, Jefferds, Millard)

and shopping. We then realized that investigating clusters of communities would provide a more accurate description of what we were doing as we collected the data.

In addition to the detailed community studies, we also gathered data on communities with approximately 15 percent or more of the population in the agricultural labor force but no Latino residents. We wanted to see how such communities differed from those with a Latino influx. The researchers also examined printed sources of data, including local and national newspapers and the holdings of local libraries.

Confidentiality and Exceptions in Cases of Public Events

We have changed the names of people and places to protect the privacy of study participants. Where necessary to maintain confidentiality, we have created a composite study participant or community by pulling together common characteristics and ascribing them to one pseudonymous person or place.

Exceptions to this approach involved the use of newspaper articles, letters to the editor, and cartoons as data for the analysis of public controversies. An illustration is Burillo and Millard's analysis of the heated controversy in the town of Shelby, Michigan, over the construction of an apartment complex for low-income families ("En Pocas Palabras II: The Battle for Chapita Hills"). Another illustration is Crane's analysis of a mayor's race in Ligonier, Indiana, in which anti-"Mexican" fervor led to an upset ("En Pocas Palabras VI: The 'Mexican Situation'"). In writing about these two controversies, we did not disguise identities of those involved because the data we analyzed are publicly available. In all cases in this work where we use interview data, however, we have taken steps to preserve confidentiality.

Qualifications of Researchers

The research team members who engaged in qualitative research had previous research experience in the rural Midwest. The two main fieldworkers in this project, Crane and Jefferds, lived in, or less than two hours' drive from, the communities they were studying, giving them some understanding of regional issues and styles of interaction. Their familiarity allowed them to collect data relatively rapidly.

At the time of the study both researchers were advanced graduate students. Crane was conducting his own dissertation research during the course of this study, while Jefferds had already carried out data collection for her dissertation.

Most members of the research team were fluent in Spanish, and many were familiar with Mexican and Mexican American culture, as mentioned in the preface. Ability to speak Spanish was crucial to understanding study participants who lacked skill in speaking English. Receiving information from them in Spanish led us to challenge many of the stereotypes about Latinos that are widespread in the Midwest. Moreover, some phases of our study would not have been possible without researchers fluent in Spanish. For example, carrying out a focus group with Spanish-speaking high school newcomers would have been impossible without Spanish-speaking staff to coordinate the group and take notes.

Familiarity with Mexican and Mexican American culture meant that researchers had some of the conceptual tools for understanding the many viewpoints of Latino newcomers. For example, it was easy for most of us to understand that many Latino newcomers would consider it a sacred mission to insist on placing the image of the Virgin of Guadalupe in a local church. In addition, the multicultural background of the research team led us to question many of the assumptions of Midwestern Anglos and to reexamine one another's assumptions in developing our analysis.

Semistructured Interviews and Focus Groups

In two community studies, we carried out semistructured interviews followed by focus groups. To identify people to interview in Fall County, Michigan, for example, Jefferds listed the relevant organizations in the community cluster. We (Jefferds and Millard) reviewed the list and prioritized the organizations for interviews according to how much contact they had with Latino newcomers and, in some cases, their power to affect the situation of newcomer families. Then Jefferds called each organization, explained the purpose of the study, and asked to interview someone who would be appropriate. In interviews, she focused on participants' knowledge of local institutions, particularly the organizations they belonged to, whether as employees or unpaid officers (see Appendix B).

Throughout the study, researchers asked how organizations were responding to the changing population and their needs. We also asked about differences among Anglos and long-term and newly arrived Latinos and the interrelationships of these groups. Interviews took about 45 minutes in most cases, although a few extended to two hours. In a few cases, the researcher visited several times over the course of several weeks. The interviews were further tailored according to the topic of a specific community study. Each researcher pursued particular topics of interest and examined the data for cultural themes related to those topics.

For example, in studying the incorporation of Latino children in local schools, Crane collected data through interviews with school administrators, teachers, and students. He spent time in classrooms and at school events, observing routines and Latino-Anglo interaction. In taking notes, he characterized the position of the interviewee regarding age, gender, class, occupation, and length of time living in the community, as these characteristics shape experience, perceptions, and discourse.

Research team members conducted focus groups in pairs or threesomes in two community clusters. As noted, Crane designed focus groups on education and ethnic relations in high school (with assistance from Flores and Millard); Jefferds conducted groups on employment, relations on the job, and ethnic diversity in different organizations (with assistance from Millard). In each case, there were three focus groups to carry out discussions separately, one each with Latino newcomers, long-term Latino residents, and Anglos (Table A.2 describes focus group members in Fox and Mapleville, Michigan). In each case, a researcher hired a local person to be the site coordinator, invite participants, and reserve space in a quiet, private place for the meeting. Once the focus group began, the site coordinator's work was over (the coordinator was paid $80). This approach was quite successful in bringing together participants in a timely way under conditions of trust. The focus groups lasted 1 1/2 to 2 hours, and participants were given a small amount of money as a gift ($20). In each group in a specific community cluster, the investigator asked the same open-ended questions (Knodel et al. 1990), because we wanted comparable data sets (see Appendix C). This aspect of the study also assisted us in putting the focus group participants at ease; knowing that we were asking the same sensitive questions about ethnic relations in each group gave those who had some anxiety a sense that the study would be fair to all sides.

Data from the project were recorded as narratives, quotes, and transcripts in word processing files. Each interviewer took handwritten notes during interviews and typed them into a word processor after the interview and the following day, along with additional comments on details and context. During focus groups, one researcher took notes continually during the discussion and augmented them after the meeting with selected portions of transcripts from an audiotape. Focus groups in English were transcribed by a professional transcriber.

We entered the field notes into computer files first in narrative form and later inserted codes at the head of each paragraph beginning a new topic. We coded data with the classification system developed by Murdock et al. (1987). This way of coding data during fieldwork was initiated by anthropologists at the Universidad Iberoamericana in Mexico City in the 1960s. The advantage of the system is that it provides a set of codes covering hundreds of topics ready for use by a research team. The disadvantages are that it takes researchers time to get used to the coding system and that the codes are not tailor-made for the project. The typology allows research team mem-

Table A.2. Characteristics of Participants in Fox and Mapleville, Michigan, Focus Groups: Anglos, Latino Old-timers, and Latino Newcomers

	Latino (N = 12)	Anglo (N = 9)
Years living in Fox or Mapleville		
<2	1	—
2–4	7	—
5–9	2	—
10–14	—	—
15–19	1	1
≥20	1	8
Education, last grade completed		
Primary school, grades 3–6	5	—
Junior high school, grades 7–9	6	—
High school graduate, 12	—	5
College or trade school, 13–15	1	3
College graduate, 16	—	1
Gender		
Female	8	7
Male	4	2
Household size (number of people)		
2	—	3
3–5	7	6
6–8	5	—

bers to use a handful of codes to pull out information relevant to a specific question; we did not use the categories as a step in the analysis but simply as keys to finding data, similar to the Library of Congress cataloging system for books.

The data from interviews and focus groups were analyzed by reviewing field notes to see how study participants described their communities and, specifically, relations between Anglos and Latinos. Researchers delineated economic, educational, and religious issues that study participants identified. We analyzed participants' statements in relation to their ethnicity, class, and how long they had resided in the community. This approach allowed us to identify patterns of agreement and disagreement among community members in and across ethnic groups. The complexity and nuances of the participants' different points of view do not represent every opinion or ex-

Table A.2. (*Continued*)

	Latino (N = 12)	Anglo (N = 9)
Employed		
Yes	10	6
No	2	1
Volunteer/Retired	—	2
Seasonal employment		
Yes	7	2
No	3	6
Current employment		
Blue collar, service, and farmworkers		
Farmworker	3	—
Food processing worker	5	—
Restaurant worker	1	—
Pink collar workers		
Day care worker	1	1
Cosmetologist	—	1
Business owners and white collar workers		
Farmer	—	1
Government service provider	—	1
Real estate salesperson	—	2
None: volunteer or retired	—	2

perience in the communities concerning ethnic relations and population changes, but they do shed light on different avenues of response to changes in their communities.

Sampling and Limitations of the Data

We did not use random sampling techniques in the community studies for two main reasons. First, the project budget would not allow random sampling of the general population in the areas we studied. Second, when we sought to interview those holding specific types of jobs, we often had little or no choice of people to interview. For example, a school system had only one superintendent, one Spanish teacher, and one bilingual aide running a bilingual classroom (actually a study hall where Spanish-speaking students could get assistance). We used social networks to recruit study participants, and this method probably introduced some bias, as did the selection of focus group members.

If the researchers had spent much more time in the communities, we would have had a better understanding of the extent to which the participants in our focus groups and interviews were typical of the larger population. Also, because of our informed consent procedures, some participants may have felt some pressure to speak better of members of another ethnic group than they would have under other circumstances; Anglo community residents may have chosen whether to participate in our study on the basis of their level of concern for Latinos. Anglos at times seemed to filter their comments to portray themselves as fair and unprejudiced; Latinos seemed to try to portray their treatment by Anglos as unproblematic. On the other hand, we still heard many comments revealing the broad outlines of ethnic tensions and injustice in every community in this study.

Unpredictability is particularly true of research projects involving participant observation and face-to-face interviewing in communities. For researchers in the field, this project, like all the others we have worked on, became a roller coaster ride of good days and bad days in the community, as various residents engaged in or avoided participation in interviews. We were really gratified to receive support in two phases of the fieldwork. One was the focus groups, which went surprisingly smoothly. The other was the work of Crane in a high school, including focus groups he carried out with Flores and Millard. Millard had anticipated that the age gap between the researchers and the high school students would create a barrier to establishing good rapport and communication. To the contrary, however, we received excellent cooperation from the students, who seemed to appreciate having older people take them seriously and really listen to what they had to say. Their cooperation would not have been forthcoming without the support of the school administration, teachers, and parents, to whom we are also quite grateful.

Data Analysis

In analyzing the data, the researcher looked for cultural themes, defined as expressions that thread through the statements of group members and that express core cultural values. For example, regarding language, we found that Latinos universally wanted to learn English, which they saw as beneficial in the job market and everywhere else in life. This view was part of a cultural theme portraying the rural Midwest as a place where they could make a better living and take steps to better their children's lives.

On the other hand, when Anglos heard Latinos speaking Spanish, they took it as a sign of a Latino desire for separatism. This perspective belonged to an Anglo cultural theme portraying Latinos as bound up in their own cultural traditions, rejecting incorporation in rural Midwestern communities. Our general approach in the analysis was to describe participants' perspectives according to their social characteristics, including ethnicity, age, gender, length of residence in the community, occupation, and class.

In addition, researchers analyzed the ways in which resources were distributed in the communities. Jefferds collected much of the data describing the division of ownership and jobs in the communities. Our analytic approach does not view either the control of resources or the governing ideology as a prime mover in local affairs, but sees people in various economic positions as drawing on social custom and, at times, forging new practices to produce a social reality. We analyze that reality as flowing in part from the statements and actions of study participants and similar community members, who also constitute part of the forces shaping the future social and economic reality of the rural Midwest.

Generally, we received great cooperation from members of both ethnic groups in responding to surveys, interviews, and focus groups. Although we are critical of some of the practices that we found in the communities, we need to make it clear that the people and communities in our study are not the ones most prejudiced and plagued with problems of ethnic conflict in the Midwest. If anything, they are more open-minded than most, as they were willing to have us carry out our research in their communities. In some cases, they welcomed our project as a way to seek solutions to conflicts involving the changes occurring where they lived.

Some of our data analysis deals with considerable prejudice on the part of Anglos and institutional discrimination by Anglo-run organizations. We should not be surprised to find these phenomena, though, as many of us on the research team can find similar views in our own families and universities, scattered across various states, cities, and rural areas. In analyzing prejudice and institutional discrimination in the rural Midwest, we focus on their specific, local characteristics and how they play out in regard to access to resources, including jobs and education.

We find it necessary as scholars to take a critical approach to the situation of Latino newcomers and the irony that they are helping to sustain rural economies and yet have become the scapegoats of some rural people and politicians. We also have a loyalty to the people who assisted our project across the spectrum of ethnicity. Out of the belief that it is possible to improve the situation, we present the plain truth as we see it. Moreover, we do not place the blame for local conflicts on local people alone; the community studies presented here reflect forces at work nationwide and need to be dealt with throughout our country and in many institutions, including our own universities.

Interview Guide for Community Study in Fox and Mapleville, Michigan

Maríaelena D. Jefferds

The focus of these interviews was on institutions and organizations in the communities, how they related to Latino newcomers, and how the new-comers related to them. The selection of questions varied according to the interviewee's job, and some questions were asked consistently in early interviews but not as often later as the focus of the study was further de-fined. These questions were modeled after Allensworth and Rochín (1999: Appendix C).

1. General perceptions of the community
   a. How would you characterize your community?
   b. How would you compare this community with neighboring communities?
   c. What have been the biggest changes in this community over the last decade?
   d. How did these changes begin?
   e. What has been the response of community members?
   f. Do all community members view these changes in similar ways?
   g. Were particular people or organizations involved in bringing about or reacting to these changes?
   h. How do you think your community will be different in another ten years?
   i. Where do people go for: groceries, medical services, dentist, optometrist, clothing, gifts, banks, insurance?
   j. What types of social organizations are available in this community? (Churches, work organizations, charitable organizations, children's clubs, athletic groups, etc.)
   k. What types of opportunities are available in this community for: jobs, education, loans, medical services?
   l. Have these opportunities increased over the last decade? Why?
   m. Do you think they will increase or decrease over the next decade? Why?

n. How would you characterize economic conditions in this community?

o. How do economic conditions in this community compare to those of neighboring communities?

p. What factors do you think have been the most influential in determining the economic conditions of this community?

q. What are the main sources of employment?

2. Different neighborhoods and groups in the community

a. What are the neighborhoods/geographic areas that comprise this community?

b. How would you characterize the different types of people in this community? (by occupation, ethnicity, political beliefs, etc.)

c. Can these groups be defined by membership in specific organizations?

d. Are they represented by different community leaders?

e. Are there many differences between long-term residents and newcomers?

f. Who are leaders in this community? (governmental, organizational, religious, etc.)

g. Whom do they represent? How did they become leaders?

h. What issues have they worked on? What do they do in the community?

i. Do you know if these leaders are also involved in larger state or national organizations?

3. Migration into and out of the community

a. Try to think of particular people you know who have moved into this community within the last decade. Why have they come here?

b. Why have people stayed in this community? What makes it attractive?

c. Try to think of people you know who have moved out of this community. Why have they left?

d. What is the community doing to attract or discourage new residents? Are there any general feelings about the ideal population growth?

4. Ethnic climate

a. How are relations in this community between Latinos and non-Latinos? Other ethnic groups mentioned in part 2? Between recent immigrants and established residents?

5. Pressing issues
   a. What are the most pressing issues in this community?
   b. Where do you feel efforts and money should be put to benefit this community?
   c. Do other members of the community share your opinion? Who might differ and why?
6. Ethnic conflict
   a. How do locals feel about the increasing presence of Latinos in this area? Good, bad?
   b. Where do most people who live here work?
   c. Do most people who work in this community also live here?
7. Personal information
   a. How long have you lived in this community?
   b. Why did you decide to live here? How did you arrive (in terms of your job and location)?
   c. Current employment
   d. Whom do you feel you represent?
   e. What groups are you affiliated with?
   f. Is there anything you would like to add to this interview?
   g. Are there other people in this community that you think I should talk to as community leaders?
   h. Can you describe any ethnic or social changes which have occurred in the recent history of this community? Positive or negative?
   i. How does this community react to the increasing presence of Latinos in this community? Do the churches go out of their way to address any concerns or conflict, problems?
8. Questions to ask at churches
   a. Historical presence of this church in this community? Of other churches?
   b. Community support for your church and others—seems to be a lot for a small population?
   c. Changes over time?
   d. What do you do to encourage people to come to this church?
   e. Latino presence in your church, others?
9. Questions to ask at the state employment agency
   a. Brief history of the agency, overview of its goals, and specific issues associated with this community.

b. Can you describe how the employment structure of this community has changed through time, if it has?
c. Describe how the increasing Latino population influences your agency.
d. Are they a significant subsection of the focus of the work you do?
e. What can you tell me about the employment of most Latinos in this community? Generally in one sector or various? Special skills or needs?
f. Do any Latinos (or other ethnic minorities) work in your office now? How many of your clients are Latino or (other ethnic minorities)?
g. Does non-Latino population growth affect this community and your agency job?

Focus Group Questions, Fall County, Michigan

Maríaelena D. Jefferds

Icebreaker Question

(1) Introduction: name and a brief description of how you came to live in
_____ [your community].

Community Description

(2) How would you describe _____ [your community]?

(3) How would you compare _____ and _____ [this community with
neighboring communities]?

(4) Try to think of particular people you know who have moved into this
community within the last ten years? Why have they come here?

(5) Why have people stayed in _____ [your community]? What makes it
attractive?

(6) Try to think of particular people you know who have moved outside
of this community? Why have they left _____ [your community]?

(7) A. What kinds of jobs are there in _____ [your community]?

   B. What are the different racial/ethnic groups in _____ [your
   community]?

   C. What jobs are associated with specific ethnic groups?

(8) What have been the biggest changes in _____ [your community] in
the last ten years? Why have these changes taken place?

(9) How do you think this community will be different in another ten
years?

(10) A. What types of social clubs, religious organizations or charity organizations are available in this community?

   B. Are Spanish people[1] members or leaders of these organizations?
   Which ones?

(11) A. What types of committees or councils exist in this community?
   For example, the Head Start Parents' Group, Village Hall Committees, library committees.

   B. Are Spanish people members or leaders of these organizations?
   Which ones?

(12) Who are leaders in _____ [your community]? (Government, organi-

zations, religious?) Are there any Spanish people who are leaders in
_____ [your community]? Why or why not?

Migration:

(13) What is _____ [your community], as a community, doing to attract or discourage new residents?

(14) Are there any general feelings in the community about the ideal population growth? (In terms of timing or ethnicity)

(15) A. Are there many differences between long-term residents of _____ [your community] and newcomers? (Clarify ethnicity and time frame involved when participants discuss this question.)

B. How are relations between established Spanish residents and newly arrived Spanish people? (Probe for tensions based on social groups, prejudice, language.)

C. How are relations in _____ [your community] between Spanish and white people?

(16) What do people in the area say about the food processing plants—do people discuss the plants in a positive way or a negative way? (How?)

School:

(17) How about the relations between Spanish kids and white kids at school? Do they get along all right? Are there cliques made up of both Spanish and white kids, newly arrived Spanish vs. long-term residents?

(18) In _____ [your community], what are the problems with kids dropping out of school?

Human and Social Service Institutions

(19) Think of the people you know in _____ [your community] who have tried to get a loan for a house, a business or a car. Did they have any problems? If so, what were they?
Were there any problems with a specific organization or agency?

(20) Try and think of people you know who have gone to see a doctor for medical care in _____ [your community]? How was the experience? Did they have any problems?

(21) Now think about people you know who went to the hospital in _____ [your community]. What were their experiences? Did they have any problems?

(22) What are the problems in trying to get service at FIA, CAAP, Head Start, Michigan Works, or any other organizations or agencies you know of in town? (Such as communication)

Notes

1. *Aquí* in the Midwest

1. On July 2, 2002, a court case filed in 1998 against DeCoster Egg Farm in Maine resulted in a settlement of $3.2 million for racial discrimination against the plaintiffs, Mexican workers who were joined in their suit by the Mexican government (Cubria 2002). It will be interesting to see whether similar suits will be filed by the Ohio workers.

2. Some readers will be familiar with the two main ethnic groups in this study as "Hispanic" and "non-Hispanic white," as designated by most government agencies.

2. Latinos in the Rural Midwest

1. For example, Griswold del Castillo and De Leon's (1996) book, *North to Aztlán: A History of Mexican Americans in the United States,* rarely refers to Mexican Americans outside of the Southwest.

2. Indeed, members of minority groups "contributed 46 percent of the absolute growth" of the nonmetro population during the ten-year period (Fuguitt 1995:94).

3. Lake County, Illinois, adjoins Chicago and is not a rural county; however, settlement in the county demonstrates that Latinos are not concentrated in only the most populated areas of the state.

4. In fact, the U.S. government did not establish the Border Patrol, an agency to monitor the U.S.-Mexico border, until 1924 (INS 2001a).

5. Massey and Espinosa (1997) find that social networks seem to motivate some undocumented migration from Mexico to the United States. It is likely that social networks would encourage domestic migration among Latinos as well.

6. Puerto Ricans were heavily recruited through Operation Farmlift to work in the sugar beet industry in the Midwest after World War II (Rochín, Santiago, and Dickey 1989; Valdés 1992), but they refused to tolerate the poor treatment given them by companies such as Michigan Sugar and soon moved to urban areas. Between 1961 and 1966, the U.S. Cuban Refugee Center assisted Cubans in settling in the Midwest, especially in Indiana, Illinois, and Michigan (Masud-Piloto 1996).

7. These explanations have also been confirmed for Mexican immigrants living in other parts of the United States (Massey et al., 1987).

8. IRCA also increased the penalties for employers who knowingly hired, recruited, or referred individuals without legal permission to work in the United States.

9. A study in the Midwest confirms that Latino poverty rates tend to be higher in counties that are dependent on agriculture than in those dependent on manufacturing (Saenz 1994).

10. Consumer Price Index (CPI) data for all urban consumers (CPI-U) is calculated for nonmetropolitan areas (Class D size, areas with less than 50,000 individuals) in the Midwest, the South, and the United States as a whole. The comparison of the three categories indicates that for every year between 1992 and 1999, the CPI for the nonmetropolitan Midwest was lower than that in the South or nationally. These data are available from the Bureau of Labor Statistics at <www.bls.gov/cpi/home.htm>.

3. Latinos and the Changing Demographic Fabric of the Rural Midwest

1. Challenges noted by others involve religious worship (Crane, Chap. 8, this volume), law enforcement, assistance with legalization for the undocumented (Grey 2001), and immigration assistance (Grey 2001).

2. Not all of this growth is attributed to Spanish speakers.

3. The median of the estimates of the undocumented Central American immigrants was an additional 1.5 million (Bean et al. 2001).

4. It is interesting to note that the metropolitan Midwestern Latinos are also disproportionately employed in the manufacture of nondurable goods but not at the same high level as nonmetro Latinos. In Midwestern metro areas, 14.5 percent of Latinos work in these industries, compared to 32.6 percent of the nonmetro Latinos.

4. Research Overview

1. Information about the Jewish colony is from Chamber of Commerce documents and interviews with members of the Ligonier Historical Society and Ligonier Chamber of Commerce.

2. Small numbers of other Latino nationalities have historically lived in Wheelerton, for example, Puerto Ricans. Factories in Wheelerton reportedly employ workers from Central and South America. However, the local school attendance clerk (a Mexican American) only knows of "Mexican" students in the school.

3. We have no independent information on availability of Small Business Administration loans.

5. "Not Racist like Our Parents"

1. Latinos recruited to work in food processing plants during poor economic times in Willmar, Minnesota, encountered substantial hostility (Green 1994).

7. Mexicans, Americans, and Neither

1. State funding for ESL subsidizes most of the program costs.

8. "To Be with My People"

1. Cinco de Mayo, or May 5, is an important holiday in Mexico commemorating the Mexican victory over the French at the Battle of Puebla.

2. "En Michigan," music composed by René Meave and lyrics by Guillermo Martínez. Recorded by Los Bandits (the CD *La Onda del Midwest*).

3. Some Catholics refer to Protestant groups whose members claim to be born again and practice a more aggressive style of recruiting new members as *evangélicos* (evangelicals).

4. As is true of many other people in this book, our depiction of Antonia is a composite of several high school students in northern Indiana, an approach that we took to protect her and other participants' privacy.

5. The Women, Infants, and Children Special Supplemental Feeding Program (WIC), administered by the U.S. Department of Agriculture, provides prenatal care and well-baby checks and food for pregnant women and young children.

6. Anderson (1979), a Pentecostal historian, claims that Pentecostalism exemplifies a movement that began in protest against the social order and became a religious force supporting it.

En Pocas Palabras VI: The "Mexican Situation" and the Mayor's Race

1. Information about the ICC comes from interviews with the mayor and his wife, a council member who served on the ICC, the editor of the local newspaper, and local press articles.

2. As in formal demography, we use the term "in-migrant" to refer to someone who moves into a community from elsewhere in the same country (in this book, typically from the Southwest to a Midwestern town. The term "immigration" refers to an international migrant (here, mostly referring to migration from Mexico to the United States). "Out-migration" and "emigration" are the opposites of these terms.

9. *E Pluribus Unum?*

1. In many ways, these changes have been incipient in the region for some time. For example, Baldemar Velasquez of the Farm Labor Organizing Committee (FLOC), a union for agricultural workers with headquarters in Toledo, Ohio, has worked with farmworkers transnationally in Mexico and interstate by expanding his organization to North Carolina, Georgia, Florida, and Virginia. He is dealing with pay, benefits, and living and working conditions for workers in the fields and food processing plants, and he is well known for his earlier creative approach to

improving conditions for workers through three-way contracts among FLOC (representing the workers), farmers, and food processing corporations, specifically Campbell's and Heinz. He may be able to extend this approach to the current situation for at least some of the food processing workers who appear in this book.

2. For example, Michigan agriculture employs at least 25,000 migrant farmworkers every summer. Among them are numerous undocumented workers, as is true of Latinos in other low-income sectors of the Michigan economy. Our field research found, however, that the INS (U.S. Immigration and Naturalization Service) had only two agents enforcing immigration law for the entire lower peninsula of Michigan outside of the Detroit metropolitan area (Chapa and Millard, field notes 1999). Enforcement of immigration laws has typically been, at best, a token effort. The probability that any individual undocumented immigrant would see either of the agents, much less be subject to any enforcement action, was extremely small. Nonetheless, there was always a possibility that an undocumented immigrant could be discovered and deported.

Appendix C. Focus Group Questions

1. Some local Anglos use this term for Mexican Americans and Mexicans, thus avoiding the word "Mexicans," possibly out of a sense that the latter has a pejorative ring as used locally.

References Cited

Actionlines (publication of Indiana Association of Cities and Towns)
2001   The Changing Face of Tomorrow's Hoosiers. February. Indianapolis, Indiana. <www.citiesandtowns.org/content/publications/actionlines _DHT.htm>.

Acuña, Rodolfo
1988   *Occupied America.* Cambridge, Mass.: Harper and Row.

Ainsley, Ricardo
1998   Cultural Mourning, Immigration, and Engagement: Vignettes from the Mexican Experience. In *Crossings: Mexican Immigration in Interdisciplinary Perspectives,* edited by M. Suárez-Orozco, pp. 283–300. Cambridge, Mass.: David Rockefeller Center for Latin American Studies, Harvard University.

Alarcón, Rafael
2000   *Migrants of the Information Age: Indian and Mexican Engineers and Regional Development in Silicon Valley.* Working Paper no. 16, Center for Comparative Immigration Studies, University of California–San Diego.

Allensworth, Elaine M., and Refugio I. Rochín
1998a   Ethnic Transformation in Rural California: Looking beyond the Immigrant Farmworker. *Rural Sociology* 63(1):26–50.

1998b   The Latinization of Rural Places in California: Growing Immiserization or Latino Power? *Journal of the Community Development Society* 29(1):119–145.

1999   *The Mexicanization of Rural California: A Sociodemographic Analysis, 1980–1997.* East Lansing: Julian Samora Institute, Michigan State University.

Alstott, Owen, ed.
1989   *Flor y Canto.* Portland: Oregon Catholic Press.

Alvarez, R. Michael, and Tara L. Butterfield
2000   The Resurgence of Nativism in California? The Case of Proposition 187 and Illegal Immigration. *Social Science Quarterly* 81(1):167–179.

Amato, Joseph A., with John W. Meyer
1996   *To Call It Home: The New Immigrants of Southwestern Minnesota.* Marshall, Minn.: Crossings Press.

Anderson, Robert Mapes

1979   *Vision of the Disinherited*. New York: Oxford University Press.

Aponte, Robert

1995   *NAFTA and Mexican Migration to Michigan and the U.S.* JSRI Working Paper no. 25, Julian Samora Research Institute, Michigan State University, East Lansing.

1999   *Latinos in Indiana: On the Throes of Growth*. JSRI Statistical Brief no. 11, Julian Samora Research Institute, Michigan State University, East Lansing.

Aponte, Robert, and Marcelo E. Siles

1994   *Latinos in the Heartland: The Browning of the Midwest*. JSRI Research Report no. 5, Julian Samora Research Institute, Michigan State University, East Lansing.

1995   *The Browning of the Midwest*. NEXO 4(1). Julian Samora Research Institute, Michigan State University, East Lansing.

1997   *Winds of Change: Latinos in the Heartland and the Nation*. JSRI Statistical Brief no. 5, Julian Samora Research Institute, Michigan State University, East Lansing.

Bacon, David

1999   INS Declares War on Labor. *The Nation*, October 25, pp. 18–23.

Barbee, Evelyn L.

1993a   Racism and Gender in U.S. Health Care. *Medical Anthropology Quarterly* 7(4):323–324.

1993b   Racism in U.S. Nursing. *Anthropology Quarterly* 7(4):346–362.

Bean, Frank D., Barry Edmonston, and Jeffrey Passel

1990   *Undocumented Migration to the United States: IRCA and the Experience of the 1980s*. Washington, D.C.: Urban Institute Press.

Bean, Frank D., Jennifer Van Hook, and Karen Woodrow-Lafield

2001   *Estimates of Numbers of Unauthorized Migrants Residing in the United States: The Total, Mexican, and Non-Mexican Central American Unauthorized Populations in Mid-2001*. Special Report, November. Washington, D.C.: Pew Hispanic Center.

Benson, Janet E.

1996a   The Effects of Packinghouse Work on Southeast Asian Refugee Families. In *Newcomers in the Workplace: Immigrants and the Restructuring of the U.S. Economy*, edited by Louise Lamphere, Alex Stepick, and Guillermo Grenier, pp. 99–126. Philadelphia: Temple University Press.

1996b   Garden City: Meatpacking and Immigration to the High Plains. Paper presented at the conference "Immigration and the Changing Face of Rural America: Focus on the Midwestern States," Ames, Iowa, July 11–12.

Bernstein, Jared, Chauna Brocht, and Maggie Spade-Aguilar

2000   *How Much Is Enough? Basic Family Budgets for Working Families*. Washington, D.C.: Economic Policy Institute.

Betancur, John J.

1996   The Settlement Experience of Latinos in Chicago: Segregation, Speculation, and the Ecology Model. *Social Forces* 74(4):1299–1325.

Binational Study on Migration (Project)

1997   *Binational Study: Migration between Mexico and the United States.* Washington, D.C.: Commission on Immigration Reform.

Bischoff, Laura A., and Dale Dempsey

2002   Egg Farm Comment Worries Groups; State Retreat Feared on Shutdown. *Dayton (Ohio) Daily News,* October 2.

Bloom, Stephen G.

2000   *Postville: A Clash of Cultures in Heartland America.* San Diego: Harcourt Trade Publishers.

Broadway, Michael J.

1991   Economic Development Programs in the Great Plains: The Example of Nebraska. *Great Plains Research* 1:324–344.

1995   From City to Countryside: Recent Changes in the Structure and Location of the Meat- and Fish-Processing Industries. In *Any Way You Cut It: Meat Processing and Small-Town America,* edited by Donald D. Stull, Michael J. Broadway, and David Griffith, pp. 17–40. Lawrence: University Press of Kansas.

Bureau of Labor Statistics

2001   The Consumer Price Index: March 2001. Washington, D.C.: Bureau of Labor Statistics. <www.stats.bls.gov/news.release/pdf/cpi .pdf>.

Burke, Sandra Charvat

2003   Destinations and Acceptance of Immigrants: Evidence from Two Surveys. Paper presented at annual meetings of the American Sociological Association, Chicago.

Burke, Sandra Charvat, and Willis J. Goudy

1999   Immigration and Community in Iowa: How Many Have Come and What is the Impact? Paper presented at annual meetings of the American Sociological Association, Chicago.

Business First of Columbus (Ohio)

2002   New State Rules Target Buckeye Egg Farm. August 19. <www .columbus.bizjournals.com/columbus/stories/2002/08/19/daily8 .html>. Accessed April 22, 2003.

Bustamante, Jorge A.

1973   The Historical Context of Undocumented Mexican Immigration to the United States. *Aztlán* 3:257–281.

1990   Undocumented Migration from Mexico to the United States: Preliminary Findings from the Zapata Canyon Project. In *Undocumented Migration to the United States: IRCA and the Experience of the 1980s,* edited by Frank D. Bean, Barry Edmonston, and Jeffrey Passel, pp. 211–226. Washington, D.C.: Urban Institute Press.

Bustamante, Jorge A., Guillermina Jasso, Edward J. Taylor, and Paz Trigueros
    1997   Characteristics of Migrants. In Binational Study on Migration (Project), *Binational Study: Migration between Mexico and the United States,* pp. 13–24. Washington, D.C.: Commission on Immigration Reform.

Bustamante, Jorge A., Clark W. Reynolds, and Raúl A. Hinojosa Ojeda, eds.
    1992   *U.S.-Mexico Relations: Labor Market Interdependence.* Stanford: Stanford University Press.

Camarota, Steven A.
    2001   Immigrants in the United States—2000: A Snapshot of America's Foreign-Born Population. Backgrounder. (January). Washington D.C.: Center for Immigration Studies. <www.cis.org/articles/2001/back101 .html>.

Cantú, Lionel
    1995   The Peripheralization of Rural America: A Case Study of Latino Migrants in America's Heartland. *Sociological Perspectives* 38(3):399–414.

Cardenas, Gilberto
    1976   Los Desarraigados: Chicanos in the Midwestern Region of the United States. *Aztlán* 7(2):153–186.

Catanzarite, Lisa, and Michael Bernabé Aguilera
    2002   Working with Co-Ethnics: Earnings Penalties for Latino Immigrants at Latino Jobsites. *Social Problems* 49(1):101–127.

Chapa, Jorge
    1988   The Question of Mexican American Assimilation: Socioeconomic Parity or Underclass Formation? *Public Affairs Comment* 35(1):1–14.
    1990   The Myth of Hispanic Progress. *Harvard Journal of Hispanic Policy* 4:3–18.
    1995   Mexican American Class Structure and Political Participation. *New England Journal of Public Policy* (spring/summer):183–198. <www.stats .bls.gov/news.release/pdf/cpi.pdf>.
    2000   Hispanic Population. In *Encyclopedia of the U.S. Census,* edited by Margo Andersen, pp. 241–243. Washington, D.C.: Congressional Quarterly Press.

Chavez, Leo R.
    1992   *Shadowed Lives: Undocumented Immigrants in American Society.* 1st ed. Orlando, Fla.: Harcourt Brace College.
    1997   *Shadowed Lives: Undocumented Immigrants in American Society.* 2d ed. Stamford, Conn.: Wadsworth, Thomson.

Cincinnati Enquirer
    2001   Buckeye Egg Cited as Air Polluter. Tristate A.M. Report, April 15. <www.enquirer.com>. Accessed April 23, 2003.

CNN.com
    2002   "Operation Tarmac" Airport Sweep Widens. April 24. <www.cnn.com/ 2002/TRAVEL/NEWS/04/24/airports.sweep>.

Cole, David

1998   Five Myths about Immigration. In *Race, Class, and Gender in the United States: An Integrated Study*. 4th ed., edited by Paula S. Rothenberg, pp. 12–14, 128. New York: St. Martin's Press.

Columbus Dispatch

1998   Buckeye Egg Farm Gets 4th President in 3 Years. Business Reporter, December 2. <www.dispatch.com>. Accessed April 22, 2003.

2002   State Crackdown. Editorial, April 23. <www.dispatch.com>. Accessed April 22, 2003.

Cornelius, Wayne A.

1998   The Structural Embeddedness of Demand for Mexican Immigrant Labor: New Evidence from California. In *Crossings: Mexican Immigration in Interdisciplinary Perspectives*, edited by M. Suárez-Orozco, pp. 114–144. Cambridge: Harvard University Press.

Cover, Susan M.

2000   Ulery Gives Up Plan for Migrant Housing; Proposal Creates Uproar in Limecrest. *Springfield (Ohio) News-Sun*, January 25, 1.

Cromartie, John, and William Kandel

2002   Did Residential Segregation in Rural America Increase with Recent Hispanic Population Growth? Paper presented at the annual meeting of the Population Association of America, Atlanta.

2003   Hispanic Growth and Dispersion in Rural America. *<srdc.msstate.edu/measuring/cromartie.pdf>*. Accessed July 8, 2004.

Cubría, José Luis

2002   Mexican Workers to Receive Settlement from U.S. Egg Company. *The News*, Mexico City, July 2, 2002. <www.thenews.Mexico.com>.

Donato, Katharine M., Jorge Durand, and Douglas S. Massey

1992   Stemming the Tide? Assessing the Deterrent Effects of the Immigration Reform and Control Act. *Demography* 29(2):3–42.

Dressler, William W.

1993   Health in the African-American Community: Accounting for Health Inequalities. *Medical Anthropology Quarterly* 7(4):325–345.

DUP (Department of Urban Planning)

1994   Community Patterns and Trends Summary: Ligonier. Muncie, Ind.: Department of Urban Planning, Ball State University.

Durand, Jorge, Emilio Parrado, and Douglas Massey

1996   Migradollars and Development: A Reconsideration of the Mexican Case. *International Migration Review* 30(2):423–444.

Economist

2003   Half an Enchilada. *The Economist*, January 23, 37–38.

Eggerstrom, Lee

1994   The New Co-ops. *Saint Paul Pioneer Press*, August 8, p. E-1.

Ehrenreich, Barbara

    2001   *Nickel and Dimed: On (Not) Getting By in America.* New York: Henry Holt.

Encyclopaedia Britannica

    2003   Mexico. <www.corporate.britannica.com>. Accessed April 30, 2003.

Eschbach, Kart, Jacqueline Hagan, Nestor Rodríguez, Rubén Hernández-León, and Stanley Bailey

    1999   Death at the Border. *International Migration Review* 33(2):430–454.

Espinosa, Kristin E., and Douglas S. Massey

    1997   Determinants of English Proficiency among Mexican Migrants to the United States. *International Migration Review* 31(1):28–50.

Feagin, Joe R.

    2000   *Racist America: Roots, Current Realities, and Future Reparations.* New York: Routledge.

Fink, Deborah

    1998   *Cutting into the Meatpacking Line: Workers and Change in the Rural Midwest.* Chapel Hill: University of North Carolina Press.

Fix, Michael, and Jeffrey S. Passel

    1994   Immigration and Immigrants: Setting the Record Straight. Washington, D.C.: Urban Institute. <www.urban.org/pubs/immig/setting>. Accessed March 11, 2003.

Flora, Cornelia B., and Jan Flora

    1999   Dealing with Reality: Community Response to the New Latino Presence in Central Iowa. Paper presented at the annual meetings of the American Sociological Association, Chicago.

Flores, Richard R.

    2002   *Remembering the Alamo: Memory, Modernity, and the Master Symbol.* Austin: University of Texas Press.

Foley, Neil

    1997   *The White Scourge: Mexicans, Blacks, and Poor Whites in Texas Cotton Culture.* Berkeley: University of California Press.

Frey, William, H.

    1987   Migration and Depopulation of the Metropolis: Regional Restructuring or Rural Renaissance? *American Sociological Review* 52:240–257.

Friedberger, Mark

    1989   *Shake-Out: Iowa Farm Families in the 1980s.* Lexington: University Press of Kentucky.

Fuguitt, Glen V.

    1995   Population Change in Nonmetropolitan America. In *The Changing American Countryside: Rural People and Places,* edited by Emery N. Castle, pp. 77–100. Lawrence: University Press of Kansas.

García, Juan R.

    1979   History of Chicanos in Chicago Heights. *Aztlán* 7(2):291–306.

1996   *Mexicans in the Midwest, 1900–1932.* Tucson: University of Arizona Press.

Garrett, Ottie A.

1996   *The Guidebook to Amish Communities across America and Business Directory.* Kalona, Iowa: Hitching Post Enterprises.

Gonzales, Manuel G., and Cynthia M. Gonzales, eds.

2000   *En Aquel Entonces: Readings in Mexican-American History.* Bloomington: Indiana University Press.

González, Juan L.

1993   *Racial and Ethnic Groups in America.* 2d ed. Dubuque, Iowa: Kendall-Hunt Publishing.

Goudy, Willis

2002   Population Change in the Midwest: Nonmetro Population Growth Lags Metro Increase. *Rural America* 17(2). <www.ers.usda.gov/publications/ruralamerica>. Accessed September 16, 2002.

Gould, Stephen Jay

1981   *The Mismeasure of Man.* New York: W. W. Norton.

Gouveia, Lourdes, and Rogelio Saenz

1999   Latino/a Immigrants and New Social Formations in the Great Plains: An Assessment of Population Growth and Multiple Impacts. Paper presented at the annual meeting of the American Sociological Association, Chicago.

Gouveia, Lourdes, Thomas W. Sanchez, and Rogelio Saenz

2001   From Arrival to Processes of Incorporation: Latinos "Sembrando Raíces" in Nebraska Agricultural Communities. Paper presented at annual meetings of the Midwestern Sociological Society, St. Louis, Mo.

Gouveia, Lourdes, and Donald D. Stull

1995   Dances with Cows: Beefpacking's Impact on Garden City, Kansas, and Lexington, Nebraska. In *Any Way You Cut It: Meat Processing and Small-Town America,* edited by Donald D. Stull, Michael J. Broadway, and David Griffith. Lawrence: University Press of Kansas.

1997   *Latino Immigrants, Meatpacking, and Rural Communities: A Case Study of Lexington, Nebraska.* JSRI Research Report no. 26, Julian Samora Research Institute, Michigan State University, East Lansing.

Greater Des Moines Community Foundation

2000   *Snapshot in Time: A Clear View of the Importance, Value and Impacts of the Latino Population in Central Iowa.* Des Moines: State Public Policy Group.

Green, Gary Paul, Leann M. Tigges, and Daniel Diaz

1999   Racial and Ethnic Differences in Job Search Strategies in Atlanta, Boston, and Los Angeles. *Social Science Quarterly* 80(2):263–278.

Green, Susan

1994   *Del Valle a Willmar: Settling Out of the Migrant Stream in a Rural Min-*

nesota Community. Working Paper no. 19, Julian Samora Research Institute, Michigan State University, East Lansing.

Grey, Mark

  1995   Pork, Poultry, and Newcomers in Storm Lake, Iowa. In *Any Way You Cut It: Meat Processing and Small-Town America,* edited by Donald D. Stull, Michael J. Broadway, and David Griffith, pp. 109–128. Lawrence: University Press of Kansas.

  2001   Welcoming New Iowans: A Guide for Citizens and Communities. Building Respect and Tolerance. University of Northern Iowa. <www.bcs.uni.edu/idm/newiowans/PDFDocument/WelcomeNew Iowans.pdf>.

Griffith, David

  1995   New Immigrants in an Old Industry: Blue Crab Processing in Pamlico County, North Carolina. In *Any Way You Cut It: Meat Processing and Small-Town America,* edited by Donald D. Stull, Michael J. Broadway, and David Griffith, pp. 153–186. Lawrence: University Press of Kansas.

Griswold del Castillo, Richard, and Arnoldo De León

  1996   *North to Aztlán: A History of Mexican Americans in the United States.* New York: Twayne.

Gutiérrez, David G.

  1995   *Walls and Mirrors: Mexican Americans, Mexican Immigrants, and the Politics of Ethnicity.* Berkeley: University of California Press.

Guzmán, Betsy

  2001   *The Hispanic Population.* Census 2000 Brief. May. Washington, D.C.: U.S. Census Bureau. <www.census.gov/prod/2001pubs>. Accessed September 17, 2002.

Guzmán, Betsy, and Eileen Diaz McConnell

  2002   The Hispanic Population: 1990–2000 Growth and Change. *Population Research and Policy Review* 21(1–2):109–128.

Hackenberg, Robert A., and Gary Kukulka

  1995   Industries, Immigrants, and Illness in the New Midwest. In *Any Way You Cut It: Meat Processing and Small-Town America,* edited by Donald D. Stull, Michael J. Broadway, and David Griffith, pp. 187–211. Lawrence: University Press of Kansas.

Hamilton, Ruth Simms

  1989   *Creating a Paradigm and Research Agenda for Comparative Studies in the Worldwide Dispersion of African Peoples.* Monograph no. 1, African Diaspora Research Project. East Lansing: Urban Affairs Programs, Michigan State University.

Harrison, Faye V.

  1994   Racial and Gender Inequalities in Health and Health Care. *Medical Anthropology Quarterly* 8(1):90–105.

Haughney, Christine

2000   Assault on Mexicans Shakes Long Island Town. *Washington Post,* November 28, p. A3.

Hayes-Bautista, David, Werner Schink, and Jorge Chapa

1988   *The Burden of Support.* Stanford: Stanford University Press.

Healy, Patrick

1995   Studying Latinos in the Midwest. *Chronicle of Higher Education* 42(3): A7.

Heiderson, Mazin A., and Edgar R. Leon

1996   *Patterns and Trends in Michigan Migrant Education.* JSRI Statistical Brief no. 8, Julian Samora Research Institute, Michigan State University, East Lansing.

Hendee, David

1997   Population Changes Worry Rural Residents: The Latest Rural Nebraska Poll Gauges Attitudes about Communities. *Omaha World-Herald,* September 4.

Hernández-León, Rubén, and Víctor Zúñiga

2000   Making Carpet by the Mile: The Emergence of a Mexican Immigrant Community in an Industrial Region of the U.S. Historic South. *Social Science Quarterly* 81(1):49–66.

Hine, Darlene

1989   *Black Women in White: Racial Conflict and Cooperation in the Nursing Profession, 1980–1950.* Bloomington: Indiana University Press.

hooks, bell

2002   Discussant on Barriers in Women's Studies. Women's Studies Program, Michigan State University, East Lansing, Mich., March 29.

Hostetler, John A.

1993   *Amish Society.* 4th ed. Baltimore: Johns Hopkins University Press.

Huang, Tzu-Ling, and Peter F. Orazem

1996   An Analysis of the Causes and Consequences of Immigrant Population Growth in the Nonmetropolitan Midwest and South-central States, 1950–1990. Staff papers. Department of Economics, Iowa State University, Ames.

Huffman, Wallace, and John A. Miranowski

1996   Immigration, Meat Packing, and Trade: Implications for Iowa. Staff papers. Department of Economics, Iowa State University, Ames.

INS (Immigration and Naturalization Service)

2001a   Act of May 28, 1924 (43 *U.S. Statutes at Large* 240). <www.ins.usdoj.gov/graphics/aboutins/statistics/legishist/471.htm>.

2001b   INS Implements Section 245(i) Provision of the LIFE Act. News release, March 23, 2001. <www.ins.usdoj.gov/graphics/publicaffairs/newsrels/life245irel.htm>.

2002   *2000 Statistical Yearbook of the Immigration and Naturalization Ser-*

vice. Washington, D.C.: U.S. Immigration and Naturalization Service. <www.ins.gov/graphics/aboutins/statistics/00yrbk_ENF_Rev/ENF 2000Excl/Table60.xls>.

Johnson, James H., Karen D. Johnson-Webb, and Walter C. Farrell

1999   Newly Emerging Hispanic Communities in the United States: A Spatial Analysis of Settlement Patterns, Migration Fields, and Social Receptivity. In *Immigration and Opportunity: Race, Ethnicity, and Employment in the United States,* edited by Frank D. Bean and Stephanie Bell-Rose, pp. 263–310. New York: Russell Sage Foundation.

Kandel, William, and John Cromartie

2003   Hispanics Find a Home in Rural America. *Amber Waves: The Economics of Food, Farming, Natural Resources, and Rural America* (U.S. Department of Agriculture, Economic Research Service) 1, no. 1. <www.ers .usda.gov/AmberWaves/Feb03>. Accessed April 4, 2003.

Kerr, Louise Año Nuevo

2000   Chicano Settlements in Chicago. In *En Aquel Entonces: Readings in Mexican-American History,* edited by Manuel G. Gonzales and Cynthia M. Gonzales, pp. 109–116. Bloomington: Indiana University Press.

Knodel, John, Werasit Sittitrai, and Tim Brown

1990   *Focus Group Discussions for Social Science Research: A Practical Guide with an Emphasis in the Topic of Aging.* Research Report no. 90-3. Population Studies Center, University of Michigan, Ann Arbor.

Kobell, Rona

2002   Lawyer Questions Arrests at BWI; Critics Say Criminal Pasts Should Have Been Caught Earlier, Working Poor Hurt. *Baltimore Sun,* April 25, 2002, final local edition, p. 1B.

Kossek, Ellen Ernst, and Susan C. Zonia

1993   Assessing Diversity Climate: A Field Study of Reactions to Employer Efforts to Promote Diversity. *Journal of Organizational Behavior* 14:61–81.

Krantz, Colleen, and Frank Santiago

2000   Minority Enrollments Double in Iowa Schools since 1985. *Des Moines Register,* November 29.

Kuthy, Maria de Lourdes, and Gloria Delany-Barmann

2000   Comunidad y Escuela: Community Change and Educational Challenges in a Rural Illinois Town. Paper presented at a joint conference of the National Association of Hispanic and Latino Studies, National Association of African American Studies, National Association of Native American Studies, and International Association of Asian Studies, Houston, Texas, February 21–26.

Leiken, Robert S.

2002   Enchilada Lite: A Post-9/11 Mexican Migration Agreement. Washington, D.C.: Center for Immigration Studies, March 2002. <http://www.cis .org/articles/2002>. Accessed March 11, 2004.

León, Luis D.

1998   Born Again in East Los Angeles: The Congregation as Border Space. In *Gatherings in Diaspora: Religious Communities and the New Immigration,* edited by R. S. Warner and E. Wittner, pp. 163–196. Philadelphia: Temple University Press.

Leslie, Charles

1990   Scientific Racism: Reflections on Peer Review, Science, and Ideology. *Social Science and Medicine* 31(8):891–912.

Ligonier (Indiana) Advance Leader, January 1, 1990–December 31, 2000.

Littlefield, Alice, Leonard Lieberman, and Larry T. Reynolds

1982   Redefining Race: The Potential Demise of a Concept in Physical Anthropology. *Current Anthropology* 23(6):641–655.

Ludington (Michigan) Daily News. March 1, 1981–October 31, 1981; February 1, 1982–June 30, 1982; January 1, 1983–September 30, 1983.

Ludlow, Randy

1998   Neighbors Battle Egg Farm. *Cincinnati Post,* August 11. <www.cincypost.com>. Accessed April 22, 2003.

MacGregor-Mendoza, Patricia

1999   *Spanish and Academic Achievement among Midwest Mexican Youth: The Myth of the Barrier.* New York: Garland Publishing.

Marbella, Jean

2001   Diversity: Longtime Residents of Tiny Postville and Their New Jewish and Immigrant Neighbors Come to Grips on How to Come Together. *Baltimore Sun,* July 10, 2001. <www.baltimoresun.com>. Accessed July 10, 2001.

Martin, Philip

1995   Proposition 187 in California. *International Migration Review* 29(1):255–263.

1996   *Promises to Keep: Collective Bargaining in California Agriculture.* Ames: Iowa State University Press. <www.agecon.ucdavis.edu/Faculty/Phil.M/promises/promises1.htm>.

1997   Immigration and the Changing Face of Rural America. Paper presented at the 1997 National Public Policy Education Conference. <www.farmfoundation.org/pubs/increas/97/martin.pdf>. Accessed September 17, 2002.

Martin, Philip, J. Edward Taylor, and Michael Fix

1996   *Immigration and the Changing Face of Rural America: Focus on the Midwestern States.* JSRI Occasional Paper no. 21, Julian Samora Research Institute, Michigan State University, East Lansing.

Massey, Douglas S.

1998   March of Folly: U.S. Immigration Policy after NAFTA. *American Prospect* 37(March–April):22–33.

Massey, Douglas S., Rafael Alarcón, Jorge Durand, and Humberto González
   1987   *Return to Aztlán: The Social Process of International Migration from Western Mexico.* Berkeley: University of California Press.
Massey, Douglas S., Jorge Durand, and Nolan J. Malone
   2002   *Beyond Smoke and Mirrors: Mexican Immigration in an Era of Economic Integration.* New York: Russell Sage.
Massey, Douglas S., and Kristin E. Espinosa
   1997   What's Driving Mexico-U.S. Migration? A Theoretical, Empirical, and Policy Analysis. *American Journal of Sociology* 102(4):939–1000.
Masud-Piloto, Felix Roberto
   1996   *From Welcomed Exiles to Illegal Immigrants: Cuban Migration to the U.S., 1959–1995.* Lanham, Md.: Rowman and Littlefield Publishers.
McCarthy, John
   2002   State Will Propose Revoking Buckeye Egg's Permits. WKYC, Columbus, Ohio, April 22. <www.wkyc.com> Accessed April 22, 2003.
McIntosh, Peggy
   1992   White Privilege and Male Privilege: A Personal Account of Coming to See Correspondences through Work in Women's Studies. In *Race, Class, and Gender,* edited by Margaret L. Anderson and Patricia Hill Collins, pp. 70–81. Belmont, Calif.: Wadsworth.
MCSSA (Michigan Commission on Spanish Speaking Affairs)
   1995   *Michigan's Hispanic Community: A Profile.* Lansing, Mich.: Department of Civil Rights, State of Michigan.
Menchaca, Martha
   1995   *The Mexican Outsiders: A Community History of Marginalization and Discrimination in California.* Austin: University of Texas Press.
Migration News
   2000   INS: Border, Detention. *Migration News* 7(1). <www.migration.ucdavis.edu/mn/jan2000mn>. Accessed May 24, 2003.
Millard, Ann V.
   1994a   A Causal Model of High Rates of Child Mortality. *Social Science and Medicine* 38(2):253–268.
   1994b   Furor in the Academy: Diversity, Cultural Relativism, and Institutional Discrimination. *Graduate Post* (Michigan State University) 2(1):10–13.
Millard, Ann V., and E. A. Berlin
   1984   Sex Ratio and Natural Selection at the Human ABO Locus. *Human Heredity* 33:130–136.
Mines, Richard, and Douglas S. Massey
   1985   Patterns of Migration to the United States from Two Mexican Communities. *Latin American Research Review* 20:104–124.
MSNBC
   2002   Neighbors Await Fate of Ohio Egg Farm. MSNBC, New York, July 24. <www.stacks.msnbc.com>. Accessed April 22, 2003.

Murdock, George P., Clellan S. Ford, Alfred E. Hudson, Raymond Kennedy, Leo W. Simmons, and John W. M. Whiting

1987   *Outline of Cultural Materials.* 5th ed. New Haven, Conn.: Human Relations Area Files.

Muskegon (Michigan) Chronicle, March 1, 1981–October 31, 1981; February 1, 1982–June 30, 1982; January 1, 1983–September 30, 1983.

1981   Shelby Farmers Oppose "Chapita Hills." August 18.

1983   Shelby Complex Is Still Vacant. By Willa Kenoyer, August 2.

1983   Chapita Hills Water Bill to Be Paid in Full Today. By Pam Lucas, September 6.

Naples, Nancy A.

1994   Contradictions in Agrarian Ideology: Restructuring Gender, Race-Ethnicity, and Class. *Rural Sociology* 59(1):110–135.

2000   Economic Restructuring and Racialization: Incorporation of Mexicans and Mexican-Americans in the Rural Midwest. Working Paper 7, Center for Comparative Immigration Studies, University of California–San Diego. <www.ccis-ucsd.org/PUBLICATIONS/wrkg7.pdf>.

National Employment Law Project

2001   <www.nelp.org>. Accessed July 27, 2001.

Nord, Mark

2003   Does it Cost Less to Live in Rural Areas? Evidence from New Data on Food Security and Hunger. *Rural Sociology* 65(1).

Oceana County (Michigan) News, March 1, 1981–December 31, 1981; February 1, 1982–June 30, 1982; January 1, 1983–September 30, 1983.

1981   Letter to the editor. By Congressman Guy Vander Jagt, with copy of letters to the congressman by Dwight O. Calhoun (acting administrator, Farmers Home Administration) and Philip Roberts (state director, USDA). May 6.

Oceana (Michigan) Herald Journal, March 1, 1981–December 31, 1981; February 1, 1982–June 30, 1982; January 1, 1983–September 30, 1983.

1981   Letter to the editor. By William Field, March 5.

1981   Letter to the editor. By Grover Merrill, March 12.

1981   Low Income Housing for Migrant Workers Held Up. March 17.

1981   Chapita Hills Foes Fall Back to Zoning as Lone Defense. By Greg Means, April 9.

1981   Letter to the editor. By Phillip Roberts, May 6.

1981   Building Permit Application Expected for Chapita Hills. By Greg Means, October 15.

1982   FmHA Suspends Chapita Loan. March 25.

1982   Judge Gives Chapita Hills Final Green Light. June 21.

1983   Chapita Hills Ready Soon for Occupancy. January 27.

Omi, Michael, and Howard Winant

1986   *Racial Formation in the United States: From the 1960s to the 1980s.* 1st ed. New York: Routledge.

1994   *Racial Formation in the United States: From the 1960s to the 1990s.* 2d ed. New York: Routledge.

Page, Helán, and R. Brooke Thomas

1994   White Public Space and the Construction of White Privilege in U.S. Health Care: Fresh Concepts and a New Model of Analysis. *Medical Anthropology Quarterly* 8(1):109–115.

Passel, Jeffrey S., and Karen A. Woodrow

1987   Change in the Undocumented Alien Population in the United States, 1979–1983. *International Migration Review* 21:1304–1323.

Peck, Vivienne

2001   Logansport Works with Community Leaders, Employers to Accommodate Hispanic Workers. *Actionlines* (published by Indiana Association of Cities and Towns), February, pp. 10–12.

Poultry Times (Columbus, Ohio)

2002   Consultants to Oversee Buckeye Egg Farms. June 24. <www.poultry andeggnews.com>. Accessed April 22, 2003.

Poyo, Gerald E., and Mariano Díaz-Miranda

1994   Cubans in the United States. In *History,* edited by Alfredo Jimenez, pp. 315–345, vol. 2 of *Handbook of Hispanic Cultures in the United States,* edited by Nicolás Kanellos and Claudio Esteva-Fabregat. Houston: Arte Público Press.

Puente, Teresa

2000   Hispanics Alter Demographics in the Heartland. *Chicago Tribune,* January 16, p. 3.

Quinn, Mike

2001   The Changing Face of Tomorrow's Hoosiers. *Actionlines* (published by Indiana Association of Cities and Towns), February, p. 9.

Rauschning, Hermann

1940   *The Voice of Destruction.* New York: G. P. Putnam's.

RMN (Rural Migration News)

2000   Vanguard and Meat Packing. Vol. 6, no. 4 (October). <www.migration .ucdavis.edu/rmn>. Accessed May 14, 2003.

2001   Northeast, Midwest. Vol. 7, no. 1 (January). <www.migration.ucdavis .edu/rmn>. Accessed April 22, 2003.

Robinson, Gregory

2001   ESCAP II (Executive Steering Committee for A.C.E. Policy II): Demographic Analysis Results. Report no. 1, October 13. Washington D.C.: U.S. Bureau of the Census. <www.census.gov/dmd/www/pdf/ Report1.pdf>.

Rochín, Refugio I.

1995   Rural Latinos: Evolving Conditions and Issues. In *The Changing American Countryside: Rural People and Places,* edited by Emery N. Castle, pp. 286–302. Lawrence: University Press of Kansas.

Rochín, Refugio I., and Rogelio Saenz

1996 *Latinos in the Rural Midwest: Community Development Implications.* Research proposal, Julian Samora Research Institute, Michigan State University, East Lansing.

Rochín, Refugio I., Anne M. Santiago, and Karla S. Dickey

1989 *Migrant Workers and Seasonal Workers in Michigan's Agriculture: A Study of Their Contributions, Characteristics, Needs, and Services.* JSRI Research Report no. 1, Julian Samora Research Institute, Michigan State University, East Lansing.

Rodriguez, Clara

2001 *Changing Race.* New York: New York University Press.

Rosenbaum, René Pérez

1997 *Migration and Integration of Latinos into Rural Midwestern Communities: The Case of "Mexicans" in Adrian, Michigan.* JSRI Research Report no. 19, Julian Samora Research Institute, Michigan State University, East Lansing.

Ruiz, Vicki L.

1987 *Cannery Women, Cannery Lives: Mexican Women, Unionization, and the California Food Processing Industry, 1937–1950.* Albuquerque: University of New Mexico Press.

1998 *From Out of the Shadows: Mexican Women in Twentieth-Century America.* New York: Oxford University Press.

Rumbaut, Rubén

1996 Immigrants from Latin America and the Caribbean: A Socioeconomic Profile. In *Immigration and Ethnic Communities: A Focus on Latinos,* edited by R. Rochín, pp. 1–9. East Lansing, Mich.: Julian Samora Research Institute, Michigan State University.

Russell, Karen K.

1992 Growing Up with Privilege and Prejudice. In *Race, Class, and Gender,* edited by Margaret L. Anderson and Patricia Hill Collins, pp. 82–87. Belmont, Calif.: Wadsworth.

Saenz, Rogelio

1994 *Latino Poverty in the Midwest: A County-Level Analysis.* JSRI Research Report no. 9, Julian Samora Research Institute, Michigan State University, East Lansing.

Saenz, Rogelio, and Cynthia M. Cready

1996 The Southwest-Midwest Mexican American Migration Flows, 1985–1990. Paper presented at the annual meeting of the Rural Sociological Society, Des Moines, Iowa.

Salgado de Snyder, V. N., M. J. Díaz-Pérez, A. Acevedo, and L. Natera

1996 Dios y el Norte: The Perceptions of Wives of Documented and Undocumented Mexican Immigrants to the United States. *Hispanic Journal of Behavioral Sciences* 18(3):283–296.

Santiago, Anne M.

1990   *Life in the Industrial Heartland: A Profile of Latinos in the Midwest.* JSRI Research Report no. 2, Julian Samora Research Institute, Michigan State University, East Lansing.

Sassen, Saskia

1990   *The Global City.* Princeton, N.J.: Princeton University Press.

Sauer, Norman J.

1992   Forensic Anthropology and the Concept of Race: If Races Don't Exist, Why Are Forensic Anthropologists So Good at Identifying Them? *Social Science and Medicine* 34(2):107–111.

Schweitzer, John H.

1993   *Graduate Admissions at MSU: An Affirmative Action Investigation.* Report, Urban Affairs Programs, Michigan State University, East Lansing.

Shanklin, Eugenia

1994   *Anthropology and Race.* Belmont, Calif.: Wadsworth.

Shapiro, Samuel

1996   Hispanics. In *Peopling Indiana: The Ethnic Experience,* edited by Robert M. Taylor Jr. and Connie A. McBirney, pp. 315–340. Indianapolis: Indiana Historical Society.

Sharp, Deborah

2002   Immigrants Encounter Red Lights at State DMVs. *USA Today,* news, final ed., p. 7A, May 10.

Sharp, Tom

2002   House Passes Changes to Driver's License Law. *Chattanooga Times/ Chattanooga Free Press,* metro sec., p. B7, May 31.

Skerry, Peter

2001   Why Amnesty Is the Wrong Way to Go. *Washington Post,* p. B10, Aug. 12.

Souhrada, Paul

2000   Clock Running Out on Trapped Hens. *Columbus Dispatch,* September 28. <www.news.uns.purdue.edu>. Accessed April 22, 2003.

Stanley, Kathleen

1992   Immigrant and Refugee Workers in the Midwestern Meatpacking Industry: Industrial Restructuring and the Transformation of Rural Labor Markets. *Policy Studies Review* 11(2):106–117.

Steele, Shelby

1990   *The Content of Our Character.* New York: St. Martin's Press.

Stull, Donald, and Michael Broadway

1995   Killing Them Softly: Work in Meatpacking Plants and What It Does to Workers. In *Any Way You Cut It: Meat Processing and Small-Town America,* edited by Donald D. Stull, Michael J. Broadway, and David Griffith, pp. 61–84. Lawrence: University Press of Kansas.

Stull, Donald D., Michael J. Broadway, and Ken C. Erickson

1992   The Price of a Good Steak: Beefpacking and Its Consequences for Garden City, Kansas. In *Structuring Diversity: Ethnographic Perspectives on the New Immigration,* edited by Louise Lamphere, pp. 35–64. Chicago: University of Chicago Press.

Stull, Donald D., Michael J. Broadway, and David Griffith, eds.

1995   *Any Way You Cut It: Meat Processing and Small-Town America.* Lawrence: University Press of Kansas.

Sullivan, Kathleen

2000   Iglesia de Dios: An Extended Family. In *Religion and the New Immigrants: Continuities and Adaptations in Immigrant Congregations,* edited by H. Ebaugh and J. Chafetz, pp. 141–152. Walnut Creek, Calif.: AltaMira Press.

Suro, Roberto

1999   *Strangers among Us: Latino Lives in a Changing America.* New York: Vintage Books.

Templo Betel, Cuerpo Ejecutivo

1996   *Templo Betel Libro Histórico, 1971–1996.* Ligonier, Ind.: Templo Betel, Assemblies of God.

Therrien, Melissa, and Roberto Ramirez

2001   *Hispanic Population in the United States: 2000.* U.S. Census Bureau, Ethnic and Hispanic Statistics Branch, Population Division. <www.census.gov/population/socdemo/hispanic/p20-535/tab08-1.txt>.

Tichenor, Daniel J.

2002   *Dividing Lines: The Politics of Immigration Control in America.* Princeton, N.J.: Princeton University Press.

Times Leader (Hazelton, Pennsylvania)

2002   Judge Orders Egg Farm to Close. July 2. <www.dfw.com>. Accessed April 22, 2003.

UPI (United Press International)

2002   Millions of Mexican Illegal Aliens Endanger U.S. Security. NewsMax.comWires,August 7.<www.newsmax.com/archives/articles/2002/8/6/143102.shtml>.

U.S. Census Bureau

1998   *Rust Belt Rebounds.* Census Brief. CENBR/98-7, December.

2000   *Annual Demographic Survey (March CPS Supplement) 2000.* [Machine-readable data files] prepared by the U.S. Census Bureau. <www.bls.census.gov/cps/ads/2000/sdata.htm>.

2001a   *Census 2000 Redistricting Data (Public Law 94-171) Summary File.* [Machine-readable data files] prepared by the U.S. Census Bureau.

2001b   *Census 2000 Redistricting Data (Public Law 94-171) Summary File.* Technical documentation prepared by the U.S. Census Bureau.

2001c   *Census 2000 Supplementary Survey (C2SS)—United States.* Tabulation from American Factfinder. <www.factfinder.census.gov/home/en/ c2ss.html>. Accessed February 11, 2004.

2001d Table 4: Difference in Population by Race and Hispanic or Latino Origin: 1990–2000, at the Census Redistricting web site. <www .census.gov/clo/www/redistricting.html>.

2002 *Census 2000 Summary File 3—United States.* Tabulation from American Factfinder. <www.factfinder.census.gov>. Accessed December 12, 2003.

2003 *Glossary: Definitions and Explanations of Terms—Decennial Census Terms.* <www.census.gov/main/www/glossary.html>. Accessed February 10, 2004.

USCIS (United States Citizenship and Immigration Services)

2003 Estimates of the Unauthorized Immigrant Population Residing in the United States: 1990–2000. Washington, D.C.: Office of Policy and Planning, USCIS, Bureau of the U.S. Dept. of Homeland Security. Released January 1, 2003. <www.uscis.gov/graphics/shared/aboutus/ statistics/Ill_Report_1211.pdf>. Accessed December 11, 2003.

U.S. Commission on Agricultural Workers

1992 *Report of the Commission on Agricultural Workers.* Washington, D.C.: U.S. Government Printing Office.

U.S. Department of Agriculture, Economic Research Service

2002 Nonmetro Jobs by Industry, 1990–1997. <www.ers.usda.gov/Briefing/ rural/Gallery/indusemp.htm>. Accessed September 16, 2002.

U.S. Department of Labor

2002 Application of U.S. Labor Laws to Immigrant Workers: Effect of Hoffman Plastics Decision on Laws Enforced by the Wage and Hour Division. Fact Sheet 48. Washington, D.C.: Employment Standards Administration Wage and Hour Division. <www.dol.gov/esa/regs/ compliance/whd/whdfs48.htm>.

Valdés, Dennis (Dionicio) Nodín

1991 *Al Norte: Agricultural Workers in the Great Lakes Region, 1917–1970.* Austin: University of Texas Press.

1992 *Divergent Roots, Common Destinies? Latino Work and Settlement in Michigan.* JSRI Occasional Paper no. 4, Julian Samora Research Institute, Michigan State University, East Lansing.

2000a *Barrios Norteños: St. Paul and Midwestern Mexican Communities in the Twentieth Century.* Austin: University of Texas Press.

2000b Region, Nation, and World-System: Perspectives on Midwestern Chicana/o History. In *Voices of a New Chicana/o History,* edited by Refugio I. Rochín and Dennis N. Valdés, pp. 115–140. East Lansing: Michigan State University Press.

Vargas, Zaragosa

1993 *Proletarians of the North: A History of Mexican Industrial Workers in*

Detroit and the Midwest, 1917–1933. Berkeley: University of California Press.

Wells, Miriam J.
1996   *Strawberry Fields: Politics, Class, and Work in California Agriculture.* Ithaca, N.Y.: Cornell University Press.

Wherritt, Irene, and Nora González
1989   Spanish Language Maintenance in a Small Iowa Community. *International Journal of the Sociology of Language* 79:29–39.

Wilson, Tamar Diana
2000   Anti-Immigrant Sentiment and the Problem of Reproduction/Maintenance in Mexican Immigration to the United States. *Critique of Anthropology* 20(2):191–213.

WKYC
2002   State Will Propose Revoking Buckeye Egg's Permits. WKYC Radio, Columbus, Ohio, April 22. <www.wkyc.com>. Accessed April 22, 2003.

Zavella, Patricia
1987   *Women's Work and Chicano Families: Cannery Workers of the Santa Clara Valley.* Ithaca, N.Y.: Cornell University Press.

Zoellner, Tom
2001   Mexico Says Legalize Crossovers or No Deal. *(Phoenix) Arizona Republic,* June 22. <www.azcentral.com/arizonarepublic>.

Index

Ball State University, 208
Banks: and discrimination, 112; Latino
    clientele of, 84; and Latino newcomers,
    197; loans, 88, 92, 118, 122, 123, 146, 147
Barbee, Evelyn L., 110
Bean, Frank D., 35, 55, 240n.3
Benson, Janet E., 39, 48, 50, 51, 52, 53
Bernstein, Jared, 91
Berryville, Michigan, 179, 182
Betancur, John J., 34
Bilingual individuals: and education, 165;
    and higher-level positions, 37, 90, 128;
    and racism, 134; and religion, 185; and
    social service workers, 93
Bilingual services: and education, 51, 53,
    116, 120, 147, 152–153, 191–192, 210,
    213; and medical services, 11, 53, 93, 147,
    210, 211; and religion, 12, 170, 174, 177,
    189; and social services, 12, 21, 92–93,
    114, 116, 117, 210, 211
Binational Study, 34, 35, 38, 105
Births, 47
Bischoff, Laura A., 16
Bloom, Stephen G., 77
Border enforcement, 57, 218, 219
Border Patrol, U.S., 57, 218, 239n.4
Bracero Program, 23, 32–33, 56
Broadway, Michael J., 14, 35, 36, 37, 39, 50,
    53, 105
Bureau of Labor Statistics, 37, 240n.10
Burillo, Catalina, 41, 44, 223, 224, 225
Burke, Sandra Charvat, 25, 26, 39, 53, 104
Bush, George W., 217–218
Businesses: and Anglo/Latino separa-
    tion, 87–92, 109, 122; and community
    problem solving, 210; of Latinos, 30, 31,
    40, 52, 84, 85, 88–89, 118, 122, 146,
    147, 204; and politics, 203. See also
    Restaurants; Stores
Business First of Columbus (Ohio), 17
Bustamante, Jorge A., 32, 34, 38, 49
Butterfield, Tara L., 39

California: Latinos migrating to rural
    Midwest from, 22, 37–38, 49, 84; and
    Proposition 187, 11, 37, 38, 39; and
    racism, 113; and rural Latino popula-

tion, 48, 62, 68, 72, 145; rural Midwest
    compared to, 10–11, 145
Camarota, Steven A., 27
Canneries, 33
Cantú, Lionel, 50
Cardenas, Gilberto, 27
Castañeda, Jorge, 218
Catanzarite, Lisa, 57
Catholic churches, 30, 87, 169–171, 172,
    174–180, 184, 191, 194
Cedar Rapids, Iowa, 48
Census 2000 Supplementary Survey
    (C2SS), 54
Central Americans, 57
Chapa, Jorge, 10, 16, 20, 62, 82, 146, 223,
    224, 242n.2
Chavez, Fred, 149, 150, 151, 154, 157
Chavez, Leo R., 25, 34, 217
Chicago, Illinois, 26, 30, 86, 125
Children: bilingual abilities of, 11–12, 18,
    148; and child care, 14, 36; immuniza-
    tion of, 51; and religion, 179, 186–188,
    193; role as interpreter, 11–12, 74, 93,
    116, 140
Churches. See Religion
Churubusco, Indiana, 107
Ciderville, Michigan, 175–177, 195
Cincinnati Enquirer, 16, 17
Cinco de Mayo, 155, 157, 158, 174, 211
Civic organizations, 31, 40, 115–116
Civil rights legislation, 112
Class. See Social class
Cleveland, Ohio, 26
Clinics: Anglo attitudes toward, 120, 121,
    122, 137; and definition of migrant
    farmworkers, 118; demand for, 105, 147;
    and interpreters, 11, 92, 93, 117. See also
    Medical services
CNN.com, 218
Cole, David, 24
Columbus, Ohio, 15–16
Columbus Dispatch, 16
Columbus Junction, Iowa, 47
Community studies: and confidential-
    ity, 224–225; data analysis, 230–232;
    interview guide for, 233–236; researcher
    qualifications, 225–226; sampling and

limitations of data, 229–230; selection of communities, 222–224; semistructured interviews and focus groups, 226–229

Congregations. *See* Religion

Consumer price index, 37, 240n.10

Cornelius, Wayne A., 58

Cover, Susan M., 46

Crane, Ken R., 76, 77, 78, 82, 84, 99, 151, 157, 174, 175, 183, 204, 222, 223, 224, 225, 226, 227, 230

Cready, Cynthia M., 33, 49

Crime prevention, 51

Crime rates, 104

Cromartie, John, 26

Cubans, 33, 49, 239n.6

Cubria, Jose Luis, 239n.1

Current Population Survey (CPS), 69

Delany-Barmann, Gloria, 14

De León, Arnoldo, 32, 33, 239n.1

Demography: consequences of rapid change, 48–53; and employment, 68–71, 72, 216; and Latino migration to rural Midwest, 1, 9–12, 58, 62–68, 73; and Latino newcomers, 105; of Latino population growth, 58–62; and public policy, 215–216; and religion, 52–53, 194

Dempsey, Dale, 16

Detroit, Michigan, 10, 26, 30, 31, 80

Dickey, Karla S., 239n.6

Discrimination: and Anglos' control of resources, 109; churches' involvement in, 194; definition of, 109–110; and economics, 31, 40; and education, 110, 162, 192, 214; forms of, 102; institutional, 102, 104, 110, 114, 115, 116–117, 124, 210, 231; and Latino newcomers, 21, 40, 123, 212; and Latino old-timers vs. newcomers, 123; Latinos' attitudes toward, 146; and politics, 110, 203; prevalence of, 12, 21, 81; progress against, 13; and refugees, 52; and Spanish language, 93; and subtle racism, 113; theoretical aspects of, 109–123; and U.S. acquisition of Texas, 28. *See also* Racism

Doctors: Latino interaction with, 104; Latino physicians, 18; and ratio of physicians to population, 53; and Spanish language knowledge, 53, 92. *See also* Medical services

Donato, Katharine M., 35

Dressler, William W., 107

Driver's licenses, 39, 55, 99

DUP (Department of Urban Planning), 80, 208

Durand, Jorge, 56

East Chicago, Indiana, 30, 31

Eastern European immigrants, 29

Economic Policy Institute, 110

Economics: and Anglo/Latino separation, 87–92, 148; Anglos' attitudes toward, 139, 142–145; and demographic changes, 48–49, 72–73, 216; and discrimination, 31, 32; and farming, 47, 50, 126, 144–145; and immigration, 57, 58; and Latino migration to rural Midwest, 23, 34, 83, 145–148; and Latino newcomers, 105, 181, 212; and Ligonier, 77; and low unemployment rates, 36; of Mexico, 56, 84; and public policy, 146–147, 221; and racism, 115, 116; rural economic change, 47–52, 69, 72–73; and standards of living, 14–18, 37, 39

Education: Anglo attitudes toward, 120; and Anglo/Latino separation, 5, 160–161; Anglo students' experiences of, 158–161; and bilingual services, 51, 53, 116, 120, 147, 152–153, 191–192, 210, 213; and community problem solving, 210–211; costs of, 57, 148; demand for, 51, 53–54, 97; and discrimination, 110, 162, 192, 214; and dropouts, 51, 152, 153–155, 167, 213, 214; and ethnicity, 155–156, 161, 165–166; grade school, 143–144, 149, 152, 153, 156, 168; higher education, 18, 144, 154–155, 156, 167, 191–192; high school, 51, 84, 102–103, 115, 149–171, 213, 214; and interpreters, 117; and Latino old-timers vs. newcomers, 154, 161, 162–168; of Latino population, 71, 72, 73, 86, 149, 215; and

Ethnography: and characteristics of villages and towns, 85–87; comparisons of rural communities, 94–98; focus group questions, 237–238; interview guide for community studies, 233–236; and Latino migration to rural Midwest, 1–2; research questions and methods, 80–82, 222–232

European immigrants, 29, 55–56, 77, 118, 174

Factories: and agricultural classification, 41; and Amish, 75, 79, 91, 97; and Anglo/Latino separation, 5, 89–91; Anglos' attitudes toward, 140; and Latino migration to rural Midwest, 79, 81; and local infrastructure, 105; and managers, 89–90; and workers, 1, 41, 90, 91, 105

Fall County, Michigan: and Anglo/Latino separation, 148; and Anglos' attitudes toward Latinos, 146; and employment, 142, 145; focus group questions, 237–238; and food processing, 11, 125, 129–131, 139, 141; and racism, 111, 113–114, 117–118, 126; and semistructured interviews, 226

Families: extended, 32, 214–215; and Immigration Control and Reform Act, 34, 84; and Latino migration to rural Midwest, 8, 30, 33, 53, 83, 84; and recruitment of Latinos, 36; and religion, 188; and repatriation programs, 32; role of children in, 11–12, 74, 93, 116, 140; stress of dual-income household, 17

Farmers' Home Administration, 43

Farm Labor Organizing Committee (FLOC), 241–242n.1

Farms and farming: and Amish communities, 94, 96–97; and Anglo/Latino separation, 91–92, 122; apple, 144; and economics, 47, 50, 126, 144–145; fruit, 91, 125, 144–145; grain, 91, 125; and Latinos as farm owners, 92, 118, 145, 146, 147; and megafarms, 17, 221; and racism, 115, 117–118; restructuring of, 50; and rural Midwest, 86; sugar beet, 23, 29, 31, 40, 239n.6; vegetable, 91, 125;

and workers, 91–92. *See also* Migrant farmworkers

Feagin, Joe R., 108, 112–115

Fertility, 48

Field, William, 42, 43

Fink, Deborah, 36

Fix, Michael, 57

Flint, Michigan, 10

Flora, Cornelia B., 26, 39, 53

Flora, Jan, 26, 39, 53

Flores, Isidore, 82, 223, 227, 230

Flores, Richard R., 112

Florida, 84

Foley, Neil, 11, 28, 113

Food processing: and Anglo/Latino separation, 127, 212; Anglos' attitudes toward, 137–142, 146; concentration of Latinos in, 69, 72; and costs to local government, 220; expansion of, 49–50, 127; and health issues, 53, 130, 131, 133; and Immigration Reform and Control Act, 138–139; Latino experiences in, 128–137; and Latino migration to rural Midwest, 10, 11, 21, 47, 48, 62, 72, 97, 146, 212; and Latino old-timers vs. newcomers, 91; and living wage with benefits, 147; and migrant workers, 118–119; and pollution, 2, 16, 17, 126, 137, 140, 146; and racism, 126, 131, 134–135; and recruitment of Latino workers, 120, 145; restructuring of, 47, 125, 126; and standards of living, 15–17, 98, 121; and working conditions, 8–9, 16, 125, 126, 128, 129–131, 132, 136, 146, 212, 242n.1. *See also* Meatpacking

Fox, Michigan: characteristics of focus group participants, 227, 228, 229; churches of, 87, 170; divisions among Anglos, 2–3; and education, 143–144; and food processing, 125, 136; and industrial parks, 142, 144; interview guide for community study, 233–236; and racism, 106, 110, 115; and social services, 121

Fox, Vicente, 217–218

Frey, William H., 33

Friedberger, Mark, 50

IBP (Iowa Beef Processing Company),
90–91, 209
Identity markers, 107, 108
Illegal Immigration Reform and Immigrant Responsibility Act (IIRIRA),
38, 39
Illinois, 13, 14, 33, 107
Immigration: and deportation in 1920s,
31, 32, 40; and deportation in 1990s, 39,
40, 200; and enforcement, 217, 242n.2;
history of, 14, 23, 174, 217; impact on rural Midwest, 83; and Latino population,
62; Latinos assumed to be immigrants,
3, 22–23, 39; and Latinos settling in
rural Midwest, 49; national context of,
54–58; and politics, 38, 201, 220; and
population growth, 9–10; and Proposition 187, 11; and public policy, 28, 32–35,
38, 39, 54, 55, 56–57, 58, 105, 205, 211,
212, 216–221; and racism, 113; and rural
California, 10; and sugar beet farming,
29; and Texas' annexation, 28. *See also*
Undocumented immigrants
Immigration Act of 1917, 29
Immigration and Nationality Act (INA),
33, 34, 38
Immigration and Naturalization Service
(INS), 23, 38–39, 99, 217, 239n.4,
242n.2
Immigration Reform and Control Act
(IRCA): as amnesty program, 34, 38, 58;
Anglos' attitudes toward, 138–139; and
employers, 240n.8; and families, 34,
84; and light industry, 17; and undocumented immigrants, 23, 34–35, 56, 57,
126, 139; and voting, 93
Indiana: and churches, 174; and employers' recruitment, 33; and manufacturing, 10, 30; and racism, 106; and racist
communities, 13, 107; and recruitment
of Latinos, 37; and religion, 193–194;
rural communities in, 1. *See also specific
cities*
Indiana Association of Cities and Towns, 78
Indiana Chamber of Commerce, 208
Industrial parks, 77, 83, 142–143, 144
Industry: and employment, 69, 70, 73,
148; growth in, 9, 30, 33; restructuring

in, 50; working conditions in, 31. *See also*
Industrial parks; Light industries
In-migration. *See* Migration
Institutional racism. *See* Racism
Intercultural Committee (ICC), 197–200,
202, 206
Iowa: and education, 53–54; INS raids in,
38; and meatpacking, 36; and racism,
104; and recruitment of Latinos, 37; and
rural Latino population, 26. *See also
specific cities*
Iowa Beef Processing Company, 90–91,
209

Jefferds, Maríaelena D., 82, 223, 224, 225,
226, 227, 231
Jehovah's Witnesses, 170
Jews, 76, 77, 78–79, 202
Jobs. *See* Employment
Johnson, James H., 104
Johnstown, Ohio, 15–16

Kammer, Jerry, 218
Kandel, William, 26
Kansas, 36
Kansas City, Missouri, 30
Kerr, Louise Año Nuevo, 10
Kimbirauskas, Kendra, 140–141
Knodel, John, 227
Kobell, Rona, 218
Kossek, Ellen Ernst, 110
Krantz, Colleen, 54
Ku Klux Klan, 13, 106, 107, 113
Kukulka, Gary, 14, 39, 53
Kuthy, Maria de Lourdes, 14

Labor force. *See* Employment
Lainge, Glenn, 173
Latin America, 108, 213, 214
Latin American immigrants, 49, 56, 108,
219
Latino newcomers: and age distribution,
215; Anglo attitudes toward, 2, 3–4, 5,
104–105, 123, 204; Anglo stereotypes of,
104, 204, 215; and community problem
solving, 209; and discrimination, 21, 40,
123, 212; and economics, 105, 181, 212;
and education, 154, 161, 162–168, 225;

and employment availability, 1, 8, 97; and English language, 23–24, 123, 148; and housing, 45, 85, 86; and immigration status, 3, 10, 19, 22–23, 104, 220; and Latino stores, 89; and politics, 197, 202, 203; and population growth, 212; and public policy, 147, 209; and racism, 12; and religion, 174, 178, 179, 180–181, 187–188, 189, 193–195, 226; and welfare, 5, 25, 204; and working conditions, 3, 20, 91, 221

Latino old-timers vs. newcomers: and discrimination, 123; and education, 154, 161, 162–168; and English language, 86, 162; and housing, 85, 86; and politics, 192, 197, 199, 202; and religion, 85, 187–188, 194

Latinos: and Anglo culture, 1–2; and Anglo/Latino separation, 87–98; definition of, 108; income level of, 20–21; myths about, 22–25, 27, 58; and perceptions of racism, 106, 107, 111–112, 113, 114, 123; political participation of, 93–94; population of, 5, 9, 26, 47, 58–68, 72, 83, 85–86, 104, 149; and race formation, 108–109; and terminology, 18, 19. See also Anglo stereotypes of Latinos; Latino newcomers; Latino old-timers vs. newcomers; Mexicans

Legal Immigration and Family Equity Act of 2000 (LIFE Act), 27, 38

Leiken, Robert, 218

Leon, Edgar R., 37

León, Luis D., 192

Leslie, Charles, 107, 110

Levanda, Archbishop, 176

Lexington, Nebraska, 37, 47, 49, 52, 53

Light industries: and employment, 8, 10, 11, 17–18, 21, 142–143; and Latino migration to rural Midwest, 48, 97, 98, 212; and recruitment of Latino workers, 120; and rural Midwest, 9–10

Ligonier, Indiana: and community problem solving, 205–209; descriptions of, 75–77, 204; ethnicity in, 76, 77, 87, 202; founding of, 76–77; Latino migration to, 82–85, 196; migration history in, 78–80, 202; and politics, 196–203, 225

Ligonier Advance Leader, 79, 82, 84, 198, 199, 200, 201, 203, 207, 208, 209

Limited English proficiency (LEP), 53, 91, 92, 152

Littlefield, Alice, 110

Loans. See Banks

Logansport, Indiana, 83, 90, 209

Longardner, Glenn, 196–203, 206

Long-term residents: Anglos as, 2–3, 5, 39, 53, 82, 104; Latinos as, 39, 82, 85, 86, 115, 123, 154, 161, 162–168, 187–188, 192, 194, 199, 202, 917

Low-income residents: Anglo attitudes toward, 81, 120, 123, 139; and Anglo/Latino separation, 88, 147, 148, 169; Anglos as, 121, 147; and assimilation, 184; and church support, 181–182; and economics, 215; and education, 214, 215; and ethnicity, 80, 81; expansion of, 148, 220; and farming, 145; and food processing, 142, 146; and housing, 46; and racism, 1; and religion, 179, 194

Ludlow, Randy, 16

Manufacturing: and employee turnover, 54, 80; geographic redistribution of jobs in, 35, 50; and Latino migration, 33, 80; Latinos employed in, 30, 53, 69, 70, 72; and recruitment of Latinos, 33, 36, 40; and working conditions, 39

Mapleville, Michigan: characteristics of focus group participants, 227, 228, 229; churches of, 170; divisions among Anglos, 2, 3; and food processing, 125, 136, 140; and industrial parks, 142, 144; interview guide for community study, 233–236; and recruitment of Latino workers, 119–120; and religion, 169–171; and social services, 121

Marbella, Jean, 77, 83, 97, 209

Marshall, Minnesota, 47, 49

Marshalltown, Iowa, 47

Martin, Philip, 10, 11, 34, 35, 36, 37, 38, 39, 49, 51, 53, 105

Martínez, Guillermo, 175

Massey, Douglas S., 10, 23, 24, 28, 33, 34, 38, 39, 55, 146, 216, 217, 239nn.5,7

Masud-Piloto, Felix Robert, 239n.6

Millard, Ann V., 8, 16, 20, 82, 88, 110, 122, 222, 223, 224, 225, 226, 227, 230, 242n.2

Milwaukee, Wisconsin, 26

Mines, Richard, 33

Minnesota, 47, 49, 51, 96

Miranowski, John A., 49

Morales, José, 172–173

MSNBC, 17

Murdock, George P., 227

Muskegon Chronicle, 43, 44

Musselman, Charles, 200–202, 203

Mutual aid societies, 30

NAFTA (North American Free Trade Agreement), 56

Naples, Nancy A., 109, 126

National Employment Law Project, 92

Native Americans, 77, 86, 108, 114, 118

Nebraska: and food processing, 11; INS raids in, 38; and meatpacking, 36; and Operation Vanguard, 39; and racism, 104; rural communities in, 1; and rural Latino population, 26, 47. *See also specific cities*

Nord, Mark, 37

North Carolina, 27, 62

Oceana County, Michigan, 41–46, 120, 225

Oceana Herald Journal, 42, 43, 44

Ohio, 1, 15–16, 26, 30, 46, 47

Omi, Michael, 102, 108, 109

Operation Gatekeeper, 38

Operation Tarmac, 218

Operation Vanguard, 39, 217

Orazem, Peter F., 48

Out-migration. *See* Migration

Pacheco, Ramón, 174, 175, 190

Page, Helán, 110

Passel, Jeffrey S., 33, 57

Peck, Vivienne, 90, 91

Pentecostal churches, 178, 182, 184–185, 187, 194, 241n.6

Pohlmann, Anton, 16

Police: and Anglo/Latino separation, 92; harassment by, 12, 100–101, 166; and

Spanish language, 92, 100; and undocumented immigrants, 99–101

Politics: and Anglo/Latino separation, 93–94, 116, 148; and benefits for migrant farmworkers, 120; and bilingual education, 213; and community problem solving, 3, 205–211; and discrimination, 110, 203; and education, 191–192, 213; and ethnicity, 80, 196–205; and housing, 41–46, 120, 225; and immigration, 38, 201, 220; and Latino voting, 93–94, 119, 202; and Ligonier, 196–203, 202; and policy changes, 205; political resettlement, 28, 33; and public space, 198; and racism, 116; and religion, 94, 169, 172, 178, 186, 188–189, 191–193, 194, 195, 199–200

Population: age distribution, 68, 69, 73, 215–216; aging, 73, 97, 216; growth in, 5, 48–49, 50, 62, 72–73, 85–86, 95–96, 104, 117–118, 173, 196, 212, 222; rural population trends, 1, 21, 26, 47, 52, 72, 83; statistics on, 59–61; and urban areas, 26, 58, 65, 66; and white flight, 146, 148

Postville, Iowa, 77, 83, 97, 209

Potawatomi Indians, 176, 186

Poultry Times, 16

Poverty: and Anglo stereotypes of Latinos, 6, 73, 114, 204; Anglos' view of, 6, 137, 146; and discrimination, 123; and food processing, 15; and Immigration Reform and Control Act, 35; and meatpacking, 51; of migrant farmworkers, 7, 118, 136; myths concerning, 24; and rural areas, 49; and rural California, 48; and working poor, 8, 24, 73, 98, 120, 121, 127, 137, 140, 146, 147, 204, 218, 219

Prejudice. *See* Discrimination; Racism

PRIDE, 208

Proposition 187 (California), 11, 37, 38, 39

Protestant churches, 87, 178–179, 182, 183, 191, 194

Public policy: and age distribution, 68; and agriculture, 119, 121; and community problem solving, 205–209, 219; and demography, 215–216; and discrimination, 81; and economics, 146–147, 221; and education, 167–168, 191–192, 212–214, 215, 216, 219, 221; and food processing, 125–126; and immigration, 28, 32–35, 38, 39, 54, 55, 56–57, 58, 105, 205, 211, 212, 216–221; and local government policies, 31, 32, 49, 52, 105, 211, 219–220, 221; and population growth, 212; as reactive, 48; and social services, 11–12, 31, 221

Puerto Ricans, 33, 239n.6, 240n.2

Qualitative research. *See* Ethnography
Quality of life, comparisons of, 94–98
Quinn, Mike, 78

Race, concept of, 107–109
Racialization, 102, 109, 123–124
Racism: and Anglo exploitation of Latinos, 5, 6, 23, 148; Anglo opposition to, 3–4, 103, 105; and Anglos, 12–14, 102–104, 105, 106, 110, 123, 148, 189, 231; blatant, 112, 113; community variation in, 12–14; covert, 112, 114–115, 124; definition of, 103, 105–108; and demographic changes, 51; and education, 102–103, 109, 115, 116, 123, 124, 155, 158–161, 166–167, 213; and ethnology, 105–108; Feagin's three types of, 112–115; and Latinos and race formation, 108–109; and Menchaca's concept of social apartness, 115–116; myths concerning, 25; and police, 101; theoretical aspects of, 109–123. *See also* Discrimination
Ramirez, Roberto, 23, 27
Refugees, 52, 76, 80, 83, 174
Religion: and Anglo/Latino separation, 5, 24, 30, 169–171, 178, 189, 215; and churches, 12, 30–31, 40, 87, 94, 97, 170, 172–179, 188–195, 211, 214–215; and church policies, 205; and community problem solving, 211; and congregations, 12, 180–191, 193–195; and demography, 52–53, 194; and discrimination, 110; and divisions among Anglos, 3, 87; and Latino old-timers vs. newcomers, 85, 187–188, 194; and Mexican Catholic

societies, 30; and migrant farmworkers, 177, 188–189; and pastors, 12, 93, 94, 214; and policy changes, 214–215; and politics, 94, 169, 172, 178, 186, 188–189, 191–193, 194, 195, 199–200; and racism, 124; and recruitment of pastors, 12; and Spanish language, 12, 24, 87, 169, 170, 174, 175, 176, 177, 178, 180, 184, 185–188; and templos, 172–174, 178–179, 183–184, 188, 194; and Virgin of Guadalupe, 30, 169–171, 186–188
Restaurants: and Amish, 97; Anglo ownership of, 88, 122; Anglo versus Mexican ownership of Mexican restaurants, 4–5; Latino ownership of, 88–89, 118, 122; Mexican restaurants prior to Great Depression, 30; and recruitment of Latino workers, 119–120; *taquerías*, 84
Retail trade industry, 69
Reza, Mary Frances, 176
Rising Sun, Indiana, 94
RMN (Rural Migration News), 16, 39
Roberts, Phillip, 43
Robinson, Gregory, 55
Rochín, Refugio I., 10, 11, 20, 26, 27, 29, 33, 35, 44–45, 48, 53, 54, 62, 145, 146, 148, 222, 233, 239n.6
Rodriguez, Clara, 108
Rosenbaum, René Pérez, 23, 29, 32, 34, 35, 104
Ruiz, Vicki L., 10
Rumbaut, Rubén, 49
Rural commuting, 64
Russell, Karen K., 110

Saavedra, Megan, 149, 150–151, 154, 155
Saenz, Rogelio, 20, 25, 33, 36, 39, 49, 122, 240n.9
St. Barbara's Catholic Church, 175–177, 179, 185, 186–189, 193, 194
St. Louis, Missouri, 30
St. Martin's Catholic Church, 172, 174–175, 179, 180–181, 190, 192–193, 194
Salgado de Snyder, V. N., 11
Salvadorans, 49
Sanchez, Thomas W., 25, 122
San Diego, California, 38

Sugar beet farming, 23, 29, 31, 40, 239n.6
Suro, Roberto, 58

Taxes: and age distribution, 73; and Anglo stereotypes of Latinos, 159, 160; and public policy, 215; tax abatements, 36, 121, 142, 220; and tax base, 48, 50, 148; and welfare benefits, 25, 57, 216–217
Temples. *See* Religion
Templo Cristo Rey, 172–174, 180, 184, 189–190, 193, 194
Texas: border with Mexico, 28, 90; colonias of, 48; and food processing, 136; and Latino population, 62; Latinos migrating to Midwest from, 5, 17, 49, 79, 84, 93; and racism, 113; and religion, 194
Therrien, Melissa, 23, 27
Thomas, R. Brooke, 110
Tichenor, Daniel J., 55
Times Leader, 17
Toledo, Ohio, 47
Topeka, Indiana, 97
Total Quality of Life Initiative (TQLI), 208–209
Trailers, 7–8, 54, 76, 85, 101
Transnationalism, 18, 58, 108, 170, 176
Treaty of Guadalupe Hidalgo (1848), 27, 28
Tuberculosis, 51

Undocumented immigrants: and amnesty program, 34; as de facto guest workers, 55, 216; efforts to decrease, 34–35, 56–57; and employers, 58, 136, 217, 220; enforcement against, 217, 242n.2; and federal legislation, 34–35, 38–39, 58, 105, 126; motivation of, 56; and police, 99–101; and politics, 197; and Proposition 187, 37; and raids, 16, 38, 200; and social networks, 239n.5; status of, 220; stereotypes of, 104, 159; stress on, 217; and taxes, 25, 57, 216–217; and welfare, 25, 57, 216–217
Unions, 10, 31, 36, 50, 119, 133, 143, 219
United Migrants for Opportunity (UMOI), 188
United States Citizenship and Immigration Services (USCIS), 56

UPI (United Press International), 218
Upper middle class, 16, 18, 111, 148, 169
Urban areas: and cost of living, 32; and education, 71, 72; and employment, 240n.4; and Latino population, 26, 58, 65, 66; and meatpacking, 35–36
Uriegas, Mike, 44
U.S. Census Bureau, 36, 55, 56, 61, 63, 65, 66, 67, 68, 69, 70, 71, 72
U.S. Commission on Agricultural Workers, 34, 35
U.S. Department of Agriculture, 35
U.S. Department of Education, 154
U.S. Department of Justice, 218
U.S. Department of Labor, 92, 219
U.S. English, Inc., 23, 213
U.S.-Mexican War, 28
U.S. Supreme Court, 219

Valdés, Dennis (Dionicio) Nodín, 10, 11, 23, 27, 29, 32, 33, 188, 239n.6
Vander Jagt, Guy, 43
Vargas, Zaragosa, 10, 23, 24, 25, 27, 29, 30, 31, 32, 40
Velásquez, Baldemar, 241–242n.1
Villa, Petra, 44
Virgin of Guadalupe: controversy over, 169–171, 226; mass celebrating, 186–188; and Mexican Catholic churches, 30, 186; and politics, 169, 186, 193

Waterloo, Iowa, 47
Welfare: access to, 57; Anglos' attitudes toward, 5, 11, 25, 31, 104, 113–114, 120–121, 122, 126, 137, 148, 204, 214, 215; Anglos' use of, 121, 137; employers as exploiters of welfare system, 5, 126, 127, 148, 204; and Great Depression, 25, 31; and undocumented immigrants, 25, 57, 216–217; and working poor, 146, 204
Wells, Miriam J., 10
Wheelerton, Indiana: churches of, 172–175, 177, 179, 180–184, 187, 195; and education, 149–171; Latino community in, 85; and Latino migration, 80, 83, 84, 240n.2; and racism, 111; and undocumented immigrants, 99–101